The Grand Hostels

Luxury Hostels of the World

gestalten

Welcome to the future of budget travel

» My aim has always been to find <u>new ways</u> to *inspire* people to travel, *challenge* the conventional ways we travel, and *discover* something new. «

I'm a hotel kind of girl. I backpacked around Europe and stayed in hostels in my 20s. Now that I have a job, I can afford my own room. I can't bear the idea of slumming it now in a 10-bed dorm with a bunch of smelly backpackers."

My date had been going really well until that moment. I had just gone through a tough breakup and, on the advice of a friend, had signed up for the dating site *match.com* (this was before the days of Tinder). I found my love for travel to be a great icebreaker on dates. Until they discovered that I wrote about budget travel, that is.

» Budget travel? Isn't that about staying in hostels? Does that mean you sleep in dorms? «

They asked me quizzically, their foreheads creased with discontent. Hostels did not just get a negative reception among my Match.com dates. I realized myself that, as I was getting older, I was finding it increasingly difficult to sleep in dorms-only hostels. The more I travelled, the more intolerant I had become of other people's travelling habits. I craved the luxury of having my own space, but I wasn't ready to graduate to the mundane, characterless, and insipid world of hotels.

Growing older had some benefits—increased wisdom made me realize that I wanted a special experience when I travel. At 39, travel was no longer about spartan rooms and sleeping in the cheapest bed available. I wanted more than just a cheap bed. I wanted an experience.

And so I began my mission to discover an alternative, more grown-up way to backpack around the world. One that would not mean sacrificing comfort.

I started to research online, reading travel blogs, and speaking to the travel community via Instagram and Twitter to ask about their experiences of hostelling. I found that, especially in my own age segment, of travellers aged 30–39, there was a trend of people "traveling younger." They were choosing hostels, previously thought to be mainstays of people in their twenties. I then discovered the new breed of design hostels that had emerged in the last few years.

These hostels are a step up from the usual hostel. They have dorms, but also offer private en suite rooms, and the design is on a par with what you would find in a boutique 4- or 5-star hotel. And the facilities are outstanding. From outdoor swimming pools to rooftop dinners, from petanque bars to in-house cinemas, from co-working spaces and tango classes to Spanish cooking lessons and sushi dinners—there is a wealth of amazing experiences to savor and enjoy in each of the 116 luxury hostels within this book. I like to think of each of them as your home away from home. Once you stay there, you'll find it hard to leave. I promise.

What started as a means of discovering a new way to travel and of rekindling my passion for backpacking, also became a great way for me to meet some amazing characters. I've had the pleasure of meeting some very creative, courageous and inspiring people through this project. For that reason, I hope that when you do decide to visit these hostels, you will have the same experience and be just as inspired by their warmth and vision. In my opinion, they are redefining the way we travel and also the way we see hostels.

On *BudgetTraveller.org*, my aim has always been to find new ways to inspire people to see the world, challenge the conventional ways we travel, and discover something new. It is my hope that this book will inspire a new generation of travelers, old and young to visit these amazing hostels and embrace this exciting new revolution in hostelling.

Welcome to the future of budget travel. Welcome to the Grand Hostels, the Luxury Hostels of the World.

Kash Dhattacharya
Founder and editor, *BudgetTraveller.org*

Types of hostels

Budget

Romantic

Foodie

Family Friendly

Party

Quiet

Boutique

Design

Lisbon: city of rugged charm

Paris and Venice, eat your heart out. Lisbon is the *world's most romantic city* for me.

Walking through the city's travessas and catching the strains of fado at every corner, I never stop admiring the beauty of the buildings that have withstood the city's countless invasions and earthquakes. Lisbon is like a journey back in time. It is a city to fall in love with again and again.

Where to eat

Walking up and down Lisbon's narrow travessas requires a lot of energy, so I often stop to refuel at one of the city's many pastelarias, enjoying the guilty pleasure Lisboetas take most pride in. The Pasteis de Nata is a cinnamon-flavored custard tart, that is customarily washed down with bica, a powerful espresso. You can find the best Pasteis de Nata in the suburb of Belém, where Vasco da Gama set sail for the New World. Antiga Confeitaria de Belém has been baking the delicious treats since 1837, following an ancient recipe that's still a highly guarded secret.

For a taste of Portuguese cuisine, venture to the Alvalade neighborhood, home of the Portuguese punk movement. Pay a visit to Adega da Bairrada, a locals-only restaurant, and try the classic bacalhau (cod) and cozido à portuguesa, a stew slow cooked to perfection. You can find a variety of meat-based specialties at O Carteiro, such as arroz de cabidela—chicken (or rabbit) cooked in its own blood and served with rice. Some Portuguese dishes are not for the faint-hearted.

For a modern take on Portuguese cuisine, check out Time Out Lisboa, which brings together some of the city's best restaurants under one roof. I love popping into Trincas, sister restaurant of the wonderful Decadente at The Independente Hostel & Suites. Trincas specializes in Portuguese petiscos (sharing dishes); my favorite is the octopus rice. For more petiscos, don't miss A Maria Não Deixa, near the famous Bica funicular. Get Santini's excellent gelato for dessert.

» As a restaurateur I have to keep up with what's happening, but I find myself preferring the classics. For a low-key, back-alley experience go to Zé da Mouraria, whose lunch menu will warm your soul. For a high-end experience with top Portuguese produce and earth-shattering wines, I recommend Coelho da Rocha. The two brothers who run it started off as waiters at their other restaurant, →

Magano, and bought the place from their former boss. They are a true inspiration. «

DUARTE D'EÇA LEAL
— The Independente Collective

Where to drink

The Portuguese are quite particular when it comes to drinking. There's drinking at meals, at the beach, and at parties, but they don't do after-work sessions that well and don't plan drinks without a purpose. Fox Trot is an exception to the norm. The owner, Mr. Joaquim, bought the place from his former boss after 20 years bartending. It has a much sought-after pool table and a lovely beer garden.

Red Frog Speakeasy, located on the stylish Avenida da Liberdade, might be the best cocktail bar in town. Reminiscent of a 1920s prohibition bar, this speakeasy is hidden behind a closed door with no signage. Ring the bell to enter. The drinks are on the pricier side, but it is a cool experience and the cocktails are very nice.

If you like a drink with a view, head to Miradouro de Santa Catarina.

Grab a bottle of beer from the local supermarket and watch a beautiful sunset by the Tagus River. The place has a great atmosphere and you can listen to the street musicians' funky tunes. Park Restaurant and Bar is another quirky choice for sunset drinks. It's a rooftop parking lot converted into a hip roof-terrace bar.

Where to party

Contenders come and go, but true icons are timeless. In Lisbon it is Lux, which has superbly curated music and decor that bares the soul of its founder Manuel Reis. One way or another, you'll wind up there.

Another favorite is the hip Cais do Sodré, also known as Pink Street, a nod to its former guise as Lisbon's red-light district. What used to be a seedy area has now been transformed into one of the city's biggest party hotspots. Musicbox is also a popular choice, hosting both Portuguese and international artists. If you're a hip-hop fan, check out Copenhagen, or Titanic Sur Mer for jazz and live music.

Going for a walk

I take great joy in wandering the streets of Alfama, capturing snapshots of local life, such as elderly women gossiping from windows. Bairro da Mouraria is one of the city's most multicultural neighborhoods and another fascinating place to stroll.

> » The Tagus riverfront is intrinsic to Lisboa. The scent of the tides, the sound of the water, the way it reflects this city's unique light. My perfect walk starts somewhere around Belém and stretches past MAAT (Museum of Art, Architecture and Technology) all the way up to Village Underground and LxFactory. «
>
> **DUARTE D'EÇA LEAL**
> *— The Independente Collective*

Getting around town

I love watching the world go by from the backseat of the Tram 28—riding it is one of life's greatest adventures. It seems to have become victim to Lisbon's rising popularity, so take a ride early in the morning to beat the crowds, and watch out for pickpockets.

> » eCooltra is the best way to travel short distances. The scooter rental system is managed through an app. You just need to download it, take a picture of your driver's license and ID card, and you are ready. Very cheap too! «
>
> **NUNO CONSTANTINO**
> *— Hub New Lisbon Hostel* →

Walking through the city's travessas and catching the strains of *fado* at every corner, I never stop admiring the beauty of the buildings. <u>Lisbon</u> is like a journey back in time. It is a city to *fall in love* with again and again.

The best place to relax

The Atlantic coastline is only 20 minutes from Lisbon. When the weekend comes, locals head out to popular Costa da Caparica and hang out with friends at bars Cabana do Pescador or Borda D'Água. If the weather doesn't allow for sand and sea, then having a relaxing picnic at Jardim da Estrela is a pleasant alternative.

> » The best place to relax is <u>Fundaçao Calouste Gulbenkian</u>. Strolling among the trees and plants, enjoying an open-air concert, or simply relaxing by the lake watching the birds—those are just some of the ways to hang out there. «

JADE PERLE LOUIS
—Destination Hostels

Best viewpoint

Lisbon is stretched across seven hills and offers many vantage points, or miradouros. Miradouro São Pedro de Alcântara, opposite The Independente Hostel & Suites, has spectacular panoramic views. Or head to The Insólito, a quirky rooftop restaurant, for an even more epic view.

Miradouro Monsanto has a restaurant that has been abandoned since 2001. It used to be visited only by curious people or street artists, but in September 2017 became an official viewpoint of the city.

> » <u>Miradouro da Nossa Senhora do Monte</u> is an amazing place to take photographs and admire the sunset, although it is a bit crowded at that time of the day. «

NUNO CONSTANTINO
—Hub New Lisbon Hostel

Secret places

Lisbon is mysterious, but it lends itself to being discovered. I recommend jumping on a boat to Cova do Vapor, an authentic fisherman's outpost with a unique beach. Your senses will be seduced by the taste of fresh fish washed down with Vinho Verde. Top it off with a dive in the cold water and a nap under the warm sun.

Village Underground is another secret spot, right next to LxFactory. Enjoy a drink in the café located in an intriguing architectural structure with stacked shipping containers and double-decker buses. This place is home to a new creative community—and perfectly Instagrammable.

> » Take the fisherman's path from Almada to Cacilhas and visit the statue of Cristo Rei. It is very beautiful and you will discover the unexplored, most typical Portugal. To return to Lisbon, take the boat from Cacilhas. «

NUNO CONSTANTINO
—Hub New Lisbon Hostel

The Independente
Hostel & Suites

Luxury hospitality with a twist

Overlooking the beautiful Miradouro de São Pedro de Alcântara, The Independente has a great location at the intersection of three of Lisbon's most vibrant and celebrated neighborhoods: Bairro Alto, Príncipe Real, and Avenida da Liberdade. The art deco-inspired hostel is the brainchild of four brothers who envisioned a different concept of hospitality, creating a meeting point where "travelers as well as locals can come together."

The interior design is a juxtaposition of Scandinavian minimalism with ornate architecture. It is a happy contradiction that works beautifully. The building was formerly the Swiss ambassador's official residence before being converted into a luxury hostel in 2011 with 90 beds spread across 11 spacious dorm rooms. The original character of the building has been preserved with its high ceilings, ornate wall moldings, and detailed wrought-iron balconies that open to a view of the Tagus River. The dorm rooms have sturdy

wooden bunk beds with private reading lights and outlets. Each dorm is tastefully decorated with a mix of antiques and family heirlooms alongside reclaimed furniture pieces. There are four private suites with balconies where guests can enjoy an espresso from the self-service coffee machine, perfect for a couple or a family that would like more privacy. The hostel hosts regular concerts from local and international artists, and the guest relations team organizes weekly events, including movie →

Good to know

PRICE RANGE
$ $ $ $ $
AMENITIES INCLUDE
Free WiFi; restaurant;
bar; rooftop bar; lounge.

Tip: The hostel hosts
regular concerts from
local and international
artists, and the guest
relations team organizes
weekly events, including
movie nights and
cooking shows, as well as
surf tours and many
other fun activities.

The Independente has a great location at the intersection of three of Lisbon's most vibrant and celebrated neighborhoods: Bairro Alto, Príncipe Real, and Avenida da Liberdade.

nights and cooking shows, as well as surf tours and many other fun activities.

Also housed within are The Decadente Restaurante & Bar, one of Lisbon's most stylish and popular venues. It is known for serving modern Portuguese cuisine using locally sourced ingredients, and guests can relax with one of their signature cocktails in the outdoor beer garden—the perfect place to chill on a hot summer day in Lisbon. The bar attracts a steady stream of trendy Lisboetas, making you feel part of the city's DNA. The free breakfast, consisting of orange juice, cereal, coffee, bread, cheese, and cold meats, is a great way to start the day.

The Independente is the perfect hostel for design lovers. Pair that with a cracking restaurant, cool bar, and friendly staff, and you have all the makings of a great experience at this very special and unique hostel.

Goodmorning Hostel

Wake up happy in the heart of Lisbon

Situated on Praça dos Restauradores in the heart of Lisbon, Goodmorning Hostel follows suit in the new breed of designer hostels. There's warm wooden flooring, bright bold wallpaper, and rooms filled with a cornucopia of vintage curios and recycled furniture pieces. The dorm rooms are spacious here. Travelers looking for more privacy can choose an en suite double on the top floor of the hostel. All rooms have a balcony with panoramic views of the city.

The staff are a truly outstanding feature of this hostel: they have a friendly, personable approach, and lots of ideas of cool, unusual things to do in Lisbon. There's a busy calendar of social events to keep guests entertained: a ramble through town up to the castle; a biking tour with highlights of the city; an excellent free walking tour; tours up to Sintra, a beautiful hilltop city neighboring Lisbon; and free sangria night on Fridays.

Another highlight event is the "Moustache Cooking Class" with Joao, a staff member with, yes, a magnificent moustache. During his class he introduces local Portuguese dishes from feijoada to caldo verde to bacalhau à brás—guests are welcome to lend a hand to cook! A free glass of red wine, port wine, or Ginginha (a ginja berry liqueur), accompanies the meal. Breakfast here is free and fantastic; with freshly-made waffles, it's something different from your standard hostel fare. There's free coffee and tea available throughout the day. If you need to stock up on food or alcohol, there's a cheap and excellent supermarket nearby.

Staying at the Goodmorning Hostel is like being invited into a friend's home. The superb central location, generous breakfast, and friendly, knowledgeable hostel staff make this a great base for exploring Lisbon.

PRICE RANGE
$ $ $ $ $

AMENITIES INCLUDE
linens; towels available; free city maps; 24-hour reception; free WiFi; power adapters; lounge area; book exchange; cable TV/DVDs; hairdryer; housekeeping; keycard access; laundry service; lockers; air conditioning; free luggage storage; individual night lamps; self-catering facilities; free tea and coffee; free city walking tours; pub crawls; bicycle rentals; bar. Breakfast included.

Tip: Check out » Moustache Cooking Class « with Joao where he introduces local Portuguese dishes.

Hub New Lisbon Hostel

A place to channel your inner child

Hub New Lisbon Hostel is located in a beautifully renovated eighteenth-century building close to the party district of Bairro Alto. With a young and energetic team led by the charismatic Nuno, a wonderful on-site bar, clean and comfortable rooms, plus an amazing ball pit, this hostel offers a cool and convenient base for exploring Lisbon.

The hostel walks the fine line of being a low-budget yet stylish hostel. It also balances the old and the new perfectly. Characteristic features of the old building, such as the azulejo tiles, fresco-painted ceilings, and original wooden floors, contrast with the modern bunk beds.

With a mix of dorms and private rooms, this hostel caters for travelers on all budgets. There is a choice of four, six, and eight-bed mixed dorms with either shared facilities or en

suites. There is also a mix of classic and modern design. The very original and colorful Cube room resembles a Rubik's Cube, and the Cross room is black and very modern-looking with bunk beds that contrast nicely with the eighteenth-century azulejo wall panels. All the bunk beds have a good degree of privacy and are fitted with a reading light and three power sockets. Large secure lockers beneath the beds are for securing personal belongings. There is an exclusive floor for →

Good to know

PRICE RANGE
$ $ $ $ $

AMENITIES INCLUDE
bar; terrace; giant ball pit;
foosball; beer pong;
playStation; board
games; dining areas;
locker rooms.

Tip: Don't miss jumping
into the Hub New
Lisbon Hostel's giant
ball pit to bring out
your inner child!
It will bring back good
childhood memories.

With a young and energetic team *Hub New Lisbon Hostel* offers a cool and convenient base for exploring Lisbon. It offers everything a modern-day backpacker is looking for in a hostel.

female travelers, and private rooms on the fourth floor have mesmerizing views of the Lisbon skyline. Bathed in light, these rooms are quiet, comfortable, and offer a good night's sleep.

Hub New Lisbon Hostel offers everything a modern-day backpacker looks for in a hostel. There is a free breakfast every morning and a communal kitchen for cooking dinner with friends or preparing snacks for the day. BUH is an on-site bar, which serves Portuguese signatures such as pastel de nata and the Brazilian classic caipirinha. ⌂

Porto: hub of tiny pleasures

I believe some cities exist not only in the physical realm but also in our *imagination*.

Even if we are not there, they are flowing through our veins and return to us in the silent moments between the stresses and strains of our everyday lives. Porto is one of the cities that stays with you long after you have said your final goodbye.

There is a word in Portuguese that comes close to describing this strange, beautiful emotion. Saudade. The word describes a deep emotional state of nostalgic or profound melancholic longing for an absent something or someone that one loves. Saudade can be described as the love that remains after something or someone is gone. So here is my saudade for Porto.

Where to eat

Choosing where to eat in Porto is a hard task. Portugal, and the northern region in particular, has a very rich food culture. When in Porto you have to try francesinha, the city's most famous dish that consists of a sandwich filled with different types of meat, covered with melted cheese and an egg on top. It is served with a special sauce and goes very well with a cold beer. Café Santiago is the undisputed king of Porto's most famous sandwich. Cervejaria Brasão and O Golfinho are equally worthy places to sample this dish. Another famous Porto dish to try is tripas à moda do Porto that consists of tripe with beans and sauce, some meat and rice. Rápido, next to São Bento train station (and The Passenger Hostel), and Tripeiro do a great version of this.

Porto's humble taverns aka tascas are a good place to seek the authentic flavors of the city. At Adega Rio Douro on Tuesday afternoons you can listen to live fado music and eat typical snacks like bifana or codfish. If you are a fan of cheese, I recommend Casa Guedes for their sandwich of pulled pork and melting Serra da Estrela cheese. Wash it down with a glass of their own rosé wine called Espadal. O Gazela is a simple café in Central Porto which is famous for its cachorrinhos da batalha, a kind of hotdog with a special type of sausage, topped with melted cheese, and an optional spicy sauce.

A Badalhoca is another place to try, a bit further away in Boavista. It serves delicious sandwiches and a special rosé wine.

One of the nicest streets in Porto is Rua de Miguel Bombarda, home to lots of independent art galleries and also to the fantastic Rota Do Chá. This is my favorite place to drink tea and chat with friends in Porto. →

They have a beautiful back garden with a huge Buddha stupa. My favorites here are the delicious champagne cassis tea and the mango cheesecake.

For a city in love with meat, there are still many options for vegetarians and vegans. Himali Bachu from Tattva Design Hostel is a vegetarian and advises:

» Being a vegetarian and not a fan of vegetarian restaurants, I love some of the pizzerias here in Porto: Casa D'Ouro, Il Fornaio—for the quality of the pizza and also the ambience of the place itself. Sushi places that specialize in veggie sushi that I would recommend for quality are Sumo (Cais de Gaia) and Kai Kou. «

HIMALI BACHU
—*Tattva Design Hostel*

Where to drink

Whenever I'm back in Porto, I love heading to Cervejaria Galiza.

This is a local version of a beer hall—they serve cold, good beer and delicious seafood: the prawns and octopus are excellent here.

If you're looking to hang out with locals head to Bonaparte, a popular Irish pub in the neighborhood of Foz by the sea. With vintage, wood-panelled decor, this bar has been serving thirsty locals and tourists since 1977. If you're keen on finding a decent cheap football bar, Clube Porto Rugby is the place frequented by Erasmus students and locals alike. They have live music, mostly local people, and a nice ambience.

If you're looking to sample a nice selection of Portuguese wines like wines from Douro and Minho, head to Capela Incomum, a wine bar located in a sixteenth-century chapel.

» On a sunny saturday or sunday afternoon you can listen to live jazz at MiraJazz with a beer or wine and enjoy amazing views of the Douro River. Adega Leonor and Adega Sports Bar are two low-priced bars where you can either drink on the street with friends or play pool and darts inside, or watch all kinds of sport on TV. «

TOMÁS GRAÇA
—*The Passenger Hostel*

Where to party

Galerias de Paris, composed of three parallel streets full of bars and discos, is the hub of Porto's nightlife. It's centrally located near the famous Lello bookshop and the Clerigos Tower. Alternative music lovers should try Gare (techno) or Maus Hábitos (a fifth-floor art gallery, restaurant and disco). For live music try Galerias de Paris and Rua, a small but multifaceted tapas bar with live music from Wednesday to Sunday.

» Coffee house and art gallery by day, music club and bar by night, split over two floors, Plano D is one of the coolest and most original night venues in Porto. «

GONÇALO NUNO
—*Gallery Hostel*

Going for a walk

Porto is a great city to walk and explore, from the old town to the river and to the sea.

Starting in Aliados in the city center I love going for a walk to the Ribeira (riverside) via Rua das Flores. If you are an art lover, check out the fantastic urban art and art galleries during a stroll down Rua de Miguel Bombarda and Rua da Madeira.

I definitely recommend hopping over to Foz which has a nice walking path, suitable for whatever you're in the mood for, be it walking, running or cycling.

Getting around town

The car is the most practical way to get around Porto. However, given how relatively small Porto is, the best way to explore the city is walking. Porto's close proximity to the Costa Verde coastline is not so well known to tourists and well worth visiting. The best way to observe the scenic coastline is by hopping on the no. 500 bus which starts from Praça da Liberdade and goes up the coast all the way to Matosinhos.

Best place to relax

As I mentioned earlier, Porto's location by the sea offers visitors a chance to relax on one of its many beaches. I love going to the large sandy beach in Praia dos Ingleses. There is a nice bar, restaurant and coffeeshop right on the beach where I love to chill with a beer and watch the world go by. Cross the majestic Dom Luís I Bridge (built by a student of Gustave Eiffel) and head over to Gaia to relax in the Jardim do Morro. Jardins do Palácio de Cristal, with its beautiful peacocks, is also a great place to relax and offers excellent views of the river. →

Porto is one of the cities that stays with you long after you have said your final *goodbye*. There is a word in Portuguese that comes close to describing this strange, beautiful emotion. *Saudade*. Saudade can be described as the love that remains after something or someone is gone.

» For me the terrace bar of the Yeatman Hotel offers the best view of Porto's skyline from Gaia. «

GONÇALO NUNO
—*Gallery Hostel*

Secret Spot

I like to go far away, either following the northern coast and going to Angeiras (the first fishing village after Porto) or following the southern coast and heading to Miramar beach.

Within the city, I really like the stairs that take you from Batalha to Rua da Madeira and vice-versa. Beyond the street art, you have an amazing view and a different perspective of São Bento train station and the city in general. Another great spot is Guindalense Futebol Clube. You can find it in Escada dos Guindais with incredible views to the bridge and river.

Best viewpoint

Not far from the river, Jardim das Virtudes is a beautiful garden to visit, especially in the summer, and offers a fantastic view of the Douro and shores of Gaia. Mirajazz, Miradouro da Vitoria and the top of the Clerigos Tower are also excellent vantage points to get a panoramic view of the river and city.

For the best views of Porto, you should hop over the Dom Luiz I Bridge to Gaia on the other side of the river. With a church and monastery, the Serra do Pilar hill offers a dreamy lookout over the city. Jardim do Morro offers an equally excellent view, especially at sunset when the city lights switch on.

The House of Sandeman
Hostel & Suites

Iconic accommodation in an eighteenth-century wine cellar

Guests of the House of Sandeman Hostel & Suites indulge in a piece of prominent wine history and contemporary lore at this branded hostel—the first such branding project in the world.

While the iconic building is 227 years old, the project to turn it into a multicultural space and luxury accommodation has only recently been completed, opening to the public in April 2018.

It started with Sogrape, one of the most prominent wine companies on the Iberian Peninsula, joining forces with the hospitality group Independente Collective to create a destination for guests visiting Porto to enjoy a whole range of experiences related to the iconic port wine brand Sandeman.

The building sits atop the Sandeman Cellars, so guests are about as close as they can get to two centuries of port history and expertise. The House of Sandeman has twelve suites, four dorms, a restaurant, a terrace, a bar / cafeteria, a guest lounge, and an event room with capacity for up to fifty people. The building's exterior has been left mostly untouched, with the exception of improved lighting design, some fresh paint on the façade, and wooden windows (now equipped with double glazing for maximum comfort), but the inside would be unrecognizable to its former occupants.

With an emphasis on the original eighteenth-century features, the interior design—by Catarina →

Good to know

PRICE RANGE
$ $ $ $ $
AMENITIES INCLUDE
free fiber optic WiFi;
self-catering facilities;
huge dorm beds; vintage
bicycle rentals; vinyl
records and turntables
available in the suites;
reading lights; hairdryer;
en suite bathrooms;
on-site restaurant;
postcard view of Porto
and the Douro River;
great music and
atmosphere; local insight
and handy guides;
friendly staff; special
homemade breakfast
available.

*Tip: Enjoy exclusive
homemade dinners
at the hostel's
private wine cellar
and kitchen!*

» We wanted to create an experience that properly celebrates the alternative, entrepreneurial, and independent spirit of Porto and Vila Nova de Gaia. «

Cabral—has chromatic references and furniture design and embellishments, which subliminally evoke the Sandeman brand and its origins.

The first floor, where the hostel dorms are located, was previously used as the Sandeman office and hosts some of the most amazing architectural features of this historic building: large double-height ceilings, stone walls and arches, and a series of stunning skylights. The dorms' outstanding feature is the astonishing wine barrel-inspired beds. Created by a Portuguese designer, they come with luxurious king single mattresses—unheard of in hostel dorms—two

power plugs, coat hooks, and a bottle holder. The rest of the first floor has five large suites overlooking the Douro River and Porto's beautiful riverfront. These rooms are predominantly black and white and with original wooden floors, double beds, and a vinyl turntable.

On the second floor, the Sandeman's boardroom and dining room has been readapted to become the "Original Suites." In these rooms, the original ceilings and wooden floors were retained and restored, and warm and comfortable amenities have been added to complete the experience. The old tasting room has

been renovated and transformed into a welcome desk as well a bar / lounge and is the epicenter of the hostel's social life. This area is also where the hostel's private wine cellar and kitchen can be found, and where guests can enjoy exclusive homemade dinners prepared by the hostel's cook using only locally sourced produce. Plans are in the making to host live concerts and DJ sets here.

The George Restaurant & Terrace is located on the opposite side of the building, just steps away from the Douro River and with a postcard view of Porto. Adjacent to the famous Sandeman wine cellars, →

the restaurant building has been restored to highlight some of the old rustic characteristics. The original stones and terracotta bricks, together with soft pastel tones, green plants, and contemporary pieces, give it a clean, cool, and laid-back look. It's inviting to travelers, guests, visitors, and even locals.

Porto-born Pedro Limão is the mastermind behind the restaurant's cuisine, backed by an incredible team of young Portuguese chefs. The produce is sourced from the Douro region, and the menu offers a combination of original and irreverent dishes with great care taken for the origin and tradition of the ingredients used as well as the authenticity of the producers who sell them. It simply doesn't get much more authentic than this!

The terrace sits on the edge of the river and features a sea container

transformed into a bar. Here they serve refreshing Port wine cocktails and delicious snacks, and host live music performances and DJ sets during the hot summer months.

Of course, the real history runs beneath the surface and guests can better understand the phenomenon of Sandeman and this incredible series of buildings by visiting the cellars on the ground floor—the Sandeman brand's wine cellars are still in operation to this day. Although the company recently decided to renovate this area as well, in order to improve the visitor's experience, changes to the cellars— where they still age the precious liquid as they did over 200 years ago—were kept to a bare minimum to maintain the original authenticity.

If you love everything port, you'll love everything Sandeman at this luxury retreat. ⌂

The Passenger

Just the ticket for a comfortable stay in Porto

The creation of The Passenger Hostel, lodged inside Porto's iconic São Bento Station, was a huge undertaking. The station, opened in 1896 and still in operation, is a UNESCO World Heritage Site.

"This was a project of enormous responsibility. We tried to preserve what existed and restore what was original—it was a huge challenge to try to create a living space worthy of the twenty-first century while preserving the original design in a non-intrusive manner," says owner Rita Correa Figueira.

The unique location paired with vintage elements of design is culturally fascinating, and guests gain a wealth of experience while staying here. As a three-story, symmetrical, imposing granite structure, discovering the architecture of the station itself is one of the delights of staying at The Passenger Hostel. Guests should pay special attention to the beautiful azulejo panel and the tiled vestibule.

You can practically walk off the railway platform and into the hostel, making The Passenger Hostel a super convenient place to stay, especially if traveling by train. Some of the most visited landmarks in the city are close by. Rua de Santa Catarina, Porto's main shopping street, is just a few minutes walk away, as is Aliados Avenue, Clérigos Tower, the Douro riverside, and Galerias de Paris—the nightlife strip. The hostel's rooms →

Good to know

PRICE RANGE
$ $ $ $ $
AMENITIES INCLUDE
free WiFi; self-catering
facilities; laundry
facilities; lounge; bar;
library; living room
with TV.

Tip: Enjoy the hostel's
super convenient
location. Rua
de Santa Catarina,
Porto's main shopping
street, is just a few
minutes walk away,
as is Aliados Avenue,
Clérigos Tower, the
Douro riverside, and
Galerias de Paris—the
nightlife strip.

The Passenger Hostel's walls are adorned with contemporary Portuguese art; guests will fall in love with the works of Marta Wengorovius, Manuel Caeiro, Miguelangelo Veiga, and Pedro Guerra.

are comfortable and cozy, and shining wooden floors and large windows illuminate the space. Every room is designed to be both beautiful and functional. Clever ideas—like wardrobes or tables that convert into an extra bed—add a combination of practicality and style. An assemblage of eclectic vintage pieces, gathered from all over the globe, add a particular unique flair to the hostel.

The walls are adorned with contemporary Portuguese art; guests will fall in love with the works of Marta Wengorovius, Manuel Caeiro, Miguelangelo Veiga, and Pedro Guerra. There are plans to take this even further, as the hostel hopes to open an art gallery in the conservatory room situated behind the clock tower of the train station. Despite the collection of vintage

items (and being housed inside an old train station), The Passenger Hostel has a remarkably contemporary feel. It's also a "green hostel." The hostel uses smart-energy appliances, LED lighting and is always on the look-out for sustainable, eco-friendly solutions in order to run efficiently.

There are both shared and private bedrooms; shared rooms often feature seating areas as well as beds. All dorms feature a private locker for each guest, a privacy curtain, a bedside power socket, and a reading light. Many dorms have sofas to sit and relax in, so guests can comfortably hang out and chat with new friends and traveling companions. Bathrooms are very clean, attractive spaces, with dark tiles, modern fittings, good showers, and hairdryers. A bar with lounge, shared kitchen,

and laundry facilities are all welcome amenities. The kitchen is spacious, with three large wooden tables that are perfect for sharing stories with fellow guests over a meal. The hostel has plans for cooking workshops in the near future.

There are two living room areas on the first and third floors. Both common living spaces are wonderfully equipped with a Bose sound system. If you're in the mood for music, the hostel has a piano located in the mezzanine lounge area from where you can see trains arriving and departing. There's also a small library where guests are encouraged to take and leave books on their travels.

Whether here to relax or explore, you will surely enjoy your stay at Porto's one-of-a-kind Passenger Hostel.

Gallery Hostel

Eco-hostel meets art gallery

Located in the trendiest quarter of Porto, between the art district and hip nightlife, the eco-friendly Gallery Hostel typifies the concept of the luxury hostel: Service, cleanliness, and facilities are top priorities here, along with a friendly and familial atmosphere.

Gallery Hostel is an excellent poster child for the stunning metamorphosis Porto has undergone. Situated in the trendy downtown quarter of Miguel Bombarda, situated between nightlife and the art scene, this privileged area beguiles with its

gourmet restaurants, art galleries, design boutiques, stylists, and vintage shops; the quarter is vibrant with a never-ending flow of activity.

However, it's the fusion of the hostel concept with an in-house gallery that gives Gallery Hostel a distinct status. The gallery contributes to the whole community by hosting diverse bi-monthly art exhibitions, concerts, and other cultural and artistic initiatives.

The hostel building is an impressive 1906 villa formerly owned by a member of the local aristocracy. Through a restoration project, the owners maintained most of the original aspects of the

traditional house and have blended it with modern decor, infusing neutral and earthy tones with unique textures and furnishings. The result is stunning—a contemporary design hostel that also functions as an art gallery. In addition, the common areas are charming and stylish, a haven of relaxation and coziness.

One of the standouts of Gallery Hostel is its staff. Hospitality is one area where hostels often excel, but at Gallery, each guest is truly looked after with great care; perhaps this can be attributed in part to the owners' training at the Ecole hôtelière de Lausanne, the school where the best go to learn the art →

Good to know

PRICE RANGE
$ $ $ $ $
AMENITIES INCLUDE
linens; free city maps;
free WiFi and internet
access; adaptors;
air conditioning; free
city tours; security
lockers; safe deposit
box; luggage storage;
24-hour reception;
24-hour security;
parking; bicycle rentals;
laundry facilities;
self-catering facilities;
housekeeping; hairdryer;
free towels; extra cots;
games room; café.
Free breakfast included.

Tip: One delightful
hostel activity is the
in-house preparation
of delicious and
affordable dinners!

It's the fusion of
the hostel concept
with an art
gallery that gives
Gallery Hostel
a distinct status.

of hospitality. On entering the hostel, there's a cozy reception area to the right with a long, narrow corridor hosting art exhibitions straight ahead. A computer room replete with huge Mac desktops is available for guests; it also has a convenient, well-stocked library, packed with books about local history.

Further along the corridor, there's an opening with a skylight, creating an airy, light atmosphere. To the right is a staircase—lined with azulejos—winding down into the lower levels of the building. Downstairs there is a cozy open-plan bar with plenty of soft cushions to sink into after a long day of roaming the winding confusion of Porto's cobbled streets. The bar serves selected Portuguese wines from their extensive wine list— a rarity for any hostel; Porto wine

tasting sessions can be organized on request. (Note: If you are a wine aficionado, the hostel organizes full-day wine tours in the nearby Douro Valley.) Opposite the bar is a tranquil winter garden, conveniently open for smokers. There is also a living room-cum-cinema with huge comfy sofas and a projector screen showing movies and the occasional local football derby. To top that off, the hostel has a karaoke machine if you feel like crooning a tune or two.

One delightful hostel activity is the in-house preparation of delicious and affordable dinners; they're a good chance to meet fellow travelers and discover traditional Portuguese dishes, like caldo verde and arroz de pato. The meals are cooked by the hostel's own chef from Brazil and are equal in taste to lovingly homemade dishes. Meals come

to 10€ including dessert and local wine. Gallery Hostel's central location makes it easy to see all of Porto's sights and sounds. Rent a bike from reception to fly solo, or take advantage of the hostel's excellent free 90-minute walking tour of all the city's key monuments and hotspots.

Forty-one beds fill the hostel's rooms—the rooms are named after local architects, writers, and artists, adding a real Porto flavor. Dorms have their own private balconies while doubles and triples enjoy garden views—perfect for relaxing at the end of a busy day of sight-seeing with a book or in the company of fellow travelers and friends. In terms of value for money, a popular choice is the spacious six-bed dorm, which comes with its own en suite bathroom complete with a stellar power shower. △

The Lights Hostel

Sit back—The Lights Hostel will take care of everything

The Lights Hostel was created by a group of four friends: two born and bred Malaga locals, and two seasoned travelers. The combination of local knowledge and travel experience has this hostel checking the entire list of a traveler's needs and desires.

In a historic building in the heart of Malaga, the space is divided into two parts: the main hostel and a separate block with hotel-style rooms. The rooms and hostel are very secure and accessible via keycard. For those on a budget, the dorms here are fantastic, with custom-made beds that have privacy curtains, personal reading lights, and storage lockers under the beds. All the dorms and doubles have lovely balconies. Air-conditioning units are provided in the summer and extra blankets in the winter months. The shared bathrooms are clean, well maintained, and feature custom-built dual head showers.

The standout feature of The Lights Hostel is the rooftop terrace. Guests gather in the terrace to watch the sunset and enjoy sundowners. Every evening, the hostel staff prepares a cheap dinner catering to all diets. The staff here make you feel at home and are always looking for ways to add to your city experience. A whole bunch of events—from free sangria evenings on the terrace to beach volleyball in the afternoons—are available for guests. The staff will show you some of their favorite bars on the local bar tour.

If you've had a long night on the town, then the free buffet breakfast is the perfect cure. Served from 7:30 a.m. to 11 a.m., there's coffee, tea, milk, orange juice, mixed fruit juice, white and black bread, butter, strawberry and peach jam, three different kinds of cereals, honey, and Nutella.

You can truly get into the Malaga spirit at The Lights Hostel, while trusting that you're always in good hands.

Good to know

PRICE RANGE
$ $ $ $ $
AMENITIES INCLUDE
24-hour reception;
free WiFi; self-catering
facilities; laundry
service; air conditioning;
rooftop terrace; bar;
daily tours. Breakfast
buffet included.

Tip: A whole bunch
of events—from
free sangria evenings
on the terrace
to beach volleyball in
the afternoons—are
available for guests.
The staff will show
you some of their
favorite bars on the
local bar tour.

Quartier Bilbao Hostel

Quartier Bilbao Hostel Boutique is in the heart of Bilbao's iconic Casco Viejo, the city's old town. This charming pedestrian area is right by Ribera Market, Santiago Cathedral, and Plaza Nueva.

Quartier Bilbao is housed inside an old building that used to be a factory store, and much of the industrial feel has been retained. Renovations have, of course, added style, design, and comfort, rendering it a sleek design hostel with an informal, social atmosphere. Some of the popular common areas include the rooftop terrace, a TV lounge with convenient vending machines, and a kitchenette facility where a self-serve continental breakfast is available. All rooms are equipped with air conditioning and crisp bed linens; bunk beds have reading lights, power sockets, and lockers.

For this price point, Quartier Bilbao is a cool boutique hostel with plenty going for it. ⌂

Good to know

PRICE RANGE
$ $ $ $ $
AMENITIES INCLUDE
linens; kitchenette; air conditioning; lockers; rooftop terrace; TV lounge with vending machines. Breakfast included (self-service, continental).

Tip: Explore Bilbao's iconic Casco Viejo, the city's old town. This charming pedestrian area is right by Ribera Market, Santiago Cathedral, and Plaza Nueva.

Boutique Hostel Forum

Situated right in the heart of Zadar's old town, guests at the Hostel Forum wake up to views of the ancient Roman Forum and over 3,000 years of history.

The hostel itself has an eye-catching design and color palette, with blue and orange featured prominently throughout the building. "Zadar blue," as it is called, reflects the cobalt blue sky above and the crystal clear Adriatic Sea below. The orange reflects the vibrant color of the sunset here, once referred to as "the most beautiful in the world" by Alfred Hitchcock.

The en suite four-bed dorms with Japanese capsule-style pods—each with pull-down blinds, power points, a reading light, and personal mirror—offer guests complete privacy. Guests who choose a dormitory receive a free breakfast packed to go. If you are traveling with loved ones, you have the choice of more intimate private twin rooms with panoramic views of the sprawling Adriatic in the distance. ⌂

Good to know

PRICE RANGE
$ $ $ $ $
AMENITIES INCLUDE
linens; towels; 24-hour reception; free WiFi; laundry service; iron and ironing board; air conditioning; vending machine; self-catering; power adapter. Breakfast included.

Tip: An excellent all-you-can-eat breakfast buffet is included in the price, enjoy a great selection of meats, cheeses, bread, burek, juice, yogurt, and coffee.

Sunset Destination Hostel

Situated in an art deco heritage building that also houses the Cais do Sodré Station, this hostel enjoys a fantastic location by the Tagus River. Surrounded by an urban garden, the rooftop pool with unrivaled views of the river below is the star feature of this hostel.

The design here is eclectic, combining offbeat contemporary items, mixed motifs, and generous accessories. The quirky dorm beds, for instance, are made from recycled wood inspired by the owner's trip to Cappadocia.

The rooms here are a mix of dorms and privates, some with views and en suite facilities. Every guest has access to a locker with key and padlock.

Sunset Destination is a fantastic hostel choice. It has a delicious free breakfast, friendly staff with insight into Lisbon, and the stylish Zebra Bar on the rooftop terrace. Enjoy a cocktail with new hostel friends while watching the sunset over the Tagus River. ⌂

Good to know

PRICE RANGE
$ $ $ $ $
AMENITIES INCLUDE
24-hour reception; free WiFi; luggage storage; laundry service; self-catering facilities; dining area; rooftop terrace; bar; swimming pool.

Tip: Enjoy a cocktail with new hostel friends at the stylish Zebra Bar on the rooftop terrace while watching the sunset over the Tagus River.

Tattva Design Hostel

Good to know

PRICE RANGE
$ $ $ $ $
AMENITIES INCLUDE
free WiFi and internet access; laundry facilities; lockers with free locks; keycard access; wheelchair access; elevator; air conditioning; large orthopedic beds; individual curtains for privacy; en suite bathrooms; heaters; individual fans; bar; restaurant; lounge; terrace.

Tip: Try Porto's most famous dish at the restaurant: francesinha. And for lucky summer travelers, be sure to take advantage of the terrace bar, where you can enjoy seasonal barbecues.

Tattva Design Hostel is in a stylish, blue-tiled building located just around the corner from São Bento station in Porto. Distilling the concept of hip hotels into an affordable hostel for budget travelers, Tattva Design Hostel took two world heritage-listed buildings and gave them a creative, contemporary makeover.

Framed around the five classical elements—earth, water, sky, fire, and air—the hostel stikes a nice balance with bold but not overpowering colors to create a sense of comfort and calm. Nice furnishings and beautiful light fixtures showcase the thought that has gone into making the hostel a comfortable and intimate living space.

With beds for 116 people, all the rooms at Tattva—from dorms to doubles—feature en suite bathrooms. Stylish dorms are a popular value-for-money option and feature orthopedic beds, individual curtains in each bed, good heaters, individual fans (depending on the season), and spacious individual lockers with free locks. The in-house lounge is pleasant and has a long aquarium showcasing exotic fish, while the restaurant serves up everything from chicken curry to Porto's most famous dish: *francesinha*. Be sure to take advantage of the terrace bar; lucky summer travelers can enjoy seasonal barbecues there. ⌂

Madrid: radiating liveliness

The soul of Madrid is its people. Their *bright and welcoming nature* will win your heart over between tapas and canas.

I will admit that I didn't love Madrid at first sight. While it doesn't share the same aesthetic appeal as other Spanish cities, such as Barcelona or Granada, Madrid's natural energy and incredible gastronomic scene certainly makes up for it. I would spend a week here now, just to explore the amazing tapas bars and nightlife, which is on par with the best cities in the world. As a culture vulture, I love dipping into Madrid's rich art scene and wonderful mix of markets, as well as relaxing in its beautiful parks. There is so much to discover, yet so little time, and Madrid always leaves me wanting more.

Where to eat

I love to start my day at Mamá Framboise in the Justicia district, just a stone's throw away from the Room007 hostel. Without exaggeration, this is possibly one of the best bakeries I have ever been to. The hot chocolate is delectable, the macarons are the finest I've tasted outside Paris, and the signature almond croissant is the bomb.

Madrid is home to some of the world's greatest tapas bars. The best way to soak up the scene (after visiting El Rastro flea market) is to amble through the picturesque streets of La Latina, joining the locals on their Sunday ritual of bar hopping. The quality of food in this barrio is amazing, so you can't go wrong. I recommend the lovingly restored Posada de la Villa and the warm and colorful La Perejila, where they serve excellent vermouth and pulpo a la gallega, which is Galician-style octopus served on a bed of creamy mashed potato and bread. →

It's food heaven, my friends. For breakfast, lunch, dinner, or a 4 a.m. bite after clubbing, do not leave Madrid without checking out Chocolatería San Ginés, which makes some of the finest churros and porras with chocolate. This stuff will blow your mind and belly, but not your wallet.

On Calle de Ventura de la Vega you'll find the lovely Saporem restaurant, next door to Room007 Chueca. It's a good place if you want a break from Spanish food. Start with one of the excellent mojitos, followed by a stone-baked pizza or delicious pasta. Great value, great service, and a beautiful post-industrial interior.

There's nothing like exploring a neighborhood through the eyes of a local, so I highly recom- mend Devour Madrid Food Tours. I took a fun and fact-filled 3.5-hour tour through the nooks and crannies of the Huertas neighborhood. Aside from a great literary heritage, Huertas has some of the city's finest and most historic eateries. It's a journey through the real heart of Spanish cuisine, from drinking the finest vermouth to tasting the most delicious jamón ibérico and savoring porras with chocolate.

Where to drink

If you like your bars laid-back and quirky, then you will love El Imperfecto in the Barrio de las Letras neighborhood. The super-cheap mojitos are some of the best in Madrid.

There is a strong culture of drinking vermouth in the Spanish capital, and one of the best places to sample this herb-steeped fortified wine is Bodega de la Ardosa in Malasaña. Serving locals since 1892, this bar also does an excellent tortilla and artichokes a la plancha.

Where to party

Nightlife in Spain is not for the faint of heart, and in Madrid it is normal to go out late in the evening and return home at 7 a.m. But what else is there to do in a city brimming with bars?

A good place for those on a budget is Malasaña, an area of small, unique bars frequented by students and others mindful of their budget. I like Café La Palma. The evergreen favorite amongst locals has friendly staff,

live music, and everything from cocktails to tea and cake. Then there is Ojalá, whose neon lights have a very Warholian feel, and where it's possible to get a glass of wine for only a few euros. For an otherworldly experience, try La Catrina Cantina, a Mexican bar with a fascinating display of statues.

Cuevas Sésamo is a piano bar hidden away in an underground cellar. Patrons sit around little red tables chatting away while waiters in old-fashioned uniforms weave back and forth from the bar. Under Franco it was a gathering place for left-wing intellectuals. Luckily for customers today, prices remain suitably socialist. For good live music, try Café Jazz Populart where I had the pleasure of seeing the unusual spectacle of a solo harmonica player giving a virtuoso jazz performance. Anyone who dared to ignore it was swiftly shushed by the staff. Entrance is free but be wary of the pricey drinks.

Going for a walk

I love going for a walk in Parque de El Retiro, where all locals come to relax. Its centerpiece is the magnificent Palacio de Cristal, a beautiful glass and metal building built in 1887, which is great to wander around at sunset. Plus, it's free! Do pop into Palacio de Velázquez next door, a beautiful building that frequently hosts art exhibi- tions, also for free. The park has a magnificent lake where you can hire and row your own boat.

The best place to relax

I find the wide, open spaces of the museums the perfect place to meditate and escape the madness of the city. Madrid is blessed with some wonderful galleries, and Museo Nacional-Thyssen-Bornemisza is probably my favorite. I love its eclectic and varied collection that includes Munch, Van Gogh, Monet, Picasso, Dalí, Tintoretto, Hopper, and Lichtenstein. It is housed in the beautiful Palacio de Villahermosa, a perfect example of Madrid's eighteenth-century neoclassical architecture. →

A s a culture vulture, I love dipping into Madrid's rich art scene and wonderful mix of markets, as well as relaxing in its beautiful parks. There is so much to discover, yet so little time, and Madrid always leaves me wanting more.

Best viewpoint

Palacio de Cibeles overlooks the iconic fountain of Plaza de Cibele—where Real Madrid supporters celebrate their victories—and it offers one of the best panoramic views of the city.

On a sunny day, I love heading up to the rooftop bar of Círculo de Bellas Artes, a nonprofit cultural organization that offers everything from classes and lectures to exhibitions and concerts. The magnificent 360-degree view of Madrid is worth the pricey drinks.

> » For one of the most iconic views of Madrid's skyline head up to the cafeteria of El Corte Inglés in Callao. «

RUT SAGRERA
— TOC Hostels Madrid

Secret places

One of my favorite secret spots is the small town of Segovia, a short train ride from Madrid and a living museum that includes a Roman aqueduct, sixteenth-century cathedral, and a castle that inspired Walt Disney. If the weather is good, there is nothing better than spending an entire day wandering Segovia's narrow, medieval streets. The bus from the train station stops at the foot of the aqueduct. To reach Plaza Mayor, follow the aqueduct and take the street on the right to head up the hill. The cathedral is hard to miss. Other sights include the old Jewish quarter and the aforementioned Alcázar castle.

TOC Hostels Madrid

Tip: If you want to go out in the town, a good spot to see and be seen is Plaza Mayor, only a short walk away from TOC. This main square is packed with tapas bars and restaurants— a nice introduction to Spanish atmosphere.

Located near Puerta del Sol, TOC Madrid is situated in a beautifully preserved heritage building dating back to the nineteenth century. The mixture of classical and modern design gives this hostel edge.

A key feature here includes a very cool on-site bar and lounge with original fresco paintings on the ceiling and preserved architecture giving the place a regal touch. During the day, the bar is a nice place to have a coffee, read a book, or catch up with friends. At night, the place becomes a lot more lively; besides beer, wine, and soft drinks, there's a nice range of cocktails. There is also a pool table in the games room adjoining the bar where you can hang out and socialize. There's an on-site mini market for essentials—and a nice communal lounge with TV. There is a choice of rooms at TOC. The six-bed dorm is great value; it's stylish and comfortable, plus guests are given large storage lockers for their belongings.

For a no-nonsense stay with a distinctly Spanish flourish, TOC Madrid is a winning stop for your holiday.

La Banda Rooftop Hostel

Good to know

PRICE RANGE
$ $ $ $ $
AMENITIES INCLUDE
self-catering facilities;
sun terrace; rooftop
garden; lounge; bar.
Breakfast included.

*Tip: Ask the staff
about an excellent
free walking tour
(tips are welcomed)
of Seville's historic
sights during the day,
and the late evening
tour around the
city's Jewish Quarter.*

Overlooking Seville cathedral, La Banda Rooftop Hostel is focused on celebrating music and the arts. The hostel's centerpiece is the amazing rooftop terrace where, every evening, guests gather together to watch the sunset over the cathedral spires in the distance whilst sipping on mojitos and enjoying performances from local bands. Then, after tucking into an excellent, affordable dinner, the hostel staff take guests on free tours of some of their favorite haunts in Seville. This is not your run-of-the-mill hostel pub crawl; think old man bars, ancient sherry bars, and smoky local haunts that haven't changed for years. There are also organized flamenco nights out; email in advance to check when they take place.

La Banda is a proper backpacker-style hostel: The on-site rooms are dorms only. They have seven mixed dorms ranging from four to eight beds. If you're looking for a superior dorm experience, definitely book a bed in one of their boutique dorms, which feature en suite bathrooms and beautiful, handmade wooden beds. If you are traveling with family or a partner, you can choose an off-site luxury apartment, they're just a few hundred yards away.

A free breakfast is provided in the downstairs lounge. There's also an excellent communal kitchen.

Ask the staff about an excellent free walking tour (tips are welcomed) of Seville's historic sights during the day, and the late evening tour around the city's Jewish Quarter. ⌂

Mountain Hostel Tarter

It's road access only at this tranquil mountain escape

Nestled in the Andorran mountains, this beautiful abode has one of the most picturesque settings in the world. Mountain Hostel Tarter is a spectacular, rural mountain retreat only a stone's throw away from Grandvalira.

In developing the hostel's ethos, the owners incorporated a great amount of respect for the natural setting the hostel benefits from, as well as the building's cultural heritage. The traditional rural mountain house that is home to Mountain Hostel Tarter is over 200 years old. Such Andorran mountain buildings are called "bordas." Built in the eighteenth century, it has been renovated multiple times over the years; at one time it was a storage facility for working animals (mules and cows), at another a place for crop storage, and now it's a hub for your Andorra adventure. The original structure has been maintained wherever possible; the beautiful stone walls, wooden beams, and slate roofs are still intact. The resulting structure merges seamlessly with the environment. Despite being two centuries old, the hostel has many twenty-first century additions and includes all manner of comforts.

New renovations include several environmentally conscious choices: The hostel's hot water is heated via solar energy, as is the water in the outdoor pool-jacuzzi. Energy-saving radiators, mainly composed of →

Good to know

PRICE RANGE
$ $ $ $ $
AMENITIES INCLUDE
free linens; free WiFi;
self-catering facilities;
outdoor heated
swim-spa (swimming
pool and hot tub);
mini-mart; chill indoor
area with fireplace; TV;
board games; outdoor
terrace; barbecue;
free tea and coffee.

Tip: Mountain
Hostel Tarter
is the perfect place
to spend some
time outdoors.
Whether you like
to ski, snowboard,
cycle, or hike!

» For us, it is not enough just to create *a perfect hostel* in Andorra, where you can enjoy mountain sports and share experiences with other travelers. For us, it is all pointless if we do not commit to our shared environment, culture and natural heritage. «

silicon and aluminum oxide, help optimize heating performance and the radiator is additionally designed to maintain heat for an extended period of time with reduced consumption. Lastly, the premises have been retrofitted to avoid unnecessary heat loss and subsequent energy waste.

Mountain Hostel Tarter is the perfect place to spend some time outdoors. The beauty of the Andorran mountains will assail you in every season, from the white-clad mountain peaks in the winter to the green verdant beauty of summer mountain scenery—be prepared to be awe-struck. Whether you're skiing, snowboarding, cycling, mountain biking, or hiking, you can be assured

of well-earned comfort back at your temporary home.

There are plenty of activities to be enjoyed at Mountain Hostel Tarter. After a long day of vigorous outdoor activity, there's simply nothing better than slipping into the hostel's heated swimming pool and hot tub. With majestic mountains looming in the distance, and the hot water soothing any aches or pains in your body, your evening will feel full of luxury.

There is also an indoor area complete with crackling fireplace; hang out on a beanbag chair, watch TV, peruse the books, or play a board game. If it's warm out, there's an outdoor terrace with hammocks and provisions for a barbecue. A fully equipped common kitchen enables

you to serve up home-cooked meals. The hostel has an on-site mini mart with a good selection of snacks, a variety of drinks and juices, sandwich ingredients, pasta sauces, and pizza. If you order a day in advance, you can even get fresh bread and croissants. Guests can also buy wine from the hostel's in-house wine cellar.

Bed linens are included and rooms are either doubles or shared dorms accommodating four to six people. Bathrooms are shared.

Mountain Hostel Tarter is a five-star experience designed for travelers by travelers. You will experience the best of the Andorran mountains here, while staying in the lap of nature's beauty.

Foodie cities

For treating your taste buds

Food is the number one reason people travel, whether it's feasting on an aperitivo buffet with locals in Milan, sipping on port and indulging in a three-course Portuguese meal, or trying a typical chicken and rice broth with fresh vegetables for breakfast in Bangkok. If you like following your belly to explore the world, these hostels are highly recommended.

Ostello Bello, Milan

*T*ake a sip of the cherry liqueur Ginjinha in Lisbon, Portugal and stay at the Independente <u>Hostel & Suites</u> (p. 8), or discover the hearty Francesinha sandwich, which was born in Porto, Portugal and stay at <u>Gallery Hostel</u> (p. 32) or <u>The House of Sandeman Hostel & Suites</u> (p. 22). Salmorejo is perfect for a hot day in Córdoba, Spain, and you can find a great one at <u>Option Be Hostel</u> (p. 54). While Aperol Spritz and aperitivo snacks can help you cool off in Milan, Italy at <u>Ostello Bello</u> (p. 140). Try lots of different tapas in Seville, Spain at <u>TOC Hostel Seville</u> (p. 65), or enjoy fresh pad thai in Bangkok, Thailand at Yim Yam Hostel & Garden (p. 284). The best barbecue with everything you could desire (including the beach) is in Cape Town, South Africa at <u>Once in Cape Town</u> (p. 214). For ice-cream lovers, there is no place like Rome, Italy, stay there at <u>The Beehive Hostel</u> (p. 143).

TOC Hostel Seville, Seville

Food is the *number one reason* people travel, whether it's feasting on an aperitivo buffet in Milan, or trying a typical chicken and rice broth for breakfast in Bangkok.

Yim Yam Hostel & Garden, Bangkok

Independente Hostel & Suites, Lisbon

Amistat Island Hostel

A trendy hangout in party central

Europe's premier party destination now has its own design hostel with the colorful and chic Amistat Island Hostel. Right in the center of Sant Antoni, 200 meters from Caló des Moro beach, and close to legendary venues such as the famous Café del Mar, Golden Buddha, Kasbah, and Ibiza Rocks—this hostel is the perfect base to explore Ibiza.

Laid-back and affordable, you'll find a mix of well-designed dorms and stylish doubles at Amistat, as well as cool common areas like the lounge and rooftop terrace—popular meeting points for guests. But the outstanding feature here is the outdoor swimming pool and poolside bar.

Each of the five hostel floors at Amistat has theme-based decor, with the iconography inspired by heaven and hell. The hostel has a fully equipped training room with a projector, screen, and sound system, a small library, a restaurant, and a community kitchen where guests can cook.

This hostel is well suited to groups and hosts a variety of activities, including: language exchanges, pilates and fitness sessions, workshops on healthy cooking, free walking tours, yoga, and sunset boat trips.

Amistat Island Hostel is a smart choice for travelers looking for an affordable, boutique experience on Ibiza.

Good to know

PRICE RANGE
$ $ $ $ $

AMENITIES INCLUDE
self-catering facilities;
laundry facilities;
bicycle rentals; bar;
pool; restaurant; cinema
room; training room;
reception; private rooms;
shared rooms.

Tip: This hostel is well
suited to groups and
hosts a variety of
activities, including:
language exchanges,
pilates and fitness
sessions, workshops on
healthy cooking, free
walking tours, yoga,
and sunset boat trips.

Option Be Hostel

A design hostel just like home

Option Be, José Fabra Garrido's second hostel in Córdoba incorporates the homely and modern, minimalist, Scandi-vibe of its sister hostel, Córdoba Bed And Be, and adds the fun factor with a rooftop terrace and plunge pool. Just like at Bed And Be, the emphasis here is not just on great design, but more importantly, on making guests feel at home.

With an emphasis on homey vibes, the place is stripped of all the fluff you tend to find in your typical boutique hostel—no velvet sofas, designer lamps, or large suites. Instead there's lots of retro-style furniture, comfy beanbags, and some quirky touches like wooden pots and bowls, and personalized key rings engraved by hand with the motto "Be At Home." These details were created in collaboration with Pontevedra-based Miolos Design who also assisted in the building's restoration. Elements from the original tenant Casa Patio were retained, such as the exposed brick arch walls and some of the old stones, which guests can view beneath the glass floor.

Guests can take sanctuary from the piercing Córdoban heat in their beautiful patio-cum-lounge covered with patterned chairs, beanbags, honesty bar, nice selection of books and magazines, plus lots of potted plants. "This is the kind of place you would love to have in your own house!" Garrido says.

Centrally situated in a historic district, hostel guests can also relax on the lovely rooftop terrace and enjoy panoramic views of the city and the Mezquita. This is the perfect place to curl up with a book and soak in the sun with a drink from the mini →

Good to know

PRICE RANGE
$ $ $ $ $
AMENITIES INCLUDE
linens; WiFi and internet
access; security lockers;
24-hour reception;
elevator; housekeeping;
common room; meeting
room; steam room;
air conditioning;
self-catering facilities;
fridge / freezer. Free
breakfast included.

*Tip: Rent a bike to get
yourself around the
city, and cross the
Roman bridge at night
to enjoy the amazing
view. Wake up early
to enjoy the Cathedral
Mosque and the
Alcazar for free!*

The emphasis here is not just on great design but more importantly on making guests *feel at home.*

bar downstairs. Or, if you're feeling the intense Andalusian heat and need to cool down, you can take a refreshing dip in the plunge pool.

Every day at 8:30 p.m., all the guests from Bed And Be and Option Be meet together for drinks and tapas with both hostels' staff members. Besides offering an authentic taste of Córdoba, this event is a great way to meet travelers and bond over a shared love of good food and travel. To feel at home when traveling is a luxury—that is where this hostel excels. This intimate hostel has just 10 rooms: a mix of en suite twins, doubles, and shared dorms for four and eight people. All the beds come

with individual lockers, a reading light, and a power point for charging gadgets. The mattresses here are really comfortable, and the bathrooms are spotless.

There's no rush to wake up here—no matter the hour, you can enjoy a free, typical Spanish breakfast of bread, coffee, jams, Nutella, and fresh orange juice.

The staff here are friendly and helpful, and with a great location in Córdoba, a fully equipped kitchen, beautiful interiors, free well-functioning WiFi, and excellent evening drinks and tapas tours, Option Be is a great hostel to call home when visiting Córdoba. ⌂

Barcelona: seaside flair

Inspiring architecture, fantastic flavors, year-round great weather, and so many *awesome things* to do any time of the day.

I recommend visiting El Nacional on glamorous Passeig de Gràcia—pricey but worth it. This venue has four different restaurants, so you can sample the full spectrum of Spanish cuisine while mingling with trendy Barcelonans.

Teresa Carles is one of the best-known vegetarian restaurants in the city—and for good reason. With lotus-flower chips, artichoke-filled crunchy crepes, and seitan burgers on the menu, there are lots of wholesome and tasty dishes to choose from at reasonable prices. The owners have also opened sister restaurant Flax & Kale a few meters away for those who prefer a flexitarian option.

Barcelona has some wonderful food markets, but I suggest avoiding the touristy La Boqueria Mercat at all costs. A good alternative is neighboring Mercat de Santa Caterina. If possible, take a look at the brightly colored roof of this building, which is truly unique. I'm also a big fan of Mercat de l'Abaceria, which remains devoid of tourists.

What to do

From beach volleyball and open-air vintage markets to street parties, fiestas, and carnivals, what is there not to love about Barcelona? Just like the great architect Antoni Gaudí, Barcelonans have a zest for challenging boundaries and living life to the fullest. Here are some tips to help you make the most of your time in the vanguardist capital of Catalonia.

Where to eat

If you are a foodie like me, make a stop at Jai-Ca, an authentic seafood bar tucked away just a few blocks from the seafront. Packed mainly with locals, it specializes in an excellent selection of thoroughly unhealthy, delicious Spanish tapas. Highlights include the pulpo (octopus), patatas bravas (potatoes), razor clams, and Jai-Ca's signature snails.

» Our favorite tapas bar is Dar Canete. This place is amazing! At the high end for the tapas scene, it is a blend of traditional tapas and luxury dining, but really not unaffordable, and certainly worth every penny. «

LEIGHTON SHUEY
— Sant Jordi Hostels

Where to drink

Barcelonans love to meet for an aperitivo before lunch, which is the perfect excuse for having a bite to eat and drinking vermouth in the middle of the day. Bar Calders is a local favorite but be warned, the delicious Gin Tonic del Diputat is so cheap it could get you drunk before noon. Order some nachos to avoid drinking on an empty stomach.

If La Barceloneta's balmy sea air is making you thirsty, you'll be glad to know that the streets to the harbor are jam packed with interesting spots to visit. I am a big fan of trippy Absenta Bar, which has a cool vibe with lots of weird and wonderful memorabilia dedicated to the nectar of the green fairy. It is certainly one of the most unique drinking establishments in town.

Moritz is one of the quintessential beers of the city and it has its own brewery, Fàbrica Moritz, which was refurbished a few years ago. It now hosts a multidisciplinary space where you can attend events, buy books, have some food, and, of course, have a beer.

My last tip is for all the football lovers. If you're out of luck scoring a ticket to Camp Nou but want to hang with the locals and watch the game, head to Nou Can Codina. They show the Barça games on the big screen and serve excellent vermouth.

Where to party

Kick off your night in style at Plaça Reial. The world-famous square has palm trees and ornate street lamps, and it's vibrant buzz makes it a perfect meeting point for travelers. Plaça Reial is also home to great bars such as Sidecar, Pipa Club, and my favorite,

Jamboree—a prime blues and jazz music venue, which, after midnight, transforms into a nightclub with two dance floors.

Sala Apolo is another icon of the Barcelona nightlife scene, hosting a different party every night of the week. It used to be an old theater, so the venue itself is amazing.

If you want to stay outdoors, keep an eye out for the various *festes de barri* (neighborhood parties) across the city. These festivals originated in the tradition of Barcelonans getting together in plazas to chat with old and new friends, listen to rumba, or dine together. Each district hosts its own party on a different weekend, so there's up to 70 of these going on throughout the year.

If you want to discover Barcelona's more unusual side, check out O'Barquiño. It may seem like an everyday dive bar, but head up to the second floor on weekends when regulars get together to dance, sing, and perform. If you don't speak Spanish it might get lost in translation, but the energy and spectacle are worth the visit.

Going for a walk

With more than 3 miles (4.5 kilometers) of coastline, a trip to Barcelona offers a city break and quality time by the sea with excellent beaches to choose from. I have to admit I am not much of a beach person, but Barceloneta is my favorite spot for a stroll. It is a beautiful place with palm trees swaying seductively in the gentle Mediterranean breeze—and the city's fishing district has a boozy, boisterous charm that is hard to resist.

Las Ramblas is another landmark. When I first came to Barcelona in 2004, walking the length of Las Ramblas was a real treat for the senses. It's a great introduction to the city, but be careful—it is also home to pickpockets, scam artists, and tacky souvenirs.

For something quieter, the hill of Montjuïc has a lot to offer. Start at Plaça d'Espanya and follow the road. You'll come across two major museums (Museu Nacional d'Art de Catalunya and CaixaForum Barcelona), an Olympic stadium, Greek amphitheater (Teatre Grec), Montjuïc Castle, and some of the best views in town. Once you've reached the top, enjoy a break from the madness of the city before walking all the way down to the port.

Getting around town

There is no better way to get around Barcelona than the metro. Almost everywhere in the city is only 30 minutes away. It's cheap and trains come every three minutes.

To navigate the port, jump on board a Las Golondrinas pleasure boat. It is one of the oldest tourist attractions and the tour lasts 40 minutes, offering a different perspective of the harbor and fresh sea breezes on hot summer days.

Where to relax

The Fundació Joan Miró, hidden in Montjuïc, is a modern art museum with beautiful architecture, lovely quiet gardens, and an impressive art collection by Joan Miró. Not many tourists make it here, especially during the week, so it's a great place to relax.

> » On a warm day, Parc de la Ciutadella is the place to go if you don't want to deal with the craziness of the beach. Lie in the sun or find a spot →

From beach volleyball and open-air vintage markets to street parties, fiestas, and carnivals, what is there *not to love* about Barcelona? Just like the great architect Antoni Gaudí, Barcelonans have a zest for challenging boundaries and *living life to the fullest.*

is where the locals go. Bring along some beers, a bottle of wine, some snacks, and friends. This place is for chilling out and enjoying an amazing atmosphere with a 360-degree view of Barcelona.

Secret places

Plaça de Sant Felip Neri is a quiet and romantic plaza in the busy Barri Gotic (Gothic Quarter). It's beautiful, but also has a lot of history. If you look closely at the walls, you'll see battle scars from the Civil War.

Gràcia, originally a village that marked the city limit of Barcelona, still retains its charming feel with narrow streets and leafy squares. It's home to the beautiful Casa Gràcia Hostel, and I love eating and drinking my way around the historic Plaça de la Vila de Gràcia, with its famous clock tower and town hall.

in the shade. The park is filled with life, jugglers, slack-liners, families, locals, tourists, a bit of everything, but it is not over-crowded and has a peaceful vibe. «

LEIGHTON SHUEY
– Sant Jordi Hostels

Best viewpoint

Head to Tibidabo, one of the oldest amusement parks in Europe. It's a world of fantasy and reality with its hanging airplane ride, carousels, and charming cathedral. Take the century-old funicular to get up the mountain and enjoy seeing the city spread out at your feet—it's a memorable experience.

If you're looking for something more chill, Los Bunkers del Carmen

Casa Gracia

At home in culture and luxury

Located at the top of Barcelona's historic Passeig de Gràcia—an avenue known for its beautiful architecture, ornate benches, and street lights—Casa Gracia is a home away from home. Within walking distance of the city center, the surrounding neighborhood is graced with iconic buildings of art nouveau fame, notably Gaudí's La Pedrera and Casa Batlló.

Casa Gracia's ethos focuses on providing guests with a homey, comforting experience. The hostel is a reasonable distance away from the chaos of La Rambla, the Gothic Quarter, and the scourge of pickpockets, providing rest and respite for weary travelers.

Casa Gracia is housed in an unassuming building, one reminiscent of older, art deco-style Manhattan apartments. Guests will feel swept back in time as they enter through a beautiful wrought-iron gate and step into the stylish, art deco elevator. Inside, snowy white walls arch up to a high ceiling and fluted Corinthian columns grace the rooms of what is otherwise a remarkably modern hostel. Guests can choose from a range of spacious rooms: shared dorms, private bedrooms, or apartments. All rooms enjoy large, luxurious en suite bathrooms. The superior rooms have balcony views of the humming, grand boulevard.

One of the most striking aspects of Casa Gracia is its identity as a gastro-cultural hostel. Guests are treated to mouthwatering fare—especially "vrunch" (brunch with a side of vermouth) on Saturdays.

The terrace is a lovely social space; candlelit in the evenings, it's the perfect place to wind down with a glass of wine. Take a seat, catch up on the latest hostel chat, and look out over the neighborhood with glimpses of rolling green hills in the distance.

Another communal place is the lounge area, De Tranquis, which is "alcohol-free, shout-free, and kid-free" for relaxed evenings.

Good to know

PRICE RANGE
$ $ $ $ $
AMENITIES INCLUDE
terrace; restaurant;
dance bar; lounge.

Tip: One of the most
striking aspects of
Casa Gracia is its identity
as a gastro-cultural
hostel. Guests are treated
to mouthwatering fare
especially vrunch
(brunch with a side
of vermouth) on
Saturdays. They also
host photography
exhibitions, theatrical
plays, and live
jazz concerts in the
basement bar.

TOC Hostels Barcelona

Good to know

PRICE RANGE
$ $ $ $ $
AMENITIES INCLUDE
linens; towels available;
24-hour reception;
self-catering facilities;
luggage storage; bar;
special events
(exhibitions, silent party,
food workshops, DJ
sets, movie nights).
Breakfast included.

Tip: _Take advantage_
of the city's warm
and long sunny days
on the glorious terrace
with outdoor swimming
pool. There are a bunch
of sunloungers around
the pool area, so, relax,
read, and sunbathe
after having a swim.

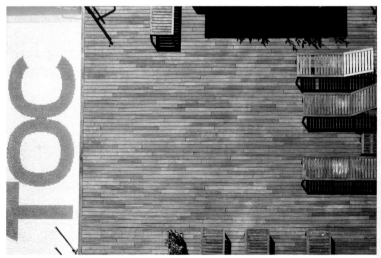

TOC Barcelona and its sister hostels in Madrid and Seville are thematically inspired by _The Dreamers_, Bernardo Bertolucci's film set in Paris during the student revolts in 1968. In line with the movie's plot and characters, the three hostels recreate the feeling of a young, restless group of people seeking space to interact with one another in order to become an active part of their own zeitgeist. Similarly, at TOC Barcelona, guests are invited to interact in a variety of social spaces. Choose between lounging on the chill-out sofas, catching up on emails on beautiful iMacs, watching a movie on the large screen, or challenging a friend to a game of pool.

Whatever budget you're on, there is a room for you here. The dorm rooms are fantastic: The bunk beds are super comfortable, and there is a large locker to store luggage. If you're traveling with friends or family, the four-person rooms are a good choice. Premium suites with a private terrace are on par with any boutique hotel.

TOC is a great place to start and end your day while exploring Barcelona.

TOC Hostels Sevilla

Previously an abandoned building dating to the 70s, this innovative hostel is centrally located right across from Seville Cathedral. TOC Sevilla is a fantastic choice for travelers who are looking for a combination of great design, friendly staff, and...tapas!

The on-site tapas bar alone is a great reason to stay at this hostel. The menu includes traditional tapas like patatas bravas, jamon serrano, croquettes, and local classics like salmorejo an remolacha. For budget-minded travelers, the six to eight-bed dorms are excellent value and don't compromise on quality. Expect en suite bathrooms, air conditioning, plugs beside your bed, reading lights, and a signature fingerprint access system—removing the hassle of carrying keys or room cards. For a bit more privacy, the hotel-style private rooms include writing desks and flat screen TVs with satellite channels.

Some rooms have a private terrace with intimate views of the cathedral. Privates also come with free scented hand wash, a vanity kit, toothbrush, and toothpaste.

The guest kitchen is cozy—small but adequate; a breakfast buffet is available. The on-site 24-hour market sells light meals and drinks. Other amenities include a fabulous mini movie theater and a very nice outdoor terrace for enjoying a drink.

Good to know

PRICE RANGE
$ $ $ $ $
AMENITIES INCLUDE
24-hour reception; laundry facilities; luggage storage; self-catering facilities; safe deposit box in private rooms; free daily walking tour; bar; special events (exhibitions, music nights); pool table; terrace; mini market.

Tip: Try one of the traditional tapas like patatas bravas, jamon serrano, croquettes, and local classics like salmorejo an remolacha at the hostel's on-site tapas bar.

Amsterdam: cosmopolitan canals

Amsterdam, *the Instagram-mable city* of concentric canals and narrow gabled houses squashed side by side, reaching for the sky.

City dwellers out and about on bicycles, snow falling on frozen canals, and scattered leaves forming rust-colored patterns. The neon signs of the red-light district, and the heady smoke from the coffee shops. This is what Amsterdam embodies to me. The heart of the historic city is found in and around the medieval and colonial canals, in the Jewish quarter of Waterlooplein, and the popular De Wallen—but if you scratch beneath the surface, Amsterdam will unveil other surprises.

Where to eat

Dutch cuisine is not all about stroopwafels and bitterballens, although admittedly these are the local foods I sample again and again whenever I visit the city. If you're feeling particularly brave, check out the abundant raw herring carts (haringhandels) scattered across Amsterdam. My favorite is Vishuisje on Herengracht canal where you can get herring with a side of pickles and onions for just three euros. If you simply can't stomach the smell, try kibbeling—bite-sized pieces of deep-fried and battered fishy deliciousness, which are available at haringhandel carts too.

No trip to Amsterdam is complete without some good frites. My search for the best ones led me to Frietsteeg. Crunchy on the outside and soft on the inside, these fries are freshly made on the premises and there is an amazing range of sauces to choose from. Mustard mayo is a winner, as is the curry ketchup.

Amsterdam is a truly cosmo-politan city, so expect to be treated to a wide variety of international cuisine. Bazar is in a converted church and it serves delicious Middle Eastern food. Hop along to Pata Negra for good Spanish tapas, and visit Fou Fow Ramen when in the mood for noodles. Soenda Kelapa is my go-to for Indonesian, and Taco Cartel is, you guessed it, the place for tacos.

→

However, if you've come to Amsterdam to sample local fare, make your way to Geflipt and order the Dutch-style burgers. For a taste of the local pub scene, try Café Slijterij Oosterling, or Bar Fisk.

> » Far from the madding crowds of central Amsterdam, Hotel de Goudfazant is nestled amongst old industrial buildings on the IJ waterfront in Amsterdam Noord. Its seasonal menu is great value, especially considering the quality of what comes out of the kitchen. «
>
> **ANNA HAFSTEINSSON**
> —*Clink Hostels*

sunny terrace at lunchtime and then, come nighttime, head inside and groove until the early hours with an eclectic mix of DJs and live music.

Where to drink & party

The Dutch are famous for their liberal take on some drugs that are restricted in other parts of the world. Therefore, it is not surprising that the cannabis coffee shops attract millions of international visitors annually. Amsterdam is a playground for those wanting to have a good time, and there are bars and parties of every kind and flavor. Some classics are De Marktkantine and Paradiso, and the clubs, cafés, and bars around Leidseplein and Rembrandtplein. Pllek is a trendy industrial hangout on the banks of the IJ River. Its built with used shipping containers and sits on a man-made beach—perfect for enjoying a cocktail or alfresco beer when the sun is shining, as well as live music and other events on offer.

Another recommendation is Pacific Parc, a great day-to-night venue. Grab a spot on its large

Going for a walk

Amsterdam has its fair share of green, open spaces. Vondelpark is undoubtedly the largest and the best known, but there are many other smaller parks where city dwellers can relax. Beatrixpark, Sarphatipark, Oosterpark, Frankendael Park, Rembrandtpark, Westerpark, Flevopark, Amstelpark, Wertheimerpark, and Sloterpark are a few of them.

Westerpark is an urban park west of the city and a perfect blend of greenery and impressive architecture. The converted Westergasfabriek gasworks hosts a number of events, including exhibitions, markets, festivals, shops, an art-house cinema, brewery, and dance club. Noorderpark is a green oasis in the heart of the Noord district. With plenty of trees and green areas, it's a great escape from the hustle and bustle of central Amsterdam.

Getting around town

The best ways to get around Amsterdam are by local tram, walking, or, even better, by bike—like the locals. Biking is quick and convenient and gives you a chance to work off those stroopwaffels!

Amsterdam, and the rest of the Netherlands, also enjoys a fantastic public transport system. The best way to navigate it is to invest in a public transport chip card (OV-chipkaart), which can be used on trams, buses, metros, and trains. You can purchase a non-personal card that can be reused and loaded with credit at any time from multiple and diverse locations.

Where to relax

Amsterdam is the city of serene canals, so what better way to relax than to take in the city's architectural glory from the water. Cocomama offers guests a private canal-boat tour during the summer.

> » There's something very calming about cruising around the city on a canal boat. We love Pure Boats, whose cozy vessels offer a welcome change from the big tourist boats. «
>
> **ANNA HAFSTEINSSON**
> —*Clink Hostels*

What about some floral therapy to inspire peace of mind? A trip to Amsterdam in the spring wouldn't be complete without visiting the tulip fields of the Keukenhof, near Lisse, and enjoying the flowers at the height of their beauty. Like a rainbow strewn across the earth, the rows of variegated colors will assail you. Visit the gardens on a weekday to avoid traffic congestion. →

City dwellers out and about on *bicycles*, snow falling on frozen *canals*, and scattered leaves forming rust-colored patterns. The neon signs of the red-light district, and the heady smoke from the *coffee shops*. This is what Amsterdam embodies to me.

Vondelpark is beautiful in all seasons. If possible, attend a free concert in the open-air theatre, held between May and early September. Listening to music in a natural setting is a great way to bring on that zen feeling.

Best viewpoint

One of the best views in Amsterdam is from A'DAM Lookout (at the top of A'DAM Tower), which is just around the corner from ClinkNOORD. The tower has a great bar where you can sip cocktails and take in the sights and sounds of the city. Not for the faint of heart, Over The Edge is Europe's highest swing and it will provide you with more than an adrenaline rush.

Noorderlicht Café on an old three-masted schooner is another great spot for views over the IJ River. It's easy to sit here for a couple of hours and watch the world go by.

The SkyLounge at Doubletree and the NEMO Science Museum Panorama Terrace are also great options, as is Westerkerk, which has the highest church tower in Amsterdam.

Secret places

Blijburg is a beachside cultural spot just outside the city, where Amsterdammers get together to play, swim, eat, and drink. With live music and festivals throughout the year, it is the best place to feel the breeze and let your hair down!

My other secret is the heavenly food spot De Hapjeshoek, a small Surinamese takeaway tucked away in the depths of Waterlooplein metro station. Whenever I am in Amsterdam, I pop in here for the delicious chicken curry sandwich a.k.a. *kipfilet kerrie broodjes*. It's a bargain!

Cocomama

A themed hostel with a racy past

A beautiful 130-year-old building with high ceilings and chandeliers, a garden complete with picnic tables and gnomes, a cuddly hostel cat called Joop, a kitchen stocked with beers for 1€, a hostel run by a bunch of energetic ladies who know the city like the back of their hands, plus an authentic, not-too-touristy location—what more could one want from a hostel in Amsterdam?

Just a 20-minute walk from Amsterdam's red-light district, Cocomama's location was itself once the site of one of the city's most famous brothels, Yab Yum. Guests can view pictures of the flamboyant former owner and his girls at the entrance, as well as a few pairs of racy, lacy underwear hanging alongside it as a tongue-in-cheek reference to the building's history.

All the rooms here are decorated with traditional Dutch themes: "Tulips," "Van Gogh," "Royal," and "Cow and Milk." If you're on a budget but still looking for a unique experience, you can stay in the "Windmill" six-bed dorm. With triple-decker, custom-made bunks, each bed in this room comes with its own privacy curtain, reading light, power outlet, and secret compartment. There is an en suite bathroom and large luggage lockers too. If you're looking for more privacy, you can choose one of the five private double rooms, which are all en suite and come with a queen-sized bed, linens, towels, toiletries by Stop The Water While Using Me!, a hair dryer, and tea and coffee making facilities.

Being a boutique hostel, Cocomama does not cater for large groups—maximum group size is four. This means that the hostel audience is primarily comprised of solo travelers who are keen to mix and socialize with other guests. Expect the style of a high-end hotel without the stiff formality and expensive prices. Guests often gather in the cozy kitchen/living room, the focal social point of the hostel.

Some hostels are a great base to explore and discover a city; some, like Cocomama, really feel like home. ⌂

Good to know

PRICE RANGE
$ $ $ $ $
AMENITIES INCLUDE
common area; awesome staff; self-catering facilities; cuddly house cat; bicycle rentals; geek book exchange; chill-out garden; theme rooms.

Tip: To give you the best possible experience of Amsterdam, Cocomama staff organize a bunch of awesome events. Ranging from tours of the red-light district to favorite nightlife hotspots on weekends— you'll be kept busy here.

King Kong Hostel

A trendy stay in Rotterdam's laid-back social hub

A hip spot combining industrial design with contemporary art, King Kong Hostel is right in the heart of Rotterdam's bustling city center. Right on the bustling Witte de Wittestraat, the hostel has infamous roots: The building dates back to 1872 and once housed a tattoo shop, an illegal casino, and a famous brothel.

One of King Kong's key features are the hip and trendy rooms. The bright colors, wood, and natural materials help create a cozy-but-cool ambience. There are 23 rooms in total with a range of dorm sizes—all with en suite bathrooms (and rain showers!)—and three private hotel-style rooms.

The rooftop Loft Dorm is a highlight. If you ever wanted a grand sleepover with all your closest friends in the world, this would be the room. With over 48 beds, it sounds quite chaotic but the beds are spread out nicely, and you feel like you have your own space. The triangular windows provide both pleasant light and views over the city center. In between are unique spaces where you can use old school gym equipment, or relax in the smattering of brightly colored hammocks or beanbags. Each bed has a nightlight, lockable storage trunk, and electrical outlet.

There are several options if you want to stay in a private room: the Full House (sleeps four) and the Kong Meis (named after a local artist duo, with access to a record player and Netflix; sleeps two). But the best one has to be the Lovers Loft. The double bed is in a loft, accessible by a →

Breakfast	
Coffee	2.20
Espresso	2.20
Double Espresso	3.00
Cappuccino	2.70
Espresso Machiatto	2.50
Soya Latte	3.40
Latte	2.90
Flat white	3.50
Regular Tea	1.30
Fresh mint tea	2.80
Chai Latte	3.50
Ice Coffee	3.50
Hand...	3.50
Ice	3.50

Good to know

PRICE RANGE
$ $ $ $ $
AMENITIES INCLUDE
self-catering facilities;
laundry facilities; movie
lounge; café; restaurant;
bar with terrace.
Breakfast not included.

*Tip: If you ever
wanted a grand
sleepover
with all your closest
friends in the world,
be sure to sleep in
the rooftop Loft Dorm.
With over 48 beds,
it sounds quite chaotic
but the beds are
spread out nicely, and
you feel like you have
your own space.*

A hip spot combining industrial design with contemporary art, *King Kong Hostel* is right in the heart of Rotterdam's bustling city center.

wooden ladder; up there you have an amazing view of Rotterdam's skyline (and a curtain for privacy).

The lobby has an excellent barista station—the coffee and homemade lemonade is great. There's a comfortable seating area where you can relax and chat with people, or simply watch the comings and goings of locals on Witte de Witt through the huge bay window.

There is a stylish open-plan kitchen-cum-dining area downstairs; kitchen facilities are open for guest use except during breakfast hours from 6:30 a.m. to 10:30 a.m. The dining area has communal picnic tables with wide benches if you're feeling social, or more intimate tables for two.

There's a fresh breakfast buffet, which includes: fresh slices of bread, croissants, scrambled eggs, yogurt, fresh juice, milk, cereal, fresh fruit, coffee, and tea.

Coffee and tea is free for guests from 8 a.m. to 11 a.m., and if you feel peckish during the day, there's a nice selection of sandwiches, wraps, salads, side dishes, and drinks to purchase.

There's a basement hangout below the kitchen with lots of pillows and a nice sofa. It's a great place to chill and watch your favorite TV shows or movies on Netflix after a long day of sightseeing in Rotterdam. There's a movie night at 8 p.m. every evening, with free popcorn.

The hostel proudly claims that their WiFi is "faster than Usain Bolt," and this is true to some extent. There's a large reading table with computers and outlets for your own laptop and other electronic appliances in the lobby. The staff at King Kong are super friendly and helpful. Besides giving you great tips on places to eat and drink, they help guests with other essentials, like printing out boarding passes and tickets, free of charge. △

Ecomama

Green, quirky, cozy, and conscious sleeping

Ecomama is the green and luxurious update to its sister hostel, the fabulous Cocomama. Whether traveling with friends, on a romantic weekend, or looking for luxury while exploring the world, Ecomama covers all the bases. The seven different types of room cater to all types of travelers on any budget. The owners have put a lot of thought into profiling guests to find the perfect room. For example, if you are a solo female traveler in need of some girl time, then the women-only dorm is perfect for you. If you're looking for an ideal romantic weekend, then the double deluxe is a good fit. For flashpackers on a budget who still

want privacy, there are windowless double cabin rooms with a shared bathroom. Ecomama's eight-bed dorm is probably the most luxurious dorm you will ever sleep in. Each room comes with fine linen and soap by Stop The Water While Using Me!

This hostel has a humanitarian aspect too. For every night you stay here, Ecomama donates 1€ to a good cause, such as Niños de Guatemala, a nonprofit organization aiming to help impoverished communities in Guatemala through education and entrepreneurship.

Ecomama is more than just a place to crash: It has impressive green credentials too. Who says sustainable living is boring? With a superlative ecological philosophy, Ecomama's environmentally minded practices

have set a high bar for other hostels and hotels. Along with a water-saving system, green roof, and cradle-to-cradle building materials, recycled materials have been used wherever possible for furnishing the interior. The hostel has a green roof and natural stone heating, and hostel cleaners use natural, eco-friendly products too.

The most eye-catching feature at Ecomama is the reception desk made out of vintage books. The communal area is an inspiring space; guests can leaf through a great selection of coffee-table books while sipping on an espresso from the on-site café.

With the perfect combination of great value for money, an eco-friendly concept, and a unique experience, Ecomama is one of the finest hostels in Europe.

Good to know

PRICE RANGE
$ $ $ $ $
AMENITIES INCLUDE
bicycle rentals;
self-catering facilities;
large luggage lockers;
city tours; custom-made
city maps; Stop The
Water While Using Me!
bathroom amenities;
skateboards; GO
OFFLINE bathrobes;
communal living room
with swings; chill cinema
teepee tent; record
player; in-house café and
bar: the FIXXX.

*Tip: Experience
Amsterdam as a local.
There's a variety of
tours and activities:
trips to an organic
beer brewery,
personalized tours of
the red-light district,
or canal boat trips.*

Generator Amsterdam

Overlooking Oosterpark, Generator Hostel is in the up-and-coming eastern side of Amsterdam. Located in an imposing brick structure dating from 1917, the hostel features elegant, grand spaces, and high ceilings.

Originally an academic institution, the designers preserved the industrial heritage character of the building while adding the quirky touches for which Amsterdam is famous.

Generator has 168 en suite twin and quadruple rooms with incredible views. The star room is an exclusive luxury apartment overlooking Oosterpark (sleeps six).

The hostel's spacious social areas are filled with creative design touches, like glass-front elevators, a raised café, and an outdoor terrace. There's an impressive lounge and bar in the former lecture hall, and the old library is now an intimate relaxation area. The on-site café is a dining destination in its own right and the university's former boiler room is one of the city's trendiest speakeasy bars.

Good to know

PRICE RANGE
$ $ $ $
AMENITIES INCLUDE
24-hour reception; free WiFi; luggage storage; laundry facilities; bicycle rentals; female-only dorms; travel shop; bar; café; chill-out areas; event space.

Tip: Explore the up-and-coming eastern side of Amsterdam outside the hostel or visit the on-site café which is a dining destination in its own right. The university's former boiler room is one of the city's trendiest speakeasy bars.

Cube Hostel

Good to know

PRICE RANGE
$ $ $ $ $
AMENITIES INCLUDE
self-catering facilities;
laundry facilities;
bar; lounge; library;
cinema room (with real
cinema seats!).

_Tip: Be sure to
visit the hostel's
boutique bar where
you can sample
everything from
owner Elizabeth's
delicious pink
lemonade to Belgian
craft beers. The
hostel is also
centrally located,
so you'll be able to
see Leuven's most
popular attractions._

A newly renovated hostel in the heart of Leuven, Cube Hostel opened to rave reviews in 2014. With a retro-chic vibe, a free pancake breakfast, a cinema, and quality, en suite rooms (with rain showers!), Cube has become a must-stay location for travelers in Belgium. The hostel is centrally located and guests have easy access to Leuven's most popular tourist attractions, including the Old Market Square—where you can visit the longest bar in Europe, the main shopping district, the famous InBev brewery, historical university buildings, and tons of interesting museums. Cube's main lounge has that vintage vibe that appeals to every travel lover. A selection of globes and travel quotes are scattered across the room, and a large library with a desk created from retro suitcases adds classic charm. Be sure to visit the hostel's boutique bar where you can sample everything from owner Elizabeth's delicious pink lemonade to Belgian craft beers.

With a variety of rooms to suit every traveler's budget and several large social areas, Cube is the perfect base to enjoy a proper slice of Flemish hospitality before exploring Leuven.

Rotterdam: edgy harbour town

A staunch maritime tradition and an uncompromising cultural scene have made Rotterdam *one of Europe's coolest cities.*

Rotterdam was one of the first cities I visited as a blogger, so I have a sentimental connection with it. Rotterdam has a cool, unpretentious vibe, and its inhabitants are down to earth and easy to chat to. It reminds me of Glasgow, another very cool port city. Rotterdam has some incredibly good hostels, the food and drink scene is one of the best in Europe, and the diverse nightlife means there is something for everyone.

Where to eat

Bertmans is a great place for breakfast, lunch, or dinner, with organic, vegetarian, and vegan dishes. The pancakes are amazing and so is the poached egg and avocado on toast. Don't miss Bertmans' lovely terrace in summer.

Speaking of outdoor terraces, Fenix Food Factory in the Katendrecht district is a must-see. Located in a former industrial warehouse, here you can enjoy fresh, delicious food from local producers. From sipping on the Kaapse Brouwers' local craft beers to sampling cheese at Booij Kaasmakers, there is a bunch of great foodie experiences to be had. Best of all, there are plenty of wooden benches outside to enjoy your food and drink while soaking in the historic view of Hotel New York and the surrounding harbor.

One of the reasons I love coming back to Rotterdam is Bazar, which specializes in North African and Middle Eastern food. I highly recommend the tavuk sis kebab, and the breakfast is one of the best I have ever tasted.

» If you haven't been to Restaurant Dierhandel De Pijp you are not a real Rotterdammer! It's nothing fancy, you just sit down with people you don't know and chat, drink, and eat. «

MONIQUE SEGEREN
— Hostel ROOM

→

Last but not least, pay a visit to Mr. Hans Bode, a Rotterdam icon who roasts delicious Rotdogs in his Hans Worst food cart. Hans loves serving them with very spicy chili, and has a special variety of habanero peppers that is apparently the second hottest in the world. You have been warned.

> » Ter Marsch & Co serve the best burgers. As it's right next door, you can simply pop into the restaurant if you are not feeling too active but still want to enjoy yourself. You don't even need to make a reservation! «

ALISA KOKORINA
— *King Kong Hostel*

Where to drink

A favorite hangout of mine is Sjatzi, an old strip club turned hipster bar that still breathes the hedonistic atmosphere of its neon-light past. Male and female dancers grease the pole on weekends, while attentive bartenders serve a nice selection of German beers, Russian vodka, cocktails, and various kinds of caviar.

If you are looking for something more upmarket, the cocktails at The Suicide Club are fantastic, and it has a great rooftop view.

Aloha Bar is home to the former Tropicana indoor swimming pool and is another popular bar amongst locals in the summer thanks to its advantageous location by the river.

> » On the outside terrace of Aloha Bar they've built swings where you can get the best view of Rotterdam's skyline. «

JOYCE BROUWER
— *Ani & Haakien*

Where to party

My happiest memories of Rotterdam are all under a blurry sheet of darkness—once the streetlights come on, the volume goes up, and you find yourself swimming in a pool of glorious humanity, and booze too. Witte de Withstraat is Rotterdam's party street and one of Europe's greatest spots—like Ibiza, but without the price tag. Check out The Performance bar, which has an organ, bathtub, and stage. They have interesting performances every hour on top of the bar, unless it's turned into a bathtub.

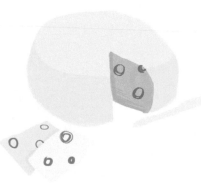

The evergreen De Witte Aap has a great selection of cocktails and beers and was once voted Europe's best bar. I also love the tropical charm of Tiki's, the New York vibe of Café LaBru, and WORM's ever-surprising experimental music.

> » If you like soul and jazz, BIRD is the best place. During the North Sea Jazz Festival in July you can see shows from big names, as they host the official after party (Doogieball) for the festival. The location under an old railway viaduct is also really cool. «

MIRJAM VERSCHOOR
— *Hostel ROOM*

Going for a walk

> » Rotterdam has lots of nice places to go for a walk and is much greener than you might think. The Kralingse Dos park is a favorite for locals. It is close to the city, and in the summer becomes the garden for many people in Rotterdam. «

MONIQUE SEGEREN
— *Hostel ROOM*

The Diergaarde Blijdorp zoo, with a fully covered oceanarium featuring sharks, penguins, and sea lions, as well as Europe's largest butterfly paradise, is also a nice place to go for a walk. Guests at King Kong Hostel get a special discount.

Getting around town

In Rotterdam everything you want to see is within walking distance. The city is also extremely bike friendly with 70,000 citizens using their bikes daily.

The best place to relax

I love the hammock in the beautiful garden of Hostel Ani & Haakien and playing with the cat, Suzy, is a plus. Parqiet is a lovely café in the Euromast tower, where you can grab a book and enjoy the views of the city.

The Dutch and water are always a good combination. Lake Kralingen, Rotte River, and the many canals are great places to spend free time, even in winter, since the locals like to go ice-skating. There are also several places where you can rent a boat or take a watertaxi—the ultimate Rotterdam thing to do.

→

Rotterdam has a cool, unpretentious vibe, and its inhabitants are down to earth and easy to chat to. It has some incredibly good hostels, the food and drink scene is *one of the best in Europe*, and the diverse nightlife means there is something for *everyone*.

Another secret spot is the Oude Nordeen, also known as the Old North neighborhood. Once seen as a problem area of the city, it is now one of Rotterdam's most dynamic places thanks to its artistic and multicultural community. In Oude Nordeen you'll find fantastic spots such as Hostel Ani & Haakien and Bertmans restaurant, and lots of beautiful houses from the 1920s and 30s.

» M4H, Rotterdam Makers District, is my secret spot. There is so much to discover in this area: Industrial sights, De Keilenderf, Joep van Lieshout's atelier, a local farm, Dakpark, and so much more! «

JOYCE BROUWER
— Ani & Haakien

Best viewpoint

If the skies are clear, the Euromast tower offers the highest viewpoint in the city, although it may not be a very good idea if you have a fear of heights.

Hop on a water taxi and go from Veerhaven to Hotel New York on the Wilhelminapier, and get a panoramic view of the Maas River. The terrace at Hotel New York also has a fantastic view with the port on one side and the city on the other.

maritime heritage that dates back to the nineteenth century. You'll find yourself walking past sailing boats and stately buildings that were untouched by the war.

Secret places

One of the most romantic and secret spots in Rotterdam is the historic Veerhaven in beautiful Scheepvaartkwartier. Veerhaven is a reminder of Rotterdam's glorious

Ani & Haakien

Community spirit fostered by and for travelers

In 2005, friends Danielle and Joyce went traveling around the world on the adventure of a lifetime. The key feature of all their favorite hostels was how they always felt at home. On their return to Rotterdam, they decided to start their own home away from home—also recognizing that, by opening a hostel, they could hold onto an eternal feeling of traveling and keep meeting interesting people from around the world.

Ani & Haakien really does feel like being invited into someone's home.

There's a large communal kitchen where guests gather for dinner every night, a beautiful garden with hammocks, and Suzy La Cubanita, a beautiful resident cat. The hostel is filled with pieces of work from friends in the local art community. There's no chance of feeling bored during your stay here. There is a packed schedule of activities written up on a daily blackboard (think yoga lessons, movie nights, and bands performing in the garden), and there's a tour for every type of traveler. Options include: a tour to the brand new Markthal, the windmills, a night walk, the graffiti scene tour, visiting the city Delft, bar tours, and the Rotterdam architecture tour.

The dorms are clean and comfortable, and the walls are painted by local artists. Doubles here are tiny—as the owners say, "You should really love your companion to book this room."

Ani & Haakien is a short walk from Rotterdam's most popular attractions including the Markthal and the famous cube houses. There are no bars neighboring the hostel so you are guaranteed a good night's sleep; however, you can find good coffee places, design shops, rooftop bars, and jazz clubs within walking distance.

If you arrive early or leave late, the hostel has free luggage storage. You can also rent bikes or store your own for free. ⌂

Good to know

PRICE RANGE
$ $ $ $ $

AMENITIES INCLUDE
24-hour access; free tours; cozy communal area; bike rentals; self-catering facilities; longboards; laundry service; personal lockers; luggage storage; indoor parking; hostel dinners; sweet hostel cat. Breakfast included.

Tip: There's a tour for every type of traveler: a tour to the brand new Markthal, the windmills, a night walk, the graffiti scene tour, visiting the city Delft, bar tours, and the Rotterdam architecture tour.

Hello I'm Local

Vintage Dutch design meets Scandi-cool

 Haarlem is a city of old Dutch nostalgia, and Hello I'm Local is right in the heart of it.

Through the names of the hostel's 12 rooms guests get to know local historical characters. There's Tante Leen a. k. a. the "Nightingale of Willemsstraat," a housemaid from the 1950s who became the voice for a generation of housewives; "Holstein Friesian," the only real Dutch dairy cows that are native to the area; "VOC," which is covered with beautiful maps named after a local mapmaker. The "Klederdracht Room" has its own swing—perfect if you are traveling with family.

Located in the Burgwal neighborhood of Haarlem and in close proximity to the famous Grote Markt and the water, Hello I'm Local is very well placed. Haarlem itself will remind you of summer holidays from the not-too-distant past.

With an increasing number of tourists seeing food as a primary reason to travel, Hello I'm Local is part of a new breed of gastro-hostels keen to share the culinary heritage of their area. The hostel takes great pride in sourcing everything from local producers, and their breakfasts are fabulous—one of the most heavenly things to wake up to. Savor traditional hand-kneaded bread with organic cheese from the local Doruveal farm.

Back at the hostel, WiFi and TV is only available in the common living area. Owner Saskia Hurd admits she is a bit old-fashioned and encourages her guests to have a conversation instead, or to play a board game. Meet some new friends by the fireplace on the patio—the perfect spot to soak up some sun during breakfast or while having an afternoon snack. Friends and guests are welcome in the living room or courtyard, but quiet time starts at 11:00 p.m., making Hello I'm Local the perfect hostel to enjoy an undisturbed night of rest. ⌂

Good to know

PRICE RANGE
$ $ $ $
AMENITIES INCLUDE
bike rentals; guest
pantry; microwave;
fridge; kettle;
free tea and coffee;
hairdryer; iron; on-site
washer and dryer.
Breakfast is not included,
but available on-site.

Tip: _Don't miss_
their fabulous locally
produced breakfasts.
They also started
a food and bike
tour—a great mix
of local culture,
beautiful
countryside &
lots of good food
and beer.

ClinkNOORD

Good to know

PRICE RANGE
$ $ $ $ $
AMENITIES INCLUDE
24-hour reception; free
WiFi; towels available;
laundry facilities;
ATM; luggage storage;
lockers; self-catering
facilities; hairdryer;
travel shop; bar; free
walking tours; atrium.
Breakfast included.

Tip: Soak up the
creative climate.
Artists are granted
accommodation
in exchange
for playing a gig
or showing their art
at the hostel's
exhibition space.
ZincBAR also puts on
regular events.

Simple Dutch design has never
reached such creative heights
as in the 1920s laboratory-turned-
hostel, ClinkNOORD.

Located "across the River IJ"
in Amsterdam Noord, ClinkNOORD
retains parts of its historic original
design, like the impressive stained
glass window running the length
of the building. Inside, the many
communal areas are cheery and bright:
a sunny and spacious atrium with
picnic tables; a café; a library with
a well-styled and well-stocked
bookcase; a bespoke self-catering
kitchen for guests; and flexible spaces
for meetings and events. A great part
of staying at ClinkNOORD is soaking
up its creative climate. They support
emerging artists to come and
"Stay & Play"—artists are granted
accommodation in exchange for
playing a gig or showing their
art at the hostel's exhibition space.
The in-house ZincBAR puts on regular
events, from DJs and karaoke nights
to talks and performances.

Hostel ROOM

Hostel ROOM is in a beautiful art deco-style building from 1923 located in Scheepvaartkwartier, a scenic district fairly close to all the main tourist attractions. There are 17 themed rooms at this hostel and all enjoy a special link to Rotterdam and the Netherlands. From the colorful, quirky Art Room to the elegant and understated Boardroom, each one has vintage furniture, oodles of character, and plenty of laid-back retro charm.

In terms of style and comfort, the favorite pick among guests is the luxury Clocktower Room. It's a private loft with a high, domed ceiling, bright walls, and huge round windows. It is also equipped with a small kitchenette, an en suite bathroom, and a private rooftop terrace with a panoramic view of Rotterdam's skyline. The friendly staff are the heart and soul of this hostel. And the spacious downstairs living room and bar are warm, funky, and super cozy; they will make you feel at home instantly. A busy roster of weekly events includes live music nights from local and international acts, quiz nights, and excellent weekly dinners—all great ways to meet new friends.

Good to know

PRICE RANGE
$ $ $ $ $
AMENITIES INCLUDE
linens; free walking tours; 24-hour reception; night security; free WiFi; lockers; self-catering facilities; laundry facilities; bicycle rentals; theme nights; fun bar with daily happy hour. Breakfast included.

Tip: Hostel ROOM has a busy roster of weekly events, including live music nights from local and international acts, quiz nights, and excellent weekly dinners.

KingKool Hostel

The brainchild of a hyper creative mind

Koning + cool = KingKool. Owner Jan de Koning created this cool hostel with the help of friends and family. From the playful lampshades to the uniquely themed rooms, everything is handmade using mainly recycled materials. Old Bordeaux wine cases have been transformed into tables and old shipping containers stacked on top of each other to create bunk beds in a Japanese-style capsule room. Besides being extremely creative, Jan has a quirky sense of humor and all rooms have a unique theme. The walls of the Bunny Room are covered with posters of naked Playmates; the Paard van Troje Room is a tribute to The Hague's iconic music venue, and the Urban Camping Suite has a full-size campervan and timber-shed bathroom. There are five types of dorm rooms with varying facilities. The deluxe dorm room has more privacy, with curtains, private power sockets, and reading lights. Dorm rooms come with lockers, but bring your own padlock. Towels are not provided, but they can be rented from the hostel.

KingKool is equipped with a multitude of facilities, including a guest kitchen, sundeck, terrace, and lounge with comfy beanbags. An on-site bar serves strong coffee and alcoholic beverages, and guests can watch movies or have fun on the PlayStation in the cinema room.

Good to know

PRICE RANGE
$ $ $ $ $

AMENITIES INCLUDE
WiFi; bar; coffee; lounge;
pool table; self-catering
facilities; designated
smoking area;
cinema; KingKool city
map; DIY walking
tour (sneakers available
for purchase).

Tip: Discover
*The Hague's most
important cultural
and historical
landmarks like
the famous Peace
Palace, which
is easily reachable
from the hostel.*

London: multicultural metropolis

London has it all—with a history that dates back to Roman times, it is currently *one of the world's most cosmopolitan cities.*

But I have a love-hate relationship with it. I love coming here for work and conferences and to meet up with old friends, but it can be expensive, and the hubbub of tourists, Londoners, and chaotic traffic can feel overwhelming—especially to a newbie. But over time, I've managed to eke out some survival strategies for making the most of my time in this multicultural city.

Where to eat

London is a melting pot of cultures and home to an impressive list of global cuisines. Head to Brick Lane for a start. It's London's curry mile and home to some of the city's best street art by Banksy, ROA, and Stik. Pop into Aladin for its excellent chicken curry and vegetable biryani. Asian sweets are the perfect antidote to a hot curry, so check out Rajmahal Sweets and try the velvety barfis and crispy jalebis. Here you'll also find the always-packed East-London institution Beigel Bake, open 24/7. Popular bagel picks are the salted beef and mustard, and cream cheese and salmon combos, as well as the simple peanut butter bagel. And they're a bargain for a slice of London history.

The British love their sandwiches. After exploring the Natural History, Victoria & Albert, or Science museums in South Kensington, I recommend grabbing a sandwich meal deal from Boots or Marks & Spencer and enjoying a picnic in beautiful Hyde Park.

Head to one of London's amazing street markets to feast on different ciders, melt-in-the-mouth cheeses, crusty breads, roasted coffee, patisseries, and so much more. My favorite is the bustling Borough Market, south of the River Thames. The chorizo roll from Brindisa is a delicious bargain.

» Only open on weekends, Maltby Street Market near Tower Bridge is a good alternative to Borough Market. A wide variety of street foods are available here, and most are centered around British food. The cheese toasties are divine. «

TITUS WILSON
— Palmers Lodge

If you want to go for dinner with great food and ambience, I highly recommend Brasserie Zédel. Located in a grand, art deco basement, the Parisian-style restaurant offers a unique yet incredibly affordable dining experience. Its marble-clad walls and extravagant light fixtures wouldn't be out of place in a Wes Anderson film, making it a particularly Instagrammable spot.

Where to drink & party

London has everything you need to enjoy a night out. You might want to indulge in a great British pastime called the pub crawl, winding your way along cobblestone streets and drinking in venues once frequented by literary greats. Both Charles Dickens and William Shakespeare were regulars at the George Inn. With oak-beam ceilings and a beautiful courtyard, this pub, standing in its current incarnation since 1676, is a great place for a proper British pale ale.

For tailor-made drinks, the mixologists at the speakeasy-style bar B.Y.O.C. (Bring Your Own Cocktail) will have what you're looking for. You bring the booze and they will concoct a tipple (or two, or three…) for you.

Lounge Bohemia is another hidden gem, especially if you like to drink your cocktails out of a mini bathtub (with accompanying rubber

ducky). Make sure to book ahead and remember ties are not allowed.

Going for a walk

World-famous Kew Gardens is a lush 132-hectare botanical paradise and home to the world's largest collection

of orchids. Be sure to visit the Great Pagoda, the Princess of Wales Conservatory, and the Victorian-era Palm House. This walk is one of life's greatest pleasures.

Some of the best walks in London are along the banks of the River Thames. Begin at the Palace of Westminster, facing Big Ben, beside the Houses of Parliament. Keep walking to the South Bank for plenty of famous sights and things to do: County Hall, London Eye, Southbank Centre, Royal National Theatre, Oxo Tower, and Gabriel's Wharf. Check out Tate Modern for the latest exhibitions or the historical Globe Theatre for a stage show. Finish by crossing the Millennium Footbridge to St. Paul's Cathedral.

» It's always a joy to wander along London's canals. Jubilee Greenway is a charming walk from Little Venice to Camden

that feels much like you're on the towpath of a countryside canal. Camden is full of street-food vendors too, so you can refuel after your walk! «

ANNA HAFSTEINSSON
— Clink78

Getting around town

The underground—or tube—and the iconic red double-decker bus are popular modes of public transport in London. The tube network runs deep and covers an extensive area. Fares depend on times and zones, as well as modes of payment.

Walking in central London is a great way to discover the labyrinth-like streets of the city, and it can often be quicker than jumping on the tube. Some underground stations are not as far from one another as they appear on the tube map.

» While it's tempting to jump on the tube to get you quickly from A to B, walking is always my favorite way to get around. The sights you see are often surprising! A trip on the River Bus is always a great way to see the city from a different perspective too. «

ANNA HAFSTEINSSON
— Clink78

The best places to relax

Green spaces in London are surprisingly abundant and a perfect place to enjoy a break from the frenetic pace of life. Stroll through Hampstead Heath on a Sunday morning, and you will meet plenty of friendly people and dogs. Afterward, head to The Holly Bush Pub and Restaurant for lunch and admire the floral displays adorning the awnings and window boxes. →

London has everything you need to enjoy a night out. You might want to indulge in a great British *pub crawl,* winding your way along cobblestone streets and drinking in venues once frequented by literary greats.

A refreshing pint of cider or a cheeky midday gin and tonic will soon have you appreciating all things London.

Best viewpoint

We always think of viewpoints as places of high altitude that inspire sweeping, panoramic views. However, alternate views of a city can be just as spectacular. Consider discovering London from one of the many bridge spanning the River Thames or take a boat tour for a different point of view.

» For a different perspective on the city, head east to ArcelorMittal Orbit, originally designed by Anish Kapoor for the 2012 Olympics. Visitors can enjoy the incredible views and then whizz down the newly attached slide, the brainchild of Belgian artist Carsten Holler. «

ANNA HAFSTEINSSON
—Clink78

For that quintessential London view, ride the London Eye. You'll have a 25-mile viewing radius in all directions on a clear day. A single rotation on the Eye takes 30 minutes—slow enough that you needn't fear motion sickness.

Secret places

It might not be so secret these days, but Wilton's Music Hall is one of London's real treasures. Hailed by The Theatres Trust as "the most important surviving early music hall to be seen anywhere," this architectural gem in London's East End hosts performances of all kinds throughout the year.

London is a treasure trove of independent and secondhand bookstores, and my favorite is Daunt Books. This Edwardian bookshop has so much history nestled in its long oak gallery, sweeping skylights, and stained-glass windows. The shop is intended to provide an alternate browsing experience for the reader, so books are arranged according to country, irrespective of the genre. It's like travelling the world via books.

Wombat's City Hostel

Relive literary history near the River Thames

Once upon a time home to the author Joseph Conrad, this seaman's hostel turned travellers palace is a stylish bolthole for travellers looking to experience a different side of London. The hostel has a chequered history. In the Victorian age it used to be a hostel for sailors, who dropped into London from the nearby docks. The house served as accommodation for sailors and seamen for a century and was known as the Red Ensign Club.

Some of the Sailors often referred to it as 'Alcatraz', because of its small cabin like, spartan rooms. It was also once upon a time home to the author Joseph Conrad. It has a great history.

The current day rooms are a lot less spartan and quite spacious. They come with comfy wooden beds, a private shower, toilet facilities and lockers for belongings. Private en suite rooms are comfortable and perfect for couples.

There are more than 20 fully equipped double rooms. Doubles and dorms come with en suite bathrooms and separate en suite toilets, plus an extra washbasin, so people can brush their teeth, even though the toilet and bathroom are occupied. The biggest dorm is a 10 bed, although most dorms are 6 bed dorms. Every bed has its own reading light, a UK power outlet and a USB port. The standout feature of this hostel can be found on the top: The 7th and 8th floors house two superior 6 bed dorms that share an exclusive living room on the 9th floor, with a balcony looking onto Tower Bridge, The Shard, Canary Wharf and the City of London.

The hostel also features a huge basement bar, courtyard, cosy hangout area in the lobby and all the amenities a backpacker could ever wish for. They have a fabulous well-equipped guest kitchen where guests can cook their own meals. There is a Sainsbury's supermarket down the road. If you are are feeling hungry, the bar serves small pizzas and snacks. They run an excellent breakfast buffet where you can help yourself to orange juice, tea and coffee, bread, spreads, cereal, fruit, cheese and meats, the perfect breakfast to kickstart your day in London.

When you arrive at the hostel you will be greeted with a small welcome drink and their very own city map with essential information with all the going-ons in town.

Even though it is a large hostel, the friendliness of the staff here make this feel more like a small hostel and less like a corporate chain hostel or hotel. Guests love the history and story of this building. Plus the location in East London is fantastic: you are a short walk from the buzzing nightlife of Shoreditch and key sights such as Tower Bridge, and the Tower of London.

Good to know

PRICE RANGE
$ $ $ $ $
AMENITIES INCLUDE
linens; towels; free WiFi; hair dryer; common area; self-catering facilities; bar; pool table; beer pong table; Nintendo 64; views over canary wharf.

Tip: Discover the buzzing nightlife of Shoreditch which is only a walk away or go visit the nearby key sights such as Tower Bridge or the Tower of London. Also check out Wombat's very own city map with all the essential going-ons in town!

Palmers Lodge Swiss Cottage

A Victorian gem set in central London

Palmers Lodge is a boutique hostel in central London, close to the underground station Swiss Cottage.

This Victorian-era home used to be the former lodge of Lord Palmer, made famous due to the largesse of a booming biscuit empire, it is now a registered historic building. The proximity to the Finchley Road shopping area makes the hostel an ideal overnight resting point for avid London shoppers.

Staying in such a well-preserved piece of history in the heart of London is an experience in itself. The period details have been retained, featuring a stunning entrance with solid oak doors, a grand wooden staircase, and a chandelier hanging above red velvet carpeting.

Palmers Lodge has a variety of accommodations, including deluxe, private, and shared rooms with en suite bathrooms. The dorm rooms come in a variety of sizes, and there are female-only options. The shining parquet floors, robust oak bunk beds, thick mattresses, nice fluffy pillows, storage, and privacy curtains make the dorms a very pleasing place to stay. The hostel linens are free and beds are premade so you can jump straight in if you arrive late. The bar and dining area are convivial communal areas that open onto an enclosed outdoor patio. The bar is open every day from 5:30 p.m. until late and is the perfect place to relax after a long day of sightseeing or shopping. With big beach umbrellas for shade, this is the best spot to enjoy a drink with friends in the summertime.

If you're staying in for the night, you can rustle up a meal in the self-service kitchen and enjoy a film from the extensive in-house DVD library on the huge plasma screen TV.

Central and convenient, Palmers Lodge Swiss Cottage is a great choice for any kind of London visit.

Good to know

PRICE RANGE
$ $ $ $ $
AMENITIES INCLUDE
24-hour reception;
free WiFi; self-catering
facilities; laundry
facilities; bar; lounge.
Breakfast available
for an additional cost.

*Tip: If you stay
during summertime,
be sure to check
out the outdoor BBQ
area where live music
events are hosted
regularly. It's the
perfect hangout
for enjoying an al
fresco drink or two
or three ...*

Palmers Lodge Hillspring

Travelers sing the praises of this cozy nook

With similar conveniences to its sister hostel (Swiss Cottage), the Hillspring Lodge sits in a quieter, residential part of North London.

In walking distance from Willesden Green Station, this hostel is just a few minutes away from Wembley Arena, making it the perfect home for groups going to see a game or a concert there.

The hostel has a quirky, eccentric sense of decor: A deer rug hangs from the ceiling, and the garden is filled with the owner's collection of over 100 motorcycles. There's a long terrace and beautiful garden to relax in after a long day of sightseeing. The popular lounge area is very cozy with tons of comfy sofas where guests can simply chill out. The dorm rooms at Hillspring come in a variety of sizes: small (sleeps up to 4), medium (sleeps up to 12), and large (sleeps up to 28). Dorms have keycard access, reading lights, central heating, and privacy curtains. Beds are premade and ready before check-in, so weary travelers can hit the hay whenever they please. Wake up and enjoy a free, simple breakfast of toast, cereal, and coffee, on offer from 7:30 until 10 a.m. The facilities at Hillspring are great:

The reception area has a few desktop PCs to use for free, the laundry amenities are sizable, plus there's an on-site restaurant with decent pub-style grub served from the evening until late at night. The fully licensed bar is a good place to meet new friends, sample some of the international beers and drinks on offer or play a game of pool. There is also a quiet reading room if that's your preferred way to unwind after a long day. With its quiet neighborhood surroundings, you'll surely get a good night's sleep at Hillspring. And it's just a 10-minute walk to 24-hour transportation so getting around to explore the city won't be an issue.

Good to know

PRICE RANGE
$ $ $ $ $
AMENITIES INCLUDE
24-hour reception;
free WiFi; self-catering
facilities; laundry
facilities; restaurant;
bar; lounge; parking.
Light breakfast included.

*Tip: In walking
distance from
Willesden Green
Station, this hostel
is just a few minutes
away from Wembley
Arena, making
it the perfect home
for groups going
to see a football game
or a concert in this
symbolic venue.*

YHA Tanners Hatch Surrey Hills

A retreat in the great British outdoors

YHA Tanners Hatch is one of the best-loved hostels in the YHA network. Set in the Surrey Hills, which has been officially designated an Area of Outstanding Natural Beauty, YHA Tanners Hatch offers a peaceful and quiet rural retreat just outside of London. It dates back to the 1940s and the picturesque cottage has plenty of character and charm.

There is no WiFi, café, or bar. Rather, guests go off-grid for the weekend and truly experience the beauty of the great British outdoors.

The hostel underwent a complete refurbishment in 2017, partly funded by donations from YHA supporters. It has been tastefully renovated without losing its history or tradition. Think exposed ceiling beams, a real coal fire in the lounge, and a wood-burning stove in the dining room. The hostel is super cozy and relaxing and there is also a double room available to book.

The Safari Tents are a new addition to the hostel. The epitome of glamping, these two-bedroom tents sleep six people and have a camp kitchen, deck, and a barbecue. Mattresses, bedding, and basic furniture is provided so there is no need to bring camping gear.

Good to know

PRICE RANGE
$ $ $ $ $
AMENITIES INCLUDE
Glamping; camping;
dining room; drying
room; lounge;
self-catering facilities;
barbecue area;
board games; gardens;
bike storage.

*Tip: Discover some
of South East
England's most
stunning and
accessible countryside,
Surrey Hills, which
has been officially
designated an Area
of Outstanding
Natural Beauty.*

YHA Keswick

Good to know

PRICE RANGE
$ $ $ $

AMENITIES INCLUDE
free WiFi; self-catering facilities; barbecue area; glamping; camping; bicycle storage; dining room; drying room; grounds; lounge; board games.

Tip: Take an early evening stroll through the town of Keswick to Friars Crag and enjoy the stunning views of the lake. You can also try one of the few long-distance cycling routes or head over to one of the nearby climbing options.

After being badly damaged by floods in 2015, YHA Keswick required extensive renovations to reopen in 2017. But the hostel has done well on its redesign, which includes an industrial chic bar and a new sleek self-catering kitchen.

The open-plan common areas have stunning balconies overlooking some of the most well-known fells in the Lake District, with big French doors opening to views over the river. The on-site restaurant serves up delicious meals in an ethereal atmosphere.

All of the bedrooms have two to six beds, making for cozy private rooms and intimate dorms where you can get a great night's sleep. There are also comfy double rooms available for couples. YHA Keswick is ideally situated in the town center with excellent access to the North Lakes Fells and a few long-distance cycling routes. There are lots of nearby options for climbing or you can take an early evening stroll through the town of Keswick to Friars Crag and enjoy the stunning views of the lake.

YHA South Downs

This beautifully converted Sussex farmhouse has stood on the gentle slope facing the River Ouse since the Middle Ages. History is still alive here, with original stone windows featuring in some of the bedrooms and a disused dairy farm on the grounds.

In a dreamy location by the South Downs walkway, this hostel offers guests a wide choice of rooms: en suite dorms, private rooms, family rooms, and a self-contained, three-bedroom family unit for exclusive use.

There's also the option of luxury camping pods. These offer all the magic of a camping experience but with the comfort of heating and electricity.

The common lounge has unpainted plaster walls and exposed brickwork, which gives the whole place a rustic feel. The hostel's on-site Courtyard Café, perfect for unwinding after a long day, has homemade cakes and coffees as well as hearty meals. The full English breakfast here is delicious and very good value.

Good to know

PRICE RANGE
$ $ $ $ $
AMENITIES INCLUDE
wheelchair accessible; self-catering facilities; laundry facilities; parking; board games; camping pods; bell tents; camping; bicycle storage; dining room; drying room; grounds; library; lounge; TV; café / bar.

Tip: Hike up to Firle Beacon. Just a short jaunt from the hostel door, take in the stunning panoramic views across the hills and out to sea—all within easy reach of the hostel.

The Rocks at Plas Curig

Top notch facilities and a great location make this one of Britain's finest hostels

Beautiful interiors, superb facilities, and stunning views of lush, green rolling fields crossed with the rugged mountainous landscape of Snowdonia make The Rocks one of Europe's best hostels. Once here, a guest's opinion of hostels will change forever.

The Rocks at Plas Curig has a dreamy location at the heart of Snowdonia, in the picturesque village of Capel Curig. Come here to escape. Spend your time snug in the lounge by the huge fireplace,

admiring the mist-shrouded views of Moel Siabod in the distance as canoeists pass by on the River Llugwy, winding its way to Betws-y-Coed. The hostel is not far away from a beautiful stretch of North Wales' coastline and the Island of Anglesey, so it's an ideal base from which to explore the great outdoors.

Capel Curig is a beautiful village to stay in this region. You can scale the mountains or go for a wander through the forest following the River Llugwy. For the more adventurous, Plas-y-Brenin Outdoor Activity Center is five minutes away, and offers a smorgasbord of

adrenaline-filled skills to master. Only 20 minutes away, there is Zip World Velocity, the fastest zipline in the world (and longest in Europe) set in the majestic Ogwen Valley, and Surf Snowdonia—the world's first inland freshwater surf lagoon—in the lush Conwy Valley.

The hostel building is an impressive space designed to be your home away from home. Even on the rainiest of days, the soft lighting, warm colors, and multitude of color-coordinated cushions give the place a cozy, cheerful ambience. An elegant, worn staircase leads you to the rooms. If you're finding it →

Good to know

PRICE RANGE
$ $ $ $ $

AMENITIES INCLUDE
free WiFi; self-catering kitchen and a large separate dining area; well-stocked library; woodstove in the lounge; huge flat screen TV; drying room; parking; Welsh craft beers; handmade fire pit; knowledgeable staff; dog friendly.

Tip: Capel Curig is a great base for exploring Snowdonia. You can scale the mountains or go for a wander through the forest following the River Llugwy. In the evening relax with a local ale from one of the two excellent pubs flanking the hostel: the Tyn-y-Coed and Bryn Tyrch Inn.

The Rocks at Plas Curig has a dreamy location at the heart of Snowdonia. Come here to escape.

hard to think of "dorms" and "luxury" in the same breath, you have to come and stay at The Rocks to see it with your own eyes. The built-in wooden bunk beds—made up before arrival—come with private fitted curtains, a personal power point, and individual reading light. The bedding here is Welsh woolen blankets and fluffy duvets that you just sink into after a long day of hiking around the countryside; crisp sheets and excellent quality mattresses ensure guests have a sound sleep.

Rooms are not en suite, but the communal bathrooms are plentiful on each floor and have nice hot showers.

The staff here are extremely knowledgeable and ready to offer lots of great tips on nearby hiking trails and places to eat. The hostel has an excellent self-catering kitchen and a large dining area—a nice way to bump into fellow adventurers from all over the world. The communal area includes a well-stocked library and seating made out of reclaimed scaffolding planks. There is a drying room for hanging up your jackets and storing hiking boots, and, if you have a vehicle, there is adequate parking space for cars. Lastly, pet owners rejoice: The Rocks is a dog-friendly hostel.

You won't be wanting for things to do here, but relaxing is always an option. If you're not on the deck, snuggled up in blankets, looking out over the Snowdon Horseshoe, you can stay warm by the woodstove and take in the scenery through the broad bay windows.

At night, relax with a craft beer or fine wine in hand and watch something on the huge flat screen TV. But only after you've enjoyed the glorious sunset behind Snowdon, the highest peak in the national park, as it changes color from red to orange to slate blue while the sun disappears out of sight.

Alternatively, you can stay outside by the fire pit or visit one of the two excellent pubs flanking the hostel: The Tyn-y-Coed and Bryn Tyrch Inn both offer a range of excellent local ales and produce.

Words can't accurately describe the experience you'll have here—you'll just have to go and see for yourself. △

The Fort Boutique Hostel

Tapas, towers, and tea at this historic fort

The Fort is a superb design hostel in Britain's ancient Roman city, York. From the hostel you can see the gothic spires of York Minster, and if you fancy a cup of warming tea, the famous Betty's Tea Rooms are just around the corner.

The Fort is York's first boutique hostel, and all has been designed with lavish attention to detail.

There are 12 bedrooms in total, including dorms and private en suites. Rooms are individually designed by young local artists who competed for the opportunity, and the result is a diverse and eclectic mix. The shared bathrooms are clean, plentiful, and separate from one another.

There is a self-catering kitchen with all the appropriate amenities, as well as free tea, coffee, and juice. Next to the kitchen is a laundry room that is free for guests to use.

Lastly, there's excellent WiFi available throughout the building.

The warm and welcoming staff at The Fort set this hostel apart, and guests are given a thorough introduction to the facilities upon check-in.

The on-site Kennedy's Restaurant and Bar is a great place to have a bite, or relax with a book and a coffee or glass of wine. Bonus: Guests get a discount on food and selected drinks here!

In the basement you'll find Sotano Charcuterie & Bar, which serves wonderful cocktails, craft beers, great wines, and delicious tapas. It's a cozy and stylish affair with candlelit ambience. Be sure to try the pan-fried chorizo served with piquillo pepper.

On weekends the bar hosts guest DJs. Be prepared to dance the night away to everything from hip hop to funky techno or Latin beats.

This boutique experience is for those who love historic charm, but remain young at heart!

Good to know

PRICE RANGE
$ $ $ $ $

AMENITIES INCLUDE
linens; towels; free WiFi;
self-catering facilities;
laundry facilities; wet
rooms; flat screen TV;
tea and coffee.

Tip: Be sure to try
the pan-fried chorizo
served with piquillo
pepper at the hostel's
basement bar Sotano
Charcuterie & Bar,
which also hosts guest
DJs on weekends.
So be prepared to
dance the night away
there, too!

YHA Hartington Hall

A rich history in a stunning landscape

A journey to YHA Hartington Hall is a journey through history. With amazing period features, loads of character, and its own beautiful honeymoon suite, this grand hostel was built as a manor house back in the seventeenth century.

With stone floors and impressive wooden beams, YHA Hartington Hall has 124 beds, with many bedrooms hiding their own historic secrets. Look out for stained glass, oak panels, and the room Bonnie Prince Charlie (may have!) stayed in during the Jacobite rising. Wooden beds, leaded windows, and winding corridors all enhance the feeling of entering a portal to the past. You'll find a mixture of dorms, family rooms, and en suite private rooms to cozy up in, as well as showers on each floor. There's also a lovely self-contained suite called The Roost—perfect for intimate holidays.

It may have been built in the 1600s, but YHA Hartington Hall has everything you need for a comfortable stay. There's free WiFi in the games room, a pool table, and Eliza's Restaurant, which is also open to the public. The hostel looks especially magical in winter, when the woodstove in the Jacobean Manor is always kept burning. Kids can burn off steam in the sprawling grounds or play a game with the giant chess pieces. There's even an outer building that can be used for wedding receptions.

Explore Peak District National Park from this cozy base, catch the annual on-site beer festival, or just relax in the atmospheric rooms—there's plenty to keep you entertained in this historic hostel. ⌂

Good to know

PRICE RANGE
$ $ $ $ $
AMENITIES INCLUDE
free WiFi; self-catering
facilities; laundry
facilities; bicycle store;
drying room; games
room; board games; TV;
library; garden; café;
licensed bar; lounge;
private rooms available;
en suite rooms available;
wedding venue; parking.

Tip: Explore Peak
District National Park
from this cozy base,
catch the annual
on-site beer festival,
or just relax in the
atmospheric
rooms—there's plenty
to keep you
entertained in this
historic hostel.

Clink78

Good to know

PRICE RANGE
$ $ $ $ $
AMENITIES INCLUDE
towels available; 24-hour
reception; free walking
tour; free WiFi; ATM;
lockers; luggage
storage; self-catering
facilities; hairdryer; trave
shop; laundry room;
internet room; TV room;
bar. Breakfast included.

Tip: Don't miss out
on one of the many
live music events
at Clink78's basement
ClashBAR, which
pays tribute to the
famous punk band
The Clash, which stood
trial at the former
courthouse.

A ten-minute walk away from King's Cross Station, in a Victorian building faced in red brick with Portland stone dressing, stands Clink78.

The sedate exterior is a guise—this lively and upbeat hostel was once a courthouse where Charles Dickens was scribe and later, the famous punk band The Clash, stood trial.

The hostel pays tribute to this with the installation of the basement ClashBAR, a venue for live music events. It's a vibrant social space with green leather sofas, multicolored poufs, and plenty of low lighting.

Clink78 exudes oodles of personality. Stay in one of the original prison cell rooms with barred windows, leaden bunks, and steel toilets (retained for show); lounge and watch a movie, play a game of chess, or read a book in one of the old wood-paneled courtrooms. Two hundred years of handing out convictions have been abolished, with conversion into a funky hostel with plenty of original character. ⌂

Jugendherberge

Nuremberg may not figure prominently on the list of top destinations to visit, but with its magical Christmas markets, difficult-but-important history, great restaurants, pedestrian-friendly cobbled streets, and relaxed easygoing vibe, it is the perfect place to visit for a long weekend. Better yet: visitors can spend the night in a 500-year-old fairytale medieval castle. Jugendherberge Nuremberg is housed in the thick walls of the city's Kaiserstellung Castle towering above the old town. The former castle stables provide high ceilings, giant square pillars, grand staircases, and wooden beams galore. Communal areas have long, low, wooden benches with square stools and tables set into red brick arches, creating great places to sip a beer or play a board game. The arched windows lead out into a courtyard with tables and umbrellas; it all comes together to provide a modern city base that feels buzzy and alive. The hostel has 93 smart bedrooms, all with en suite showers and bathrooms. ⌂

Good to know

PRICE RANGE
$ $ $ $ $
AMENITIES INCLUDE
self-catering facilities;
a multi-vision room
for educational projects;
and many family-
friendly extras including
play room; facilities
for warming baby food
and drinks; bottle
warmer; highchairs, cots
and a toilet seat for
children; bathroom stool;
diaper changing pad and
diaper bin.

*Tip: There is an
excellent bar on-site
with good German
beers and cocktails,
as well as a bistro
offering canteen-style
meals and a generous
breakfast buffet.*

Great outdoors

For connecting with nature

If you are looking to disconnect from the rest of the world and reconnect with yourself and nature, travelling off the beaten path is the best. Your perfect day might consist of a long mountain hike, snowboarding, swimming in a lake, or taking a dip in a hot tub to relax your tired muscles. You could also grab a beer and sit by the firepit to watching the sunset over the sea. Of course, you don't need to be alone—these hostels are all about friends and community and bringing outdoor lovers together.

Midgard Base Camp, Iceland

*S*ki at Les Trois Vallées Les Menuires, France at *Ho36 Les Menuires (p. 118)*, soak in the hot tub in Andorra at *Mountain Hostel Tarter (p. 46)*, Enjoy a Welsh craft beer in Snowdonia, Wales at *The Rocks at Plas Curig Hostel (p. 106)*, or swing by celebrities such as George Clooney or check out where Star Wars was filmed in Lake Como, Italy at *Ostello Bello Lake Como (p. 142)*. Visit the home of Beatrix Potter and England's most beautiful national park or smell the daffodils and hop on a steamboat tour in Ambleside in the Lake District, England at *YHA Ambleside (p. 209)*. Bask in the scenic mountain views and ride on Icelandic horses through the indescribable landscape around Hvolsvöllur, Iceland at *Midgard Base Camp (p. 208)*.

» Your *perfect day* might consist of a long mountain hike, snowboarding, swimming in a lake, or taking a dip in a hot tub to relax your tired muscles. «

stello Bello, Lake Como, Italy

Rocks on Plas Curig, United Kingdom

Ho36 Les Menuires, France

ho36 Les Ménuires

A lively ski-in/ski-out stay in the heart of the Three Valleys

"We've been dreaming of the mountains from the very beginnings of ho36," says Frank Delafon, co-founder of ho36 hostels.

Until now there hasn't been an affordable option for winter sports enthusiasts to book accommodation in the French Alps for shorter stays or on short notice; most accommodations require week-long bookings and often well in advance—more reasons ski holidays remain out of reach for travelers. ho36 is changing that. A twenty-first century take on the mountain refuge, ho36 is the first ski-in/ski-out hostel in family-friendly Les Ménuires, the heart of the Three Valleys. Featuring 35 individual or shared bedrooms, and four private loft apartments, accommodations at ho36 suit travelers of varied budgets. All rooms offer breathtaking views of the mountain peaks in Vanoise National Park. The hostel's twelve dorms (for four or six guests) can accommodate up to 74 snow-sport fans. They feature custom-made designer plywood bunk beds with an integrated curtain system for complete privacy. The use of exposed materials gives these rooms real personality, as do the retro-chic bathroom designs. Space-saving storage, extra large drawers for luggage and backpacks, a wardrobe for all-weather jackets and ski suits—everything has been cleverly thought through to optimize space without compromising comfort.

The icing on the cake is the in-house restaurant that serves up the best of local Savoyard fare. And, for après-ski enthusiasts, there are two bustling bars with live music and regular DJ nights to keep the party going until late.

Good to know

PRICE RANGE
$ $ $ $ $
AMENITIES INCLUDE
restaurant; bar; outdoor
terrace; ski cellar.

*Tip: Dine at the
in-house restaurant
that serves up the
best of local Savoyard
fare. For après-ski
enthusiasts, there are
two bustling bars with
live music and regular
DJ nights to keep the
party going until late.*

Les Piaules

Hip, arty, cozy: welcome to Paris's alternative hostel

Les Piaules is a fab new design hostel situated in a renovated 1930s art deco building in Paris's up-and-coming district of Belleville. With a hip bar, custom-made bunk beds, and a rooftop terrace that offers unparalleled views of the Paris skyline, the hostel reflects the Belleville neighborhood's vibe: fun, bubbly, and arty. The founders, three young entrepreneurs from Paris, traveled for more than a year to the world's best and worst hostels and used that experience to design rooms. The experience shows: Their custom-made bunk beds have privacy curtains, a reading light, power plugs, private lockers, and, most importantly, a comfy mattress. The rooftop terrace overlooking the Sacré Coeur and the Eiffel Tower adds to the hostel's fantasy factor. Four of the bedrooms also share the stellar view, and one of these is a dorm with custom-made bunk beds. The private rooms are luxurious with wooden parquet floors, espresso coffee machines, and cozy white linen sheets. If you like modern and minimalist design, you will love these rooms.

The hostel has the coolest bar in town with a carefully curated selection of local beer, coffee, and French specialty drinks. Enjoy a beer on tap from Brasserie de Saint Omer, one of the biggest brewers in the north of France, take a selfie in their photo booth, work off steam with the punching bag, or challenge a local on their foosball table. The bar opens up again at 7 a.m., and guests can choose from a range of breakfasts to kick start the day. The menu includes hand-roasted, locally sourced coffee, croissants, eggs and bacon, creamy 24-month-aged Comté, French cheeses from local producers, or muesli and organic yogurt.

Les Piaules is conveniently located near most of the must-see attractions in Paris. From here, you're within a 10-minute walking distance of the historical center of Paris, including: Le Marais, Châtelet, République, Notre Dame, and Saint Germain des Prés, as well as the Champs Elysées, Moulin Rouge, Père Lachaise, and more.

Good to know

PRICE RANGE
$ $ $ $ $

AMENITIES INCLUDE
free WiFi; 24-hour
reception; travel desk;
multilingual staff;
rooftop terrace; local
food & drinks;
custom-made bunks.
Breakfast not included.

Tip: _The hostel offers_
a customized map,
which has some
tips on things to do
and places to eat.
It also has the coolest
bar in town with
a carefully curated
selection of local beer,
coffee, and French
specialty drinks.

Generator Paris

The best of Paris in one location

Formerly a derelict office block in the heart of the city, Generator Paris is in Belleville, just a few steps from Canal Saint-Martin and Parc des Buttes-Chaumont, and a 15-minute stroll from Gare du Nord train station.

Unique local elements like bathroom tiles supplied by Paris Metro have been incorporated into the hostel. The social spaces are filled with furniture sourced from vintage Parisian fairs along with artwork from local artists. This hostel is huge, giving guests a great deal of choice for accommodations. All rooms here come equipped with en suite bathrooms, fluffy towels, hair dryers, and complimentary toiletries. Custom-made bunk beds in the dorms have a built-in USB port, personal charging socket, and lockable storage space. If you're looking to splash out, the stylish terrace rooms have private balconies, hammocks, and deep tubs—the ultimate in hostel comfort. Guests love the quirky layout of the lounge here. It has a playful vibe, Moorish-inspired sofas and chairs to sink into, and ping pong and foosball tables.

Kick off your evening soaking in views of the city's skyline with a freshly made cocktail in hand. From noon until 10:00 p.m., guests can chill in Khyama, the hostel's rooftop bar. Open all year round, it offers guests unrivalled views of Sacré-Cœur and Montmartre. If you're looking to continue the party later, head down to the vaulted ceilings of Le Club, the on-site basement nightclub inspired, again, by the Paris Metro.

There are a ton of awesome places to eat along Canal Saint-Martin, but if you're looking for a quiet night, pop into the hostel's in-house diner, Café Fabien, which serves a nice selection of new and classic French fare—think foie gras burgers, beef carpaccio, and old-time favorite, escargot.

With everything under one roof, don't forget to leave and see the city itself!

Good to know

PRICE RANGE
$ $ $ $ $

AMENITIES INCLUDE
24-hour reception; free
WiFi; laundry facilities;
luggage storage;
complimentary toiletries;
hair dryer; female-only
dorms; travel shop;
chill-out areas; roof
terrace; basement bar;
event space; bar; café.

*Tip: If you're looking
for a quiet night,
pop into the hostel's
in-house diner, Café
Fabien, which serves
a nice selection
of new and classic
French fare—think foie
gras burgers, beef
carpaccio, and old-time
favorite, escargot.*

Gastama Hostel

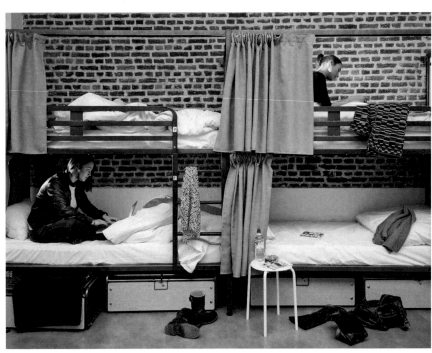

Good to know

PRICE RANGE
$ $ $ $ $
AMENITIES INCLUDE
150 hostel beds;
bar; restaurant
(The Shack); terrace;
24-hour reception
(and dedicated team!);
kitchen; luggage
storage; co-
working space.

Tip: This is a hostel for beer lovers. With over 40 local and international beers on tap, including the Gastama, their very own organic beer, which is brewed in the suburbs of Lille, you are really spoilt for choice here.

Since 2012, travelers have been able to experience Lille from an old, charming house that is a reflection of the city's Flemish-French architectural heritage. Exposed brickwork and dark wood beams give the hostel a cool, industrial-chic vibe.

The word Gastama means "welcoming" in Esperanto and you really feel welcomed from the get go.

The staff are all foodies—you will get some great tips on places to eat (with 800 restaurants to choose from in Lille, this is handy!) Thanks to their connections with the local music community, guests can get discounted tickets to intimate live gigs at places like the famous Le Peniche.

Their stylish gastro-bar-meets-pub brings locals and tourists together in a musical and friendly atmosphere. And with over 40 local and international beers on tap including the "Gastama," their very own organic beer, you are spoilt for choice here. The hostel also prides itself on being sustainable—bread is sourced from a local French bakery while their tea, coffee, and juices are organic.

Hostel Fish

Located in Denver's historic Airedale Building, Hostel Fish is an eclectic base camp for travelers exploring everything the Mile High City has to offer. In a space that was previously a brothel and saloon, the hostel is furnished in a style that captures the building's racy history. Guests are invited to recline on vintage couches or pluck at the parlor piano in the common space and bar area. Be sure to explore the entire hostel, including the balcony and the quirky "donut wall."

Ophelia's Electric Soapbox, a popular burlesque-themed bar serving crafty cocktails and small plates, is just downstairs. The bar at Hostel Fish also functions as an independent venue for social events like open mic nights and art exhibitions. Locals and tourists mingle easily here, sipping on a wide variety of Denver's famous craft beer, and the bar serves shots of absinthe to those embracing the roaring 1920s ambience. Of course, you should also hike, bike,

climb, or raft out in the Rockies while you're here. The Hostel Fish staff will help you get out into the mountains by organizing carpool options or instructions for public transport. Denver clearly offers plenty of things to do, but what Hostel Fish offers is plenty of things to feel. The blend of locals and guests here creates a welcoming atmosphere without compromising style, eccentricity, or a sense of adventure—making Hostel Fish the ideal place to stay in Denver.

Good to know

PRICE RANGE
$ $ $ $ $
AMENITIES INCLUDE
free towels; free WiFi;
charging stations
at each bunk; lockers;
free coffee.

Tip: Ophelia's Electric Soapbox, a popular burlesque-themed bar serving crafty cocktails and small plates, is just downstairs! The bar at Hostel Fish, however, also offers open mic nights and art exhibitions.

Away Hostel

Nordic cool and eighteenth-century architecture

Located in Lyon's hipster and artsy neighborhood, Croix-Rousse, Away Hostel & Coffee Shop is the follow-up to the city's other new generation luxury hostel, Slo Living. Away Hostel is a perfect blend of Nordic cool and eighteenth-century architecture; the moment you step inside you are swamped by this cozy, *hyggelig* atmosphere thanks to Lyonnais designer Charlotte Bollard's soothing wood-and-white design. Everything from the open-plan kitchen and dining area, comfy Fatboy beanbags, foosball table and reading area, to the on-site coffee shop with its cabin-like counter comes together to give you the same feel of a design hotel or potentially your impossibly hip uncle's new bachelor pad.

On a tree-lined street in an area formerly known for silk manufacturing, the hostel is a five-minute walk from downtown Lyon and right across the street from the Croix-Paquet metro station. Here, at the bottom of the Croix-Rousse hill, you can explore and discover some great boutiques plus a bunch of world food restaurants and stylish bars. Away is a short walk from the Museum of Fine Arts of Lyon, and close to the Opéra National de Lyon.

Like its sister hostel Slo Living, Away is a gastro-hostel, perfect for foodie travelers. Its menu—which changes daily—features traditional French cuisine, and everything down to the granola and cookies is homemade. Everything, that is, but the coffee, which comes from two local roasters: Extrait and its big brother Mokxa. Start the day with Away's 3€ breakfast, then end it with a three-course dinner and glass of wine for 10€—one of the best value meals in Lyon. The hostel's Sunday brunch is also a popular event: Currently on offer is a Sunday Yoga Brunch package where guests can enjoy an hour of relaxing yoga before the meal. In the evenings guests hang out with the locals in Away's basement cocktail bar, Groom ("lobby boy" in French), which established itself as a popular venue for live concerts and DJ sets in Lyon just a few months after opening. If you're looking to go out on the town, the hostel also organizes an excellent gastronomical walking tour of the city and wine tastings.

The rooms here are a mix of private en suites and dorms. The dorms feature pod-style beds equipped with a reading lamp, a plug, and a nightstand. The high ceilings, broad bay windows, and original French parquet floors give the rooms a clean and cheerful vibe even on cloudy days.

If you are a light sleeper, please note that the nights can be a little bit noisy when windows are left open in the dorms but the hostel offers free earplugs. There is also free high-speed WiFi and many locals come here simply to enjoy the coffee shop and internet connection.

Good to know

PRICE RANGE
$ $ $ $ $
AMENITIES INCLUDE
linens; reading light; free
WiFi; security lockers;
self-catering facilities;
dishwasher; microwave;
hairdryer; washing
machine; iron/ironing
board; steam room.
Breakfast not included.

Tip: This is a place
for foodies! Their
Sunday brunch, for
example, is a popular
event; currently
on offer is a Sunday
Yoga Brunch package
where guests can
enjoy an hour of
relaxing yoga before
the meal.

Hôtel OZZ

Minimalist coziness by the French seaside

Hôtel OZZ, a new hotel-hostel hybrid concept launched by HappyCulture Collection in October 2016, is situated near the train station, Gare de Nice-Ville, and the main shopping artery of the city, Avenue Jean Médecin.

Antoine and Thomas, two young Frenchmen, are the brains behind the hostel. After traveling around the world, they wanted to establish a hostel in Nice, incorporating the best of their favorite accommodations. One of their key goals was to make Hôtel OZZ feel like a home away from home. The design of the hostel achieves this with a homely and modern Scandinavian vibe. The white tiled walls, large pipes, immense wooden tables, steel and marble handrails and staircase are smart and minimalist but also cozy and welcoming.

Guests can relax and chill out in the common areas, which have a good selection of board games, plus a ping pong table and foosball table. Retro-style furniture, comfortable leather sofas, wooden floors, and a stylish outdoor patio add to the homely vibe. Dorm rooms have a breezy Mediterranean blue-and-white color scheme that is a refreshing change from the norm. Metal- and wood-framed bunk beds come with privacy curtains, individual lockers, a reading light, and a power point for charging electronic devices.

A typical French breakfast is available for a small charge. Guests can enjoy croissants and pastries, bread, jams, Nutella, coffee, and fresh orange juice. Free tea and coffee are available around the clock This is a social but quiet hostel so don't expect too much in terms of activities, but if you are looking for a stylish, economical base for exploring the Cote d'Azur, then this hostel is perfect for you.

Good to know

PRICE RANGE
$ $ $ $ $
AMENITIES INCLUDE
24-hour front desk;
WiFi; luggage room;
free coffee and
tea; concierge service;
breakfast; bar open
during summer;
bathroom in every room;
lockers in every room;
towels and padlocks
available for purchase
from the front desk; tour
organization; vending
machine; daily
housekeeping.

Tip: Go shopping
and grab some lovely
souvenirs in Nice's
main shopping
artery, Avenue Jean
Médecin, which
is close to the hostel.

Rome: the streets of timeless glory

Being almost 2,800 years old, Rome, *the eternal city,* has many hidden secrets.

Being almost 2,800 years old, Rome has many hidden secrets. Below I've revealed a few.

Where to eat

There are many articles on where to find the best carbonara or artisan gelato, but sometimes visitors overlook other local dishes such as the Roman classic cacio e pepe (cheese and pepper). Try it at the namesake trattoria Cacio e Pepe in the Prati district. Another Roman must is trapizzino, a pizza pocket stuffed with delicacies like aubergine and parmigiana. For more classics check out Flavio al Velavevodetto, especially if you are in a group. And visit Emma for its great suppli (rice ball) and pizza alla Romana— a thinner and crispier pizza than the classic one.

> » At Il Duchetto you'll find yourself in a simple and authentic environment that will transport you to the past. It is run by a family and the service is quick and simple. If you're a fan of fancy furniture, don't go there,

My first impression of the eternal city was not the best, I found it noisy and crowded with tourists. But falling in love with Rome is like enjoying a bottle of fine wine—the older you grow, the better it tastes and the more you appreciate its gnarled beauty. One way I grew to love Rome was by wandering around at sunrise. There's something almost illicit about the beauty of the empty streets bathed in the light of dawn.

but if you love a local experience, this is the place for you. They don't take reservations but the queue is usually never too long, just grab a beer while waiting. «

LORENZO BUSI
— *The RomeHello*

To get off the beaten track, hop over to the not so well known Da Emilio, a family-run, wood-paneled trattoria with no tourists and great food in the neighborhood of Porta Pia.

If you get up early, you can also pick up freshly baked bread at one of the city's old bakeries, just like the Romans do. My preference is Antico Forno Roscioli.

Where to drink & party

From chocolate bars to mystic cocktails, let's go on a crawl of Rome's best drinking spots! I suggest an aperitivo bar to kick your evening off in style (and on a budget). The concept is simple: Buy a drink and help yourself to a buffet of food that can include pasta, pizza, and slices of salami, mortadella, or cheese. Sample this tradition in Enoteca il Covino, a wine shop where you can enjoy a nice aperitivo for a good price.

If wine and chocolate make sense to you, pop into Said, a converted chocolate shop in the student quarter of San Lorenzo. Al Vino Al Vino is a bar in the Monti area with great wine choices and a caponata to die for.

» Freni e Frizioni is a bar in Trastevere created from a former clutch-and-brakes auto shop. It has lots of creative cocktails on one of the funkiest menus I've ever seen, and

an excellent, mostly vegetarian, all-you-can-eat buffet in the back room. Salotto 42, not too far from the Pantheon, is an elegant option for a cocktails night out. «

LINDA BRENNER
— *The Beehive*

If cocktails are your thing, head to The Sanctuary between the Colosseum and Monti district. Surrounded by nature and softly illuminated by torches and neon lights, this place has a very spiritual vibe. Enjoy a drink and lose yourself to the groove of electro house beats.

» If you feel like continuing your evening on the dance floor, try Lanificio, a multifunctional space that represents the creativity of Roman designers and is dedicated to art and new artistic musical forms. An informal and peaceful environment for people who know how to have fun. «

PIA LAURO
— *YellowSquare*

Head to Bar Fondi for an after-dinner negroni served by Alessandro, the bartender, and bond with the local characters. For live music, San Lorenzo is a good choice, with

Le Mura and Wishlist Club. There are other great live-music venues depending on your musical taste, including Blackmarket in Monti and Quirinetta near Trevi Fountain. If you want to meet fun people, head over to Yellow Bar in one of our featured luxury hostels, YellowSquare.

Going for a walk

Walking in Rome is a magical experience. Take a walk along Fori Imperiali on a Sunday or around Monti, one of the most picturesque neighborhoods. What about a stroll in the pedestrian area downtown? And not only because it hosts some of the city's most beautiful monuments—St. Peter's Square, Colosseum, Imperial Forum, Piazza Navona, Spanish Steps, and the Pantheon, but also because it will allow you to discover the real essence of Rome

Getting around town

Rome has the highest number of registered scooters in the world. If you're not afraid of the traffic, jump on one through scooter-sharing company Zigzag or eCooltra.

» If you're looking for more than the bare minimum, and have experience driving a scooter, scooter-sharing companies are probably worth looking into. «

STEVEN BRENNER
— *The Beehive*

Even though Rome is not a city for cyclists, there are some well-marked areas in the historic center that make it very easy to discover the city's alluring alleyways by bike.

Falling in love with Rome is like enjoying a bottle of fine wine—the older you grow, the better it tastes. One way I grew to love <u>Rome</u> was by *wandering around* at sunrise. There's something almost illicit about the *beauty* of the empty streets bathed in the light of dawn.

The best place to relax

Bursting with galleries, centuries-old ruins, and historic churches, Rome can be an overwhelming city. Disconnect from the chaos at Villa Doria Pamphilj, home to the largest urban public park in Rome and former residence of the noble family Doria Pamphilj. It is located on the scenic Gianicolo hill, which offers one of the best views of Rome.

Villa Borghese is another beautiful green spot. Rome's largest central park, it overlooks the National Etruscan Museum. Other places to relax include Villa Celimontana and Villa Torlonia.

Best viewpoint

Rome with a view? My favorite is the terrace of Viale del Belvedere in Villa Borghese. Lo Zodiaco restaurant at Monte Mario is an ideal place to enjoy the city lights and spot the stars on a clear night. It is a magical experience for the locals as well.

I also recommend grabbing a drink at one of the rooftop terraces of Rome's many 5-star hotels. The views are breathtaking—and you don't have to be a guest to enjoy them.

Secret places

You would think a city as ancient as civilization would hardly have any secrets, but Rome has the ability to surprise. The inner courtyard of Palazzo Venezia, in busy Piazza Venezia, blocks out all the traffic noise leaving you with the sound of birds and water. And despite hosting popular exhibitions, Chiostro del Bramante, near Piazza Navona, is a beautiful and calm place to have a coffee.

> » I'd say there isn't any one secret destination, but loads of secret, or easily overlooked curiosities along the way unless you get to know the city well. «

STEVEN BRENNER
— The Beehive

For more surprises, go to Monti and discover Michelangelo's Moses— go up a flight of stairs through an ivy-covered wall and enter Saint Pietro in Vincoli. An unexpected addition to the list is the Monte dei Cocci's 2,000-year-old archeological mound of waste, visible from the glass windows inside Flavio al Velavevodetto in Testaccio. Some restaurants preserve remnants of ancient Rome beneath them, such as Piazza del Teatro di Pompeo, where you can visit the wine cellar that dates back thousands of years.

Finally, visit the top of Tiber Island. If you sit there with a beer and close your eyes, you might just feel like you're on the prow of a ship.

Don't miss one of the most crowded spots in Rome: Piazza della Rotonda, where hundreds of people stand every day by the majestic façade of the Pantheon. Looking at its details, you can easily become mesmerized by its beauty, and the surrounding noise suddenly disappears, transforming this busy place into an intimate one.

YellowSquare

A raucous Roman adventure

YellowSquare is possibly the greatest party hostel on earth. Designed to provide guests with the wildest night of their lives, this hostel is a fun and exciting place with several cool spaces within the "Square" to facilitate meeting fellow guests.

With that in mind, it would be a huge mistake to label YellowSquare as just a party hostel. It has a bold concept of hospitality where guests can eat, party, sleep, and work in one space, and it caters to all types of travelers (albeit the more social type).

With YellowSquare as your base, you can do it all: catch a show with a local band, go on a food tour of Rome, enjoy a cooking class of something typically Roman like pasta guanciale, or get your hair done at the on-site salon. There are even plans for building an escape room attached to the hostel. If you're traveling for work, the hostel has a brand new co-working space to work in.

If you're traveling solo and want to meet people and party in Rome, then the dorms here are perfect (you can choose between shared bathrooms or en suite). They are comfortable and clean, and beds are equipped with a reading light, power socket, and lockers. Most importantly the en suite dorms have air conditioning in the summer. If you're looking for something more peaceful and relaxed, the newly launched Yellow Hotel has great private rooms across the road. Private rooms are equipped with an en suite bathroom, direct-dial →

Good to know

PRICE RANGE
$ $ $ $ $
AMENITIES INCLUDE
bar; self-catering
facilities; laundry
service; arcade; escape
room; hair salon.

Tip: See a show from
a local band, go
on a food tour of
Rome, enjoy a cooking
class of something
typically Roman like
pasta guanciale,
or go for drinks at the
YellowBar. There is
also a regular program
of DJ nights in their
basement nightclub.

Designed to provide guests with the *wildest night* of their lives, this hostel is a fun and exciting place.

phone, independent air conditioning, heating, a safety deposit box, hair dryer, mini fridge, and internet access.

All the party action happens at the Yellow Bar, across from the hostel. It has some of the cheapest drinks in town and a regular program of events that includes great local bands and DJ nights in their basement nightclub, Arcade. The cherry on the cake is the downright bizarre yet entertaining Tonika. If that doesn't get your pulse racing, you can reserve a seat on the Rollin Bar: a magical mystery tour of Rome by night. This van, complete with strobe lights and half-crazed backpackers knocking back the unlimited drinks on offer, will give you a front seat to surreal, beautiful views of Rome by night.

The hostel serves an à la carte breakfast with proper coffee at a range of price options. There is also an all-day menu with burgers and salads.

Be sure to dine at least once at nearby Mamma Angela's Trattoria. Choose from a great selection of antipasti, bruschetta, and more—the Roman classic cacio e pepe here is fantastic!

YellowSquare offers a variety of great walking tours and organizes cooking classes in the new basement kitchen of the hotel area. The kitchen is also available for preparing individual meals.

If you're not going out, visit the "movie garden" in the new hotel building. It's a hidden inner courtyard where you can watch classic movies or just relax with a book during the day.

YellowSquare is amazing for so many reasons, but if you are not the social type, you may want to look elsewhere. If you feel young at heart and want to party, then you will love this place; it is an experience that will stay with you for years to come.

The RomeHello

A socially conscious artist's lair

The RomeHello has the unique distinction of being Rome's—and possibly the world's—first street art and social enterprise hostel. Famous street artists from all over the world, such as Alice Pasquini, Facte, and Victoriano, were invited to decorate the walls of this hostel, and the end result is both colorful and inspiring.

The idea of inviting street artists to decorate the walls of the hostel came from owner Lorenzo Busi. A former graffiti artist himself, Busi witnessed firsthand the power these artists and their work have to inspire change. Inspiring change is a theme at The RomeHello. It has the unique identity of being both hostel and social enterprise. Rome has high unemployment rates among the city's youth and those from disadvantaged backgrounds; this situation inspired Busi to focus on employing people from those demographics.

The rooms at The RomeHello are awesome. There's a mix of spacious dorms and private rooms, all with extremely comfy beds and en suite bathrooms. Dorms have personal reading lights, USB chargers, plus spacious storage lockers beneath every bed (bring your own lock).

There's a guest kitchen on the ground floor and a cozy lounge complete with Nintendo Switch and sofas to sink into with a travel guide from the bookshelf. Prefer to chill with a beer? Socialize in The Barrel Bar—an American, post-industrial style-bar which features great live music from the Roman and international music scene. There's also a very generous buffet breakfast with fruit, fresh bread, beans, bacon, scrambled eggs, coffee, tea, and cake for an extra 8€ (6€ if you book in advance).

Good to know

PRICE RANGE
$ $ $ $ $
AMENITIES INCLUDE
self-catering facilities;
induction hobs; Nintendo
Switch console; foosball
tables; ping pong table;
inner courtyard; guest
computers and printer;
bar; buffet breakfast
available; en suite dorms.

Tip: Socialize in
The Barrel Bar—
an American,
post-industrial
style-bar that
features great
live music from
the Roman
and international
music scene.

Ostello Bello

An Italian sanctuary with exceptional staff

Ostello Bello is a hostel with distinct Italian flair. Guests here can enjoy a free Mediterranean breakfast, lazy afternoons on a bright terrace, and an evening aperitivo with locals at a traditional Italian-style bar.

With a welcome drink on arrival, guests can sip on a Peroni or an Aperol spritz while filling out passport details in the common room, one of the coziest a hostel can have. The excellent Mediterranean breakfast here is included in the price of a night's stay and, impressively, is available on demand. The common room is also home to a traditional Italian-style bar and restaurant. After work, locals pile in and join the hostel's international guests for their extremely popular aperitivo hour. Hostel guests can help themselves to food and grab a glass of wine or beer from the bar. The bar is open almost 24 hours a day.

Rooms here are bright and spacious. The dorm rooms have well-spaced beds with drawers beneath to secure valuables. All rooms are en suite and there's air conditioning in every room and common area.

Another thing to love about Ostello Bello is the large and bright terrace, complete with hammocks and barbecue facilities. Guests can also access a kitchen on the second floor and help themselves to free pasta prepared by the chef earlier in the day. Free coffee and tea is always available.

Last but not least, the staff at Ostello Bello are very friendly— a massive incentive for staying at this hostel. They make Ostello Bello feel like a sanctuary where travelers can relax and enjoy Milan.

Good to know

PRICE RANGE
$$$$$

AMENITIES INCLUDE
24-hour reception;
free WiFi; self-catering
facilities; free tours
and info; USB plug near
each bed; lounge with
TV (incl. DVD, Wii, PS3);
board games; ping pong
table; foosball; arcade
games; musical
instruments; free cultural
activities (flea markets,
live music, exhibitions,
tastings, etc.); free
breakfast at any time;
free dinner during
happy hour (7–9 p.m.);
bar; free coffee and tea.

Tip: Try some
of the free pasta
prepared by
the in-house chef
each day.

Ostello Bello

▷ *Good to know*

PRICE RANGE
$ $ $ $ $
AMENITIES INCLUDE
air conditioning; book exchange; hot showers; cots available; dishwasher; fridge / freezer; dryer; outdoor terrace; reading light; hair dryer; iron / ironing board; safe deposit box.

Tip: Try the hostel's free evening aperitivo where you can feast on pasta, couscous, or risotto. Ostello Bello for the win!
◁

Luxury at Lake Como is no longer reserved for the likes of George Clooney and other celebrities. Ostello Bello offers stylish accommodations with funky furnishings at a backpacker's price.

Housed in a 1920s townhouse, the hostel has a vintage industrial chic vibe thanks to the preservation of the original patterned floor tiles that contrast nicely with bright, colored chairs, unfinished walls, and exposed pipes. The courtyard hammocks and secret garden also give it an elegant touch.

The rooms—a mix of cozy privates and stylish dorms with metallic yellow bunk beds—all enjoy en suite facilities and air conditioning. Dorms feature reading lamps, private lockers, and USB charging points as standard. Additional features here are similar to other Ostello Bello hostels and include an amazing all-day breakfast buffet, a free welcome drink (a proper pint or glass of wine), plus the favorite: the free evening aperitivo where you can feast on pasta, couscous, or risotto. Ostello Bello for the win!

The Beehive

A hybrid of a hostel and a holistic retreat, The Beehive is the perfect place to unwind after a day of exploring Italy's bustling capital and to mingle with fellow guests while enjoying a glass of organic wine from Umbria. The hostel has elements of contemporary design, warm-colored interiors, and beautiful family portraits from the owners, Steve and Linda Brenner, who will make you feel right at home. Passionate locals, the Brenners have some great tips to share, like recommending the best gelateria in town (a subject of fierce debate among Romans). Breakfast is not included in the room price, but if you do splash out, it's a real treat. The exciting options range from scrambled tofu with veggies, juk (a Korean rice porridge), or French toast with fruit and honey. The owners also host pop-up dinners, lunches from local chefs, a yummy weekly vegan aperitivo buffet, cooking classes, and a monthly storytellers' event. There's an option here to suit every type of traveler and budget: an eight-bed dormitory, stylish private rooms, and guest rooms with self-catering facilities off-site. The private rooms are brightly colored and have huge windows that breathe in light. With lots of wardrobe space plus your own private sink and locally sourced, handmade vegetable soaps, the private rooms are definitely the top pick for travelers!

Good to know

PRICE RANGE
$ $ $ $ $
AMENITIES INCLUDE
an organic vegetarian café offering generous portions of locally sourced, home-cooked goodness; lounge; blissful garden area. Breakfast not included.

Tip: The owners host pop-up dinners, lunches from local chefs, a yummy weekly vegan aperitivo buffet, cooking classes, and a monthly storytellers' event.

Dopa Hostel

A gathering place built on positive vibes

Centrally located in the historic university quarter of Bologna, Dopa Hostel is situated in a charming sixteenth-century building that the owner fell in love with after three years of backpacking his way across the world. In a city that is not traditionally known for great hostels, the owner's dream was to create a place that would become a meeting point between Bologna and the world. The name "DOPA" is derived from dopamine, the chemical substance our body produces in moments of excitement, happiness, and positive energy. Thanks to the friendly multilingual staff and the incredible attention to detail, the surge of positive energy lives within the walls of the hostel.

Ninety-nine percent of what you can see and touch inside the hostel has been handmade by locals. A mix of Reggio Emilia icons and objects using materials like wood and steel have given the hostel a warm yet distinctive style. Besides a few private en suites, the hostel offers a mix of four, six, and eight-bed mixed dorms featuring stylish pod-style bunk beds and curtains to offer maximum privacy. There are personal reading lights in each bed and private cabinets with clothes hangers. Rooms come equipped with private lockers with individual power sockets, allowing you to charge your electronic items without having to worry about them.

Dopa has a spacious kitchen; every morning guests are served a generous, free buffet breakfast with coffee, tea, biscuits, cereal, bread, jam, fresh cheese, and local Italian specialties such as mortadella.

Good to know

PRICE RANGE
$ $ $ $ $
AMENITIES INCLUDE
free WiFi and internet
access; free printing;
laundry facilities;
self-catering facilities;
bicycle rentals; free
coffee and tea.
Breakfast included.

Tip: The hostel
organizes a dinner
twice a week
with the aid of local
chefs. For a small
fee you can have
a really nice Italian
dinner with the
added opportunity
to mingle with fellow
guests. Delizioso!

We_Crociferi

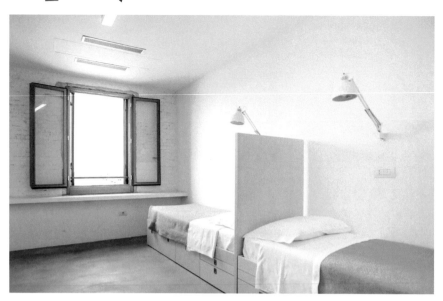

Good to know

PRICE RANGE
$ $ $ $ $

AMENITIES INCLUDE
laundry facilities;
library; meeting room;
bar; cloister.

Tip: We_Crociferi's
location is just
around the corner
from the boat
terminal, making
travel and sightseeing
a breeze. Plus
you can enjoy an
Italian aperitivo
on their sunny
terrace along one
of the many canals.

Sleeping in an ancient twelfth-century convent in Venice's Sestiere Cannaregio, guests of We_Crociferi will be transported back in time. Newly renovated, We_Crociferi doubles as a student residence during school terms, but transforms into a hostel for culture-loving visitors in the summer.

The ancient convent's architectural details have been preserved on the outside, but on the inside it's a modern hostel with all the necessary conveniences. The cloisters are now open communal spaces, where guests can sip on drinks from the lively hostel bar. A large dining area is decorated with colorful maps of the world and the library, study hall, and auditorium are all great places to convene.

The hostel is divided into twin rooms, studios, apartments, and beds in shared rooms. Rooms are white and basic with simple furnishings, but sometimes the history of the building breaks through and catches the eye. This is evident in the old frescoes that adorn the ceilings, the exposed brickwork, and tall fluted columns. On the functional side, each unit has an en suite bathroom with shower and some rooms have a kitchenette with induction hob.

Dock Inn Hostel

It may seem strange, but the novelty of sleeping in discarded shipping containers, with a unique view of the historic Warnemünde shipyard and its hulking cranes, has a stylish charm. Dock Inn Hostel is built out of old shipping containers welded together to make up 64 rooms of four and eight-bed dorms. Backpackers visiting the Baltic Coast will love the laid-back and maritime appeal.

The distinctive oblong shape is all that remains to remind you of the containers' former purpose. Each unit contains a sleeping area, bathroom, and a cozy living room corner with flat screen TV. The interiors have been furnished with comfortable furniture upholstered with natural materials and decorated with muted colors. The industrial theme continues throughout the building with concrete walls and exposed pipes forming part of the decor.

The facilities here are fantastic and on par with some of the best hostels in the world. If you want to cook, there is a fully equipped guest kitchen. Every second Thursday of the month the hostel hosts a "Sushi Session," inviting guests to take part in a three-hour professional sushi-making workshop. On other days you can also choose to dine at the in-house restaurant-bar.

The hostel offers bicycle rentals so guests can explore the beautiful, sandy Baltic coastline. And, thanks to the stiff breeze, this is also an ideal place for surfing, kiteboarding, and windsurfing.

Providing all important essentials, yet remaining easygoing, Dock Inn is the perfect hostel for active holidaymakers, design enthusiasts, families, and backpackers. ⌂

Good to know

PRICE RANGE
$ $ $ $ $
AMENITIES INCLUDE
24-hour reception; self-catering facilities; laundry facilities; rock climbing hall; sauna; cinema; meeting room; foosball, pinball, and more; restaurant.

Tip: Those who wish to burn off excess energy during bad weather periods can pay a visit to the rock climbing wall in the adjoining building. Dock Inn also has a spa on the roof including a sauna!

Upcoming destinations

For avoiding the crowds

Hektor Design Hostel, Tartu

Olomouc is is a perfect alternative to visiting Prague. The Czech Republic's sixth largest city is remarkably well preserved with eye-catching pastel facades and stunning architecture. The price of eating out and drinking is far cheaper due to the large student population. Located in the old town, the historic yet modern design hostel <u>Long Story Short Hostel</u> (p. 258) is the perfect place to stay in Olomouc. Instead of visiting Amsterdam, consider staying in the sleepy historic town of Haarlem. It is just 20 minutes away from the capital city and in close proximity to the beach. Haarlem has a wealth of well-preserved heritage buildings, plus a fantastic local brewery, Jopen, located in an old church. <u>Hello I'm Local</u> (p. 86) is a boutique hostel in Haarlem with 12 beautiful rooms, an outdoor patio, and lovely staff. If the

crowds of tourists in Paris overwhelm you, hop on the train to nearby Lille for something more relaxed. It has a great live music scene, thanks to the large student population, and the beautiful seventeenth century half-timbered houses and cobbled streets make it a very worthwhile stopover. You will find one of Europe's most welcoming and fun hostels in Lille. The very central <u>Gastama Hostel</u> (p. 124) has an outstanding on-site bar with 14 thirst-quenching beers on tap. If you are a foodie, then a visit to Bologna, one of Europe's oldest university cities, is a must. Besides sampling dishes such as tagliatelle ragù and experiencing the Italian tradition of aperitivo, this city offers beautiful red brick architecture and a lively, affordable bar scene. The centrally located <u>Dopa Hostel</u> (p. 144) is a great place to stay here. The Estonian city of Tartu is a fab pick for a weekend away or pitstop when hitting the Baltics. There are museums, cultural events, great nightlife, and the recently opened <u>Hektor Design Hostel</u> (p. 192).

Every year, the peak season in Europe's most popular destinations brings with it an ever higher tide of tourists. This often leads to increased prices for hostel rooms, overcrowding, long queues at visitor attractions, and a host of other problems that come with over-tourism. As a traveler, you can make a difference by visiting other places where you can have a positive impact on the local economy. There are plenty of places that can benefit from tourism, so head to smaller towns and villages for a glimpse of Europe away from the hordes of mainstream tourists. You will not only be welcomed, but you will also find it much easier to book affordable accommodation. Food and drink prices are cheaper, and often there is a good live music. With this in mind, we have compiled a list of off-the-beaten-path and upcoming destinations that are relatively untouched by mass tourism.

Hello I'm Local, Haarlem

Long Story Short Hostel, Olomouc

Head to smaller towns and villages for *a glimpse of Europe* away from the hordes of mainstream tourists.

Superbude St. Pauli

Unearthing Hamburg's maritime heritage one night at a time

Located in a beautiful brick building slap bang in the heart of Hamburg, Superbude (bude is "digs" in German) stands out as one of the most exciting design concepts in the budget accommodation sector. A reflection of the city's past and present, the hostel's design pays respect to the maritime heritage of Hamburg. A rope pattern motif pops up everywhere, from wooden panels on the bathrooms and corridors to the carpets. Superbude's signature yellow color is derived from the brand colors of the former resident of the building: Deutsche Post.

The hostel's designer, Armin Fischer of Dreimeta, created some unique features—ideas you may be inspired to apply in your own home. Old water pipes have been screwed together to create the most amazing magazine rack you will see in any hotel or hostel; chairs have been created from old wheelbarrows; old Astra beer crates have been up-holstered with old jeans from past residents; and the hostel key rings are made from old skateboards. From plunger coat hangers to tiny metallic anchors in the bathrooms and mousetraps used as pin boards, the level of detail in this hostel is incredible.

Room interiors cleverly mix the outlandish with the contemporary. The wallpaper is a collage of news stories from Hamburg's past and present; Konstantin Gricic's Mayday lamps hang from the goal-netting headboards of the beds—a nod to the city's local cult football club, St. Pauli; and a third of the hostel's 89 rooms feature stackable beds by Rolf Heide. All rooms have a TV, wireless internet and a bathroom with a hairdryer. The best room in the house is no

Good to know

PRICE RANGE
$ $ $ $ $
AMENITIES INCLUDE
24-hour reception; WiFi
and internet access; free
printing; common room;
Kitchen Club; bar.
Breakfast not included.

Tip: Make sure not
to miss one of the free,
local mint-concerts
performed at the hostel.
Guests also gain access
to the best live music
clubs in the area
thanks to the hostel's
close connections
with local clubs and
live music venues.

The *Superbude* is superbly located. Everything Hamburg has to offer is at your fingertips.

doubt the epic Astra Rockstar Suite, which can be rented out for private parties. The room has a stage that folds up into a sleeping area, and Astra beer is available in the headboards. There is also a self-service kitchen.

The musical theme continues in the hostel's lounge, where local bands perform free mini-concerts. Guests also gain access to the best live music clubs in the area thanks to the hostel's close connections with local clubs and live music venues.

The hostel common room is pretty much your perfect living room.

There's plenty of comfy sofas and upholstered leather chairs for relaxing and enjoying all the latest magazines. The self-service fridges in the lobby and the equipped Kitchen Club are free for guests and make you feel right at home. There's WiFi throughout the hotel and iMacs in the lobby lounge, all free of charge, available 24/7—the perfect way to stay in touch with the rest of the globe.

Breakfast is not included, but a pretty filling buffet is served from 7:00 a.m. until 12:00 p.m. with a choice of cappuccino, espresso, latte, or organic fair-trade tea, and a variety

of cereals, fresh fruit, boiled eggs, hams and cheeses, or waffles (preferably with a good dollop of Nutella).

The Superbude is superbly located. It's close to the Reeperbahn, Schanzenviertel, and Karoviertel districts as well as concerts, clubs, bars, cafés, culture, street art, and lifestyle: Everything Hamburg has to offer is at your fingertips.

With a cool, unique vibe, the beautiful communal lounge, the fantastic, functional design, and a focus on supporting the local music scene, this is the place to be if you are coming to Hamburg.

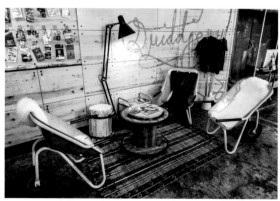

Superbude St. Georg

A colorful hostel designed by creative collaborators

Superbude Hamburg St. Georg is a convenient base for discovering the city's sights and sounds. It is within close proximity to the central station, Hamburg Hauptbahnhof; the famed shopping mile of Mönckebergstraße; magical Miniatur Wunderland; and the former docklands of HafenCity.

Armin Fischer of Dreimeta helped with the refurbishment of the property, having worked on the design of Superbude Hamburg St. Pauli. The design of St. Georg similarly reflects the city's maritime heritage and draws on key travel themes, such as the longing for freedom, home, and perpetual wanderlust.

There are a lot of clever and interesting details packed into this hostel. Each floor is differentiated by color—blue, red, beige, green, pink, and grey—and the noise-absorbing carpet is printed with imagery of container ships with cargo, booth number, and origin. Longboards by Madrid Skateboards feature as shelves on the walls.

There is a diverse range of accommodation options, from single and en suite doubles to four and six-bed dorms for those on a budget. All rooms have a large flat screen TV and free WiFi. Book the Palomabude studio for a night of fun

nostalgia. Designed in collaboration with Paloma Lemonade, the suite is decked out in bright pinks and yellows, and features bunk beds plus plenty of comfy corners (not to mention a top-of-the-range entertainment system). It's like a childhood sleepover but with a local Astra beer in hand. Local Hamburg brand fritz-kola also converted one of the six-bed dorm rooms into the fritz-bude studio. It has scaffold bed frames and a vinyl room with a record collection and record player. The St. Georg Kitchenclub is open for breakfast from 7:00 a.m. to 1:00 p.m. There is a range of facilities for guests to enjoy.

Outside of the hostel, port cruises and nights out on the Reeperbahn are Hamburg highlights.

Wombat's City Hostel

▷ *Good to know*

PRICE RANGE
$ $ $ $ $
AMENITIES INCLUDE
free WiFi; self-catering
facilities; laundry
facilities; pool table;
nailing game; (hair dryer
travel guidebooks,
umbrellas, available with
deposit); bar.

Tip: Get your free
drink on arrival,
which you can enjoy
at the excellent
womBar. The womB
also has special
drink offers, three
different happy hour
each day, and many
special events. And
don't miss out on the
free walking tour
of Vienna, which
starts right from the
◁ hostel lobby.

Situated in a former residential building, Wombats City Hostel in Vienna overlooks Vienna's most famous market Naschmarkt. With the hostel's emphasis on a social atmosphere, Viennese design agency Lucy.D designed the rooms and spaces to allow guests to mingle and interact with each other. The open-plan lobby with mismatched furniture pieces, feels more like a lounge than just a reception for check-in. Stocked with lots of brochures, travel guides and maps of the city, this is a great, cozy area to read, relax, or socialize with old or new friends.

The rooms varying from private en suite doubles to four and six-bed dorms are stylish with a modern, minimalist design—kind of like that IKEA showroom that you can just never get your own room to resemble. All of the rooms come with comfy wooden beds and en suite bathrooms. The female-only dorms have full-length mirrors and come with a hairdryer in the bathroom. Cleanliness is next to godliness for this hostel staff—they take it very seriously here and have twice won the HostelWorld award for the Cleanest Hostel Chain Worldwide.

Wombats is very secure with keycard access for the front door, each floor, the rooms, and personal lockers. Free WiFi access in the common areas is excellent and they started extending it to the guest bedrooms, which is great news. Linen is included, as is luggage storage. The hostel offers a free drink on arrival, which you can enjoy at the excellent womBar. The womBar also has special drink offers, three different happy hours each day, and a lot of special events. There is a small kitchenette for guests to use. Plenty of supermarkets can be found in the neighborhood, making it perfect if you're looking to cook and save money. Wombats offer an excellent breakfast—one of the best you will find in a hostel. The all-you-can-eat breakfast offers a very generous spread which includes coffee, bread, selection of cheese and cold meats like prosciutto and salami, hard-boiled eggs, yogurts, fruit, honey, cereals, and lots of Nutella. There is also the opportunity for guests to join a free walking tour of Vienna, which starts right from the hostel lobby.

Grand Hostel Berlin

Grand Hostel Berlin combines a bit of old world charm with great modern hospitality. It's situated in a former bishop's Palace (dating back to 1874) in the trendy Friedrichshain-Kreuzberg district, and its location and many great features—a stunning library bar, friendly staff, and spacious bunk-bee dorms—make this hostel a great choice for exploring Berlin.

The standout feature is the 1920s-style library bar. It's impossibly cool with volumes of old dusty books from floor to ceiling that you can leaf through while enjoying a coffee.

The rooms have broad bay windows that open out to the tranquil Landwehr Canal, and the surviving original ceilings, decorated with beautiful stuccowork, exude

a historical palatial quality. The double rooms are beautifully furnished with a bit of old-fashioned charm: potted plants, a dressing table, and a walk-in wardrobe.

You're just a short walk away from Mustafa's kebab heaven. Warning: The line tends to be long, so grab a bottle of beer to ease the pain of a long wait. It's worth it in the end.

Good to know

PRICE RANGE
$ $ $ $ $
AMENITIES INCLUDE
guest events; bar; terrace; bicycle rentals; tour guides; German lessons; specially priced public transport tickets; beer tastings; pub crawls. Breakfast.

Tip: Discover the trendy area of Friedrichshain-Kreuzberg around the hostel or spend a cosy evening at the hostel's stunning library bar. It's impossibly cool with volumes of old dusty books from floor to ceiling.

Berlin: a city celebrating freedom

As the *second biggest city* in the European Union and the capital of Germany, you might think Berlin would be an expensive place to visit, but it doesn't have to be.

There are plenty of wonderful things to do for free, especially if you plan on visiting in summer, which I highly recommend. Here are some of my favorite tips to make the most of your trip.

Where to eat

Berlin is home to a population made up of more than 190 nationalities, and no other city in Germany matches the city's rich culinary diversity. Boasting one of the world's largest Vietnamese communities, this is a great place to enjoy the Asian cuisine. I'm a fan of the Vietnamese bánh mì, a sandwich that mixes French and Vietnamese ingredients. My favorite is at the wonderful, unassuming Cô Cô bánh mì deli.

Berlin is also home to the biggest Turkish community outside Turkey, which is known for the döner kebab. Personally I am not a fan, but I do recommend trying a köfte sandwich at Izmir Köftecisi near the dingy Kottbusser Tor. Head to the Turkish Market on Maybachufer on Tuesdays or Fridays to buy fresh vegetables, sample Turkish specialties such as gözleme, and discover an assortment of colorful fabrics. It's right next to

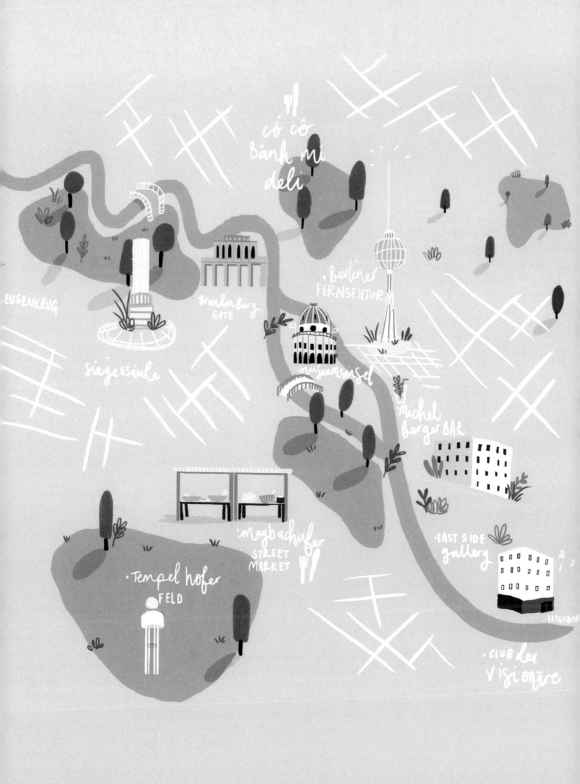

cô cô
bánh mi
deli

• berliner
FERNSEHTURM

EUSENKRUG

Brandenburg
GATE

siegessäule

museuminsel

Michel
Burger BAR

maybachufer
STREET
MARKET

• Tempelhofer
FELD

• EAST SIDE
gallery

• BERGHAIN

• CLUB der
VISIONÄRE

Neukölln, Berlin's most multicultural area and a cool food hub.

Here, Azzam is the place to go for cheap, authentic Arabic food, and there's a tiny piece of Scotland around the corner. The bar Das Gift is owned by Scottish musician Barry Burns from the band Mogwai, here you can sample Irn Bru and Tunnocks Caramel Wafers.

Where to drink

When the weather is nice, locals love to grab a beer from the iconic späti (late-night store) and go to the park. Even though Berlin is not known for its beer gardens, there are Bavarian-style brauhäuser you might enjoy, such as the Austro-German tavern Weihenstephaner Berlin. On the edge of Berlin's green lung, Tiergarten, you'll find Schleusenkrug, an outdoor biergarten, perfect for a late afternoon beer.

Ever thought of finding a perfectly palatable craft beer at a hostel? No, me neither. That is until I stepped into the basement of the Circus Hostel, which has a microbrewery. Pop into the David Hasselhoff Museum next door while you're there.

Entering many bars can almost feel like walking into someone's apartment. Bohnengold has that down-to-earth feel with beautiful people spread out across its

two rooms. I'm also a huge fan of the style-conscious Michelberger Hotel. Pick your drink of choice from their Book of Booze (gin and tonics are great here) and enjoy the cool decor, with lampshades made out of book covers, vintage chairs, and big sofas surrounded by piles of books.

Where to party

There's no city with a nightlife scene quite like Berlin. First of all, there's no official closing time for clubs, so you can often enter on a Friday night and leave on a Monday morning...

On Tuesdays I love going to the jam sessions at Das Edelweiss, a brick behemoth in Görlitzer Park. The atmosphere is electric, and you can smell the sweat, cigarette smoke, and anticipation when you're walking up the stairs. They also open the floor to the audience—if you're musically inclined.

Berlin's techno scene is legendary, and Berghain, Tresor, and Watergate are three of the best clubs in the world. But be aware of the often long queues and notoriously fickle door policy, especially in Berghain.

In summer I highly recommend Club der Visionaere, a riverside bar by Landwehr Canal. It has a relaxed atmosphere, and you can dance outdoors on the wooden deck or pull up a chair with friends.

Going for a walk

My favorite walk is a few hours long and is perfect for anyone visiting Berlin for the first time as it takes in all the sights. I start at Museum Island, where you can pop into the Pergamon Museum to see the famous Pergamon Altar and beautiful Ishtar Gate.

Don't forget to take a picture from the enchanting Friedrichsbrücke before walking up the grand boulevard of Unter den Linden. To the right you will see the Neue Wache and Käthe Kollwitz's sculpture *Mother with her Dead Son*. It's one of my favorite monuments. Keep strolling to the left and you'll find Lustgarten, with the majestic Berliner Dom in the background. This green oasis is the perfect place to relax with a book. The more haunting Bebelplatz is nearby; it's where the Nazis burnt the books of those they persecuted.

Walking west past the Neue Wache brings you to the historic Brandenburg Gate. Once a symbol of a divided city, it is now an icon of Berlin and reunified Germany. It's worth hanging around the elegant Pariser Platz to watch the flow of tourists and the colorful characters that congregate here.

Move on through the Brandenburg Gate and you will see the Reichstag building with its beautiful glass dome. The views from here are fantastic. Continue to your left for the Holocaust Memorial, another moving and symbolic architectural gem of Berlin. You can learn more about the Jewish victims of the Holocaust in the memorial's subterranean museum.

Now head straight to the lively Potsdamer Platz, and end the journey at the Ritz Carlton's fabulous Curtain Club for one of the best cocktails in town.

There's no city with a *nightlife scene* quite like <u>Berlin</u>. First of all, there's no official closing time for clubs, so you can often enter on a Friday night and leave on a Monday morning ...

Getting around town

Berlin has a transport system that is extensive, user-friendly, and reasonably reliable. It's also not that expensive given its size, especially compared to other European cities. I love taking the bus when I have time to spare. It can be a scenic way to take in all the main sights, especially if you manage to get a seat up front on the upper deck. The routes 100 and 200 take in many of Berlin's key landmarks, from Alexanderplatz to the Reichstag or Schloss Bellevue.

The best place to relax

I love spending time in Tempelhofer Feld, a former airfield in the middle of the city and a public park since 2008. You won't find much shade here, but it's a great place to cycle, rollerblade, or even windsurf. Another classic spot is by the Landwehrkanal to watch the sunset. On a warm evening, it's full of people hanging out, drinking beer, and enjoying each other's company while the sun goes down. Grab a spot amongst the crowd and soak up the atmosphere—it's the perfect way to end a day in Berlin.

Best viewpoint

One of my favorite viewpoints in Berlin is from the Siegessäule (Victory Column), nicknamed Goldelse by locals, which translates to Golden Lizzy. Climb the 285 steps to admire the panoramic views of Tiergarten, the Soviet War Memorial, and the Brandenburg Gate. Germany's tallest building and Berlin's most prominent landmark, the Fernsehturm, also known as the TV Tower, is a must visit. It has a viewing platform and revolving restaurant offering a stunning 360-degree view of the city.

Secret places

Teufelsberg is a place like no other, and its rarely visited because of its hidden location near Grunewald. This former spy station served as a listening post for British and American intelligence officers during the Cold War. Stripped bare by thieves and with every available surface covered with graffiti, the place has a post-apocalyptic feel. From the top of the tower you'll have the surreal view of large radar domes (nicknamed Berlin's Balls). The site was only very recently officially opened to the public, not that it deterred visitors previously. Now, thanks to the efforts of volunteers, the place is protected and an unexpected hidden gem that is well worth the trip.

The Circus

Where history is made and celebrated

With a museum dedicated to "The Hoff" (yes, think superlative *Baywatch* paraphernalia); a basement microbrewery; organized tours to abandoned spy stations; plus breakfast served until 1 p.m. (and also the most delicious currywurst pies!), the Circus Hostel is truly a hostel like no other in the world.

"When we started the Circus Hostel back in 1997," Tilman Hierath, one of the founders, says, "the concept of hosteling was still new to Germany. The only thing we firmly believed was that we wanted to welcome travelers to our hostel in a way that we would like to be welcomed when we travel ourselves."

This refreshing perspective is a welcome antidote to the arcane and outdated concepts of traditional hospitality. As a very well-traveled bunch of people, but with no formal qualifications in tourism or hospitality, the founders' understanding is a pretty simple but effective one:

"We believe our guests want a safe and secure home during their time in the city. Plus a good cup of coffee. That's what we aim to provide to guests coming to the Circus." Located on Rosenthaler Platz in Berlin's central Mitte district, guests of the Circus Hostel have a direct link to the heart of the city and can feel its everyday rhythms. The Circus takes great pride in its surroundings and this is reflected in the hallways where a number of slideshows share the history of Rosenthaler Platz and its many phases of development. The hostel also organizes an excellent monthly program called the Circus Talks where you can hear a variety of speakers, such as former U.S. Air Force personnel on what life was like in the divided city, and locals sharing stories of growing up on Rosenthaler Platz between 1935 and 1953. Another special feature of this hostel is

Good to know

PRICE RANGE
$ $ $ $ $
AMENITIES INCLUDE
bar/brewery; café; free
WiFi; bike rentals;
exclusive "Behind The
Curtain" tours; late
check-out; no curfew;
hairdryer; chargers to
borrow; organized
events (free walking
tours, karaoke at the bar,
trivia night, etc.).
Breakfast not included.

*Tip: Have a beer
at their basement
microbrewery, take
a tour to abandoned
spy stations or visit
the hostel's museum
dedicated to David
Hasselhoff.*

The Circus Hostel offers a perfect balance of great value, funky vibes, and really nice accommodations.

their basement microbrewery. It's a really nice place to meet fellow guests and have a cheeky on-site beer.

An amazing—albeit, unusual—feature of the hostel is their museum dedicated to David Hasselhoff. "The Hoff" is a bit of a cult hero in these parts thanks to his hit single, "Freedom", and his claimed role in the fall of the Berlin Wall. The small museum is complete with Hoff memorabilia and chest hair.

The Circus Hostel offers a perfect balance of great value, funky vibes, and really nice accommodations. Medium-sized dorm rooms are amazing value: no bunk beds here. You have four or five single beds, spaced out, and each has a reading light, fluffy pillow, and duvet. Shared bathrooms are clean and well maintained and locker space is available for valuables, or there's

the option of private en suite rooms. If you're looking for something more luxurious, rent the penthouse apartment, which comes with a full kitchen and stunning panoramic views of Mitte and the TV Tower in the distance.

The Circus Hostel welcomes a nice mix of travelers—backpackers, flashpackers, students, and also couples and mature travelers. It's not strictly what one might call a "party hostel," but has a nice communal vibe and social atmosphere. The reception area is a fun place for guests to chill and dip into an abundance of tourist literature on the city. Or, if you need technology, you can rent an iPad, iPod, or laptop there too. Staff, like their international guests, come from a wide variety of cool backgrounds and are really helpful and friendly. Their attention to detail,

like the awesome DIY walking tours (starting and ending at the Circus), and stock of bikes, Segways, and even rollerblades for rent, shows how they've thought of all their guests' possible needs.

The on-site bar and café area, Katz & Maus, does a great selection of food including an excellent all-you-can-eat buffet breakfast served daily until 1 p.m. For lunch or dinner, try their twisted Katz & Maus burgers served with potato salad or their delicious currywurst pies. The coffee here is excellent; the beans come from Costa Rica and the hostel gives 10 percent of coffee revenue to charity.

All in all, this place is so much more than just a bed for the night—it provides a real experience and feel of the city. The world definitely needs more hostels like the Circus.

Multitude Hostel

Homey charm in historical Leipzig

After studying and traveling, friends Georg and Jonas decided to build a small hostel and bar in an abandoned building in Leipzig's west end. They renovated the century-old building over several years before opening what is now a homey space for locals and travelers alike, and a great base for exploring Leipzig.

A lot of traditional materials, such as the wooden floors, brick walls, and original wooden doors, have been kept in the hostel's design.

And much of the furniture, from the kitchen to the beds themselves, has been upcycled or custom built. The whole place has been decorated with prints designed by local artists; that are available to buy as souvenirs.

The bunk beds feature blackout curtains, lockable drawers with built-in sockets, reading lights, and charging points. Comfort here is guaranteed: The mattress brand has been top-rated by the most renowned German testing institute. Fully equipped bathrooms are right next to the rooms. The double rooms have private balconies. For city tips, most of the staff live on-site and

are able to give guests advice on exceptional exhibitions or the locations of Leipzig's best parties. But staying on-site is an option too. The hostel has an in-house bar and beer garden which is popular with locals. Multitude Hostel hosts plenty of events there, from parties to quiz nights, and sometimes concerts.

In the summertime you can look forward to spending relaxing afternoons in the beer garden here, and in winter there's a fireplace in the bar you can snuggle up to, making Hostel Multitude a fantastic place to visit any time of year.

Good to know

PRICE RANGE
$ $ $ $ $

AMENITIES INCLUDE
linens; towel rentals;
free WiFi; self-catering
facilities; laundry
service; luggage
storage; library; board
games; bar; beer garden.

Tip: For city tips,
most of the staff live
on-site and are able
to give guests advice
on exceptional
exhibitions or the
locations of Leipzig's
best parties. The hostel
bar hosts plenty of
events too, from parties
to quiz nights, and
sometimes concerts.

Eden Hostel & Garden

Embrace transformation in Germany's eastern cultural hub

Young, green, and creative, Leipzig appears to be the quintessential bohemian paradise at first glance. But to really understand what the city is all about, you need a little guidance from the locals who helped make it the cultural hub it is today. That's why Eden Hostel & Garden is the place to stay in Saxony's coolest city.

Since the early 2000s, artists and creators from Germany and beyond have flocked to Leipzig with new ideas for the city's old—and frequently vacant—buildings.

Among them a group of four young women, who transformed an abandoned low-rise that used to house GDR apprentices into a local landmark. Now one of Leipzig's preeminent hostels, Eden houses travelers who wish to visit one of Germany's fastest growing and culturally rich cities.

Contrary to what critics have said, Leipzig is not about "the hype." It's about the people, an ambitious community, and the freedom to orchestrate and support creative grassroots projects in a communal way. Whether it's pop-up art installations in one of the East's abandoned buildings or a secret

open-air party in the woods, it seems like nothing in Leipzig is permanent. Staying at Eden Hostel & Garden demonstrates what can be done with the creative opportunities Leipzig offers. The four hosts also have inside knowledge of what events people are currently hosting (before they quickly disappear and are replaced by something just as exciting).

Hostel & Garden Eden is located in the central west, one of Leipzig's most happening and artistic areas. It's only a five-minute walk away from Karl-Heine-Strasse, a street filled with various bars, interesting shops, and the Westwerk Gallery and Nightclub. From here you are →

Good to know

PRICE RANGE
$ $ $ $ $

AMENITIES INCLUDE
self-catering facilities;
barbecue; lockers;
luggage storage; bicycle
rentals; lounge/TV area;
garden; sun terrace;
fantastic coffee. Pets are
allowed on request for an
additional charge.

Tip: The beautiful
garden at the rear
of the building is often
used to host outdoor
cinema nights, art
exhibitions, and
parties for the entire
community, locals
and guests alike.

Staying at *Eden Hostel & Garden* demonstrates what can be done with the creative opportunities Leipzig has to offer.

only a 10-minute walk away from the famous Spinnerei, an old cotton mill converted into numerous open art galleries showing locals' works and international exhibitions. There's a tram station right next to the hostel if you're going further afield. An alternative way to discover the city is to rent a canoe and glide along the many canals.

For party people, Institut fuer Zukunft is widely regarded as one of the best clubs in Germany. If there are any club nights taking place there when you visit, don't miss it!

If you want to get out of the city, a 30-minute bike ride through the countryside will get you to the idyllic Cospudener See, perfect for swimming or relaxing on the beach with a beer. Eden Hostel & Garden offers the laid-back and trendy

lifestyle of Leipzig with an affordable price tag. Each room has been individually styled by local artists; guests can choose to stay in a variety of uniquely themed rooms. For example, one of the double rooms has a bed built into an old Fiat Fiorino (complete with a working radio) and walls painted with scenes of daily life in the Lindenau neighborhood. Alternatively, you can stay in a twin room inspired by the Scottish designer and architect Charles Rennie Mackintosh.

The pick of the dorm rooms is the six-bed female dorm, where each bunk bed has its own design, from Japanese sleeping pods to a space shuttle cockpit. Each bed has a large luggage locker, a bed lamp, and curtain for privacy. The common area is spacious,

with plenty of room to sit and dine with large groups or new friends. There are also books and board games for rainy days or quiet evenings. The guest kitchen is complete with all cooking and storage essentials; complimentary cornflakes, milk, coffee, and tea are available at all times.

Eden Hostel & Garden's name hints at its best feature: the beautiful garden at the rear of the building, complete with a shed, lawn chairs, and a sandbox for children. It is hugely popular with locals, too, who regularly pop by to chill in the garden with a coffee or beer. The garden is often used to host outdoor cinema nights, art exhibitions, and parties for the entire community, locals and guests alike.

Die Wohngemeinschaft

16 rooms à la *Choose Your Own Adventure*

Die Wohngemeinschaft (translated loosely as "shared flat") started out as a café-bar in the middle of Cologne's creative heart, the Belgian Quarter (Belgisches Viertel). After a number of flat-share requests from customers who never wanted to leave the bar, the owners relented and opened it up as a hostel in 2008.

All of the hostel's 16 rooms have been individually decorated with tons of charming details and their own unique stories. In the aptly named "Tom's Room" you will discover Tom, who moved to Canada after the death of his great aunt. He lived in her log cabin in Lake Tagish and sailed across the lake on her boat. On returning to Europe, he decided to make a bed from the boat. In the winter he comes and stays at the hostel, but his boat bed is yours if you visit Cologne. The fabulous Compagnie de Résisdanse is a ballroom-inspired female dorm and a favorite choice for lady travelers. The dorm beds here are the biggest in any hostel in the world (over 4½ feet,

1.4 meters!). Each bunk has a curtain and is completely separated from the other, so you have complete privacy. In addition, each bed has a reading lamp, plug socket, and a shelf to keep small belongings or loose change. The rooms at Die Wohngemeinschaft do not have en suite facilities; however, there are bathrooms on each floor, and they're inspected and cleaned regularly.

Die Wohngemeinschaft's original café-bar is still running, as popular as ever and packed with locals. It's a fantastic place to hang out →

*Tip: You are on the
doorstep of some of the
city's best and most
authentic places to eat.
Enjoy the best brunch
in town at Theater
in Bauturm and
the juiciest burgers
at Beef Brothers.
Also pay a visit to
the hostel's versatile
theater space.*

After a number of flat-share requests from customers who never wanted to leave the bar, the owners of *Die Wohngemeinschaft* relented and opened it up as a hostel in 2008.

and meet people; you can enjoy delicious coffee and wonderful pastries during the day and sample a traditional Mühlen Kölsch beer in the evening. Another cool feature is the hostel's versatile theater space. Open to the public and seating up to 70 people, the theater hosts events such as concerts with local and international bands, book readings, plays, and film screenings.

Inside the hostel, guests can relax in a common lounge, which has a cool retro-chic vibe. There's also a selection of DVDs and books, and bicycles and skateboards can be rented at reception.

An organic buffet breakfast is available in the lounge from 8 a.m. to 11 a.m. Most of the breakfast items are organic. Bread is sourced from a local bakery and all cold meats are sourced from a local organic farmer. ⌂

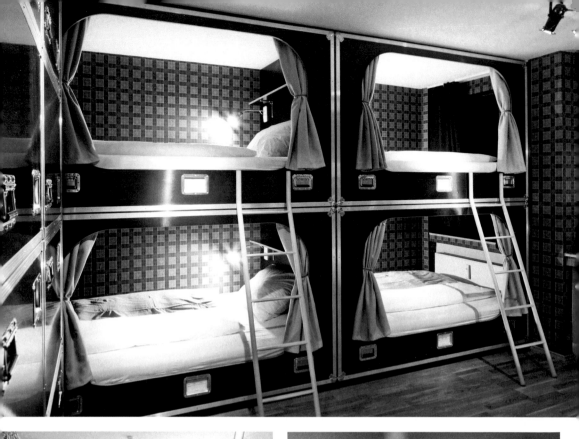

Copenhagen: Scandi finesse

Denmark has long been an inspiration in culture, politics and well-being, and wonderful *Copenhagen* is the perfect place to experience it.

I love Copenhagen. The Danish city has an emotional pull for me because it was the first place I visited on a memorable Interrail tour back in 2012. I love the beautiful architecture, eating my weight in hotdogs at the classic pølsevogn (hotdog stands) across the city, and discovering the incredible arts scene, including my favorite museum in the world, the wonderful Louisiana. The vast presence of beautiful parks and water makes you feel so close to nature, and last but not least, the hostel scene is amazing here. Copenhagen has so much to offer, and based on my past experiences and with the help of a few friends in the hostel world, I have a bunch of fun tips for you.

Where to eat

To me, there's nothing more typically Danish than the humble smørrebrød, an open-faced sandwich made with buttered rye bread. Nip into Domhusets Smørrebrød to sample one of the best in town. My favorite is the stjerneskud with egg, shrimp, caviar, a potato with a dollop of mayonnaise, and fried onions on top.

Torvehallerne is a wonderland of food stands with more than 60 selling everything from gourmet chocolate to organic, locally grown vegetables. Visit on Sparkling Wednesdays (every Wednesday) when you can taste reasonably priced bubbly.

Kødbyen— or the meatpacking district in Vesterbro—is one of Copenhagen's most popular places to go out, and Tommi's Burger Joint, an import from Reykjavik, is just one reason why. Expect quality burgers and thin-cut fries with a buffet of hot sauces and relishes to douse them in plus tasty milkshakes and craft beers, all served with a generous dose of Icelandic flair.

If you're looking for a premium dining experience, I definitely recommend visiting Hanzo, which is part of the Madklubben chain

of restaurants. The culinary focus is on Japan, Thailand, China, and Vietnam, but the chefs sometimes borrow inspiration from Laos and Cambodia as well. Choose the Hanzo experience: you are served 13 courses selected by the kitchen—all small dishes from the menu with a few surprises.

Where to drink

You are allowed to drink in public in Denmark if you behave. So, buy some drinks and go sit somewhere nice, like Nyhavn harbor, to enjoy the company of friends and watch people go by.

Blågårdsgade is one of my favorite streets. It has a festive feel, lined with basement bars and people drinking outside. Head into rock/metal bar Escobar for cheap whiskies and beers, and enjoy the quirky interior decor with lampshades made from industrial-sized baked bean cans. You can feel the hygge in Det Ny Scala, a cozy bar on Ravnsborggade. It is popular among locals and you can get well-priced gin and tonics. Finish your night in Bevar's with a coffee or beer, and an excellent program of live music ranging from jazz to swing.

» You should try the traditional *bodegas* (taverns), or bodega hopping, in Copenhagen. Start at Palæ Bar, then Do-Di Dar, then ask the guests where to go next. And the rest will be history. «

CHRISTOPHER ALM
— *Generator Copenhagen*

Where to party

The Generator Copenhagen, Steel House Copenhagen, and Urban House Meininger bars offer some of the cheapest drinks in town and a regular program of social events that draw the locals too.

But if you want to go really local, the city has an eclectic and varied party scene. Culture Box is perfect for electronic music lovers, and Rust features live music acts, R&B, and pop-heavy club nights. Shabby-chic Jolene Bar is also a big local favorite, as is the giant KB3 nightclub, which plays all kinds of music with a focus on electronic. If none of those appeal, try one of the many local pubs for a beer before bed.

Going for a walk

I love walking the streets parallel to the Strøget shopping street. The small pop-up cafés, one-of-a-kind stores, and locals-only restaurants will give you an experience of the true Copenhagen.

» In the morning and evening you will find Copenhageners walking around one of the city's many lakes. Remember to stop and hang out with young locals at Dronning Louises Bridge on a warm summer evening. Other nice places include the beach of Amager Strandpark,

Orstedsparenk, The King's Garden, and Frederiksberg Gardens. «

JEP FRIIS EGEFJORD
— *Steel House Copenhagen*

Getting around town

Copenhagen is a city made for biking, with cycle routes on almost every street. All three featured hostels in Copenhagen have bikes to rent in their backyard. I also recommend exploring town on foot. Bring your daypack, don't rush, enjoy the small gems, and experience all that Copenhagen's street life has to offer—it's one of Europe's most vibrant capitals.

Another cool way to discover the city is by taking a cruise along the idyllic canals. Tours last an hour and take in all the key sights, including Christiansborg Palace, Christianshavn, the Royal Library, Opera House, Amalienborg Palace, and the Little Mermaid statue.

The best place to relax

I love going to the Ny Carlsberg Glyptotek art museum to spend a few hours enjoying the fine collection of sculptures by Auguste Rodin—the largest collection outside of France. The museum also has a fantastic rooftop garden with great views of the city skyline and an excellent café in the Winter Garden, with free entry on Tuesdays!

To relax by the water, head to the harbor front by Skuespilhuset, the Royal Danish Playhouse. Islands Brygge, the botanical gardens, sauna, and outdoor hot tubs in Refshaleøen are also good places to go during summer.

I love the beautiful architecture, eating my weight in hotdogs at the classic *polsevogn* (hotdog stands) across the city, and discovering the incredible arts scene, including my favourite museum in the world, the wonderful *Louisiana*.

Best viewpoint

In summer I head up to the green-domed tower of the awe-inspiring Marble Church for panoramic views of the city. I also love the view of Copenhagen's old town from seventeenth-century Rundetårn tower, which is also the oldest functioning observatory in Europe.

> As you walk through the city, go into any tall hotel building and ask if you can take a picture from the rooftop terrace for your blog. You will be surprised how many will say yes. And for free. «

JEP FRIIS EGEFJORD
— *Steel House Copenhagen*

Secret places

I love visiting Christianshavn, an area of small islands in the heart of the city and one of Copenhagen's most interesting neighborhoods. It houses the alternative community of Freetown Christiania, as well as the popular Copenhagen Street Food marketplace.

> Christianshavn Boat Rentals and Café is my secret spot in Copenhagen. It's a floating bar on the canal where I can always enjoy a few hours of sunshine. This place really hits this spot. «

CHRISTOPHER ALM
— *Generator Copenhagen*

Other secret spots to check out include Damhussøen, a lake on the western periphery of the city. With football pitches, barbecue areas, nature playgrounds, and a well-marked track for walkers and runners, this is the perfect escape from the hustle and bustle of the city.

Steel House

Where industrial design meets Nordic hygge

Situated in Vesterbro, Copenhagen's most hipster area, and housed in the distinctive steel-clad building that was once home to the Danish Union of Metalworkers, this stylish design hostel launched in the summer of 2017, complete with a gym and a pool.

True to the roots of the hostel, the English designer Mike Duncalf has gone for an "industrial chic" vibe with the 253 rooms rooted in raw elements, soft textures, and rustic interiors. Reminiscent of New York-style, modern industrial lofts, expect wrought iron columns, exposed pipes, concrete, brick, and ductwork. The open-plan layout means there's plenty of communal spaces for guests to mingle and relax, from the spacious lounge with hardwood floors and leather Chesterfield sofas to the games rooms where you can try your hand at shuffleboard or have a beer at the on-site bar during its excellent value happy hour. In the basement lounge, the hostel hosts local acts and also throws a fab Karaoke night. Various bars and clubs are within walking distance, and Steel House guests get free entrance to the legendary local nightclub RUST.

This is a hostel that takes great pride in convenience and making their guests feel *hyggelig*—at home. From 6 a.m to 11 a.m. the hostel offers a Grab 'n' Go breakfast bag with tea or Fairtrade coffee included. Guests can download the hostel app that allows them to check in online and get their key directly on their mobile so that they can go straight to their rooms on arrival.

Good to know

PRICE RANGE
$ $ $ $ $

AMENITIES INCLUDE
WiFi; bar; pool; gym;
cinema; kitchen; lounge;
games room; TV room;
laundry, bike rental.
Breakfast not included.

Tip: Visit Tivoli
Gardens, The City
Square Hall, and the
famous pedestrian
shopping street,
Stroget, which are all
nearby. To explore the
city as a real
Copenhagener, Bicycle
rentals are also
available at the hostel.

Steel House Copenhagen is a hostel that takes great pride in convenience and making their guests feel *hyggelig*— at home.

Both staff and the amazing facilities create a nice, warm, and friendly atmosphere to make guests feel comfortable.

Choose from their luxurious six-bed or four-bed dorms with ready-made, pod-style cabin beds that come with individual power sockets and reading lights. For more privacy, there are intimate en suite rooms, with or without a private terrace. All rooms in the hostel have private bathrooms and include linen and towels. Dorm rooms also have personal lockers. Steel House Copenhagen is only a five-minute walk from Tivoli Gardens, The City Square Hall, and the famous pedestrian shopping street, Strøget. Bicycle rentals are also available, giving guests the perfect opportunity to explore the city as a real Copenhagener. Free guided walking tours are offered every day if you want to experience the city by foot together with fellow guests.

Tired from sightseeing or had a rough night out? Stay in and enjoy a movie or your favourite Netflix show in their fabulous in-house cinema for free. If you're looking to get active, join the staff for a morning run or one of the hostel's yoga classes for free. Or you could also go for a workout in the state-of-the-art gym or enjoy the fabulous indoor swimming pool.

Last but not least, the well-equipped, spacious communal kitchen is the ultimate in hostel kitchens with lots of shared tables for guests to congregate and chat.

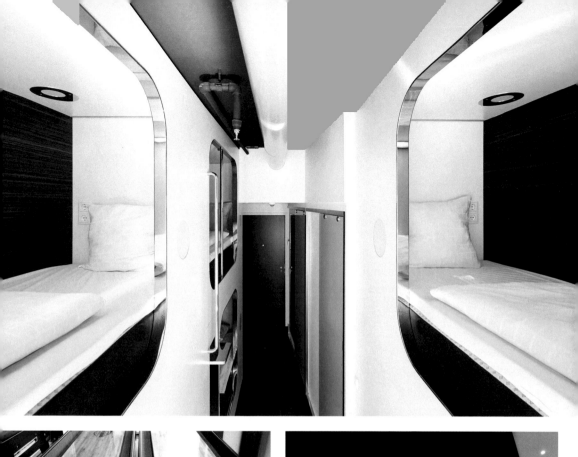

Generator Stockholm

Taking the design hostel concept to the next level

Opened in 2016, Generator Stockholm is a stylish addition to the group's unique breed of hostels spread across Europe.

The building is located in the thriving technology hub of Torsgatan 10, between the Norrmalm and Vasasten districts, a central location for shopping, visiting museums, or having a night on the town.

The lofty 11-story building has unassuming architecture with the addition of colorful window art created by Swedish design studio Amanda & Erik, and there is art and design to spark interest and enthusiasm throughout the hostel. The lounge has laid-back, minimalist decor with an industrial vibe, creating a trendy, cozy ambience. A light installation and communal table on the first floor complete the effect. A former walk-in-safe has been converted to a tattoo studio, and vintage pieces, such as an old-fashioned arcade and pinball machines, give an old-school feel to the bar.

Generator Stockholm's eatery, Restaurant Hilma, is an exciting new addition to the Stockholm culinary scene. It is open to hostel guests and locals, and the design blends Scandinavian and contemporary design. Celebrity chef Luke Thomas is head of the kitchen, which serves global cuisine and traditional Swedish dishes. Architecture agency Tengbom designed Bar Hilma, which takes much of its inspiration from nineteenth-century Swedish artist and mystic Hilma af Klint, a pioneer of the Abstract Movement. Multicolored flooring, art installations, and murals by Jacob Erixson are also of particular interest.

In addition, Generator Stockholm is perfectly equipped to host all sorts of events, from music to business, making it a chamaleonic and dynamic space that everyone, from visitors to locals, can profit from.

Good to know

PRICE RANGE
$ $ $ $ $

AMENITIES INCLUDE
WiFi; 24-hour reception; female-only dorm; travel store; bar; café; chill-out areas; restaurant; meeting rooms; bike hire; laundry; luggage storage; event space.

Tip: If you're a foodie, try some traditional Swedish dishes at Generator Stockholm's eatery, Restaurant Hilma, which is run by celebrity chef Luke Thomas. Generator Stockholm is also a great place for art and design lovers.

Dream Hostel & Hotel

Nature and serenity on a budget

Dream Hostel and Hotel exudes a wonderfully serene Nordic atmosphere. Newly renovated, the hostel is housed in an old industrial building in Tampere's vibrant Tulli district, about a 10-minute walk from Tampere Central Station. Considered a university neighborhood, Tulli is in the hub of the city's nightlife: trendy bars, local restaurants, an outdoor market, secondhand stores, and a grocery store are just a stone's throw away. Additionally, several well-known Tampere landmarks—including the much-loved Moomin Museum—

are nearby. Dream Hostel and Hotel is not your usual busy hostel, but more of a "quiet but social" home where you can relax and meet people. This hotel-hostel was a welcome addition to the Finnish accommodation scene, which, until Dream opened, had remained a relative backwater in the backpacking community because of the lack of good quality hostels; Dream Hostel and Hotel changed that. Now, with the slogan "Something different"—which could easily apply to Tampere itself—it continues to be successful, innovate, and grow.

The structural character of the building (with a variety of previous industrial tenants) has been used to

great effect to create an open, spacious and airy hostel. The common areas have bright white walls with gray, cool blue, and green accents. The open-plan communal areas have comfortable and functional furniture. Natural materials have been used extensively in the hostel, with locally sourced wood and carpeting made from sisal fiber.

The kitchen—a lovely communal space serving an ample breakfast—is the heart of the hostel and a wonderful space to meet fellow travelers.

Whatever your budget or travel style, there are rooms to suit all types. The dorms are air conditioned and expansive with beds nicely spaced out. The beds are sturdy and come

Good to know

PRICE RANGE
$ $ $ $ $

AMENITIES INCLUDE
self-catering facilities;
free WiFi; books and
games; airport shuttle;
restaurant; gastropub;
public sauna; co-working
space; meeting rooms;
group facilities; full
board available; free
popcorn on Fridays or
when it's raining.

Tip: Discover
the hostel's lively
neighborhood: trendy
bars, local restaurants,
an outdoor market,
secondhand stores,
and the much-loved
Moomin Museum
are nearby.

Dream Hostel and Hotel exudes a wonderfully serene Nordic atmosphere.

equipped with discreet reading lights and power sockets to juice up your gadgets. Big heavy doors and thick walls keep the rooms quiet and peaceful. In the hotel section there are 20 en suite rooms with a calm, natural ambience and elements of organic detailing, such as slim strips of timber lining the walls behind the beds. Features include: spotless white-tiled bathrooms, fluffy white towels, and spa-type showers and fixtures. The hanging baskets and potted plants lining the corridors mix with the smell of wood, evoking the sense of being in a forest. The true Finnish experience is completed by the hostel-hotel's brand-new public sauna.

A perfect mix of traditional and modern design, accompanied by the best gastropub in town serving authentic modern Finnish cuisine, Dream Hostel and Hotel is the place to meet locals and new friends alike. ⌂

The Yard

Get the full Helsinki experience at this concept hostel

Situated in an iconic building in the heart of Helsinki, The Yard is part of a new wave of design hostels that has recently emerged in Finland. The hostel building is from 1912, but has been modernized with Finnish craftsmanship and decorated with local art.

"Although The Yard is brand new our values are traditional: We welcome travelers and treat them the way we would wish to be treated when abroad. Our goal is to be your home away from home!" says Lina,

The Yard's owner. And it's true— Hospitality comes first here. The staff are passionate and knowledgeable, and truly love the city; they're keen to make guests fall in love with it too and will give you all the necessary tips to do so.

With 11 beautiful rooms, guests can choose a stylish private or a comfortable dorm. But the lounge—filled with Finnish design objects like locally sourced furniture and a rainbow LED ceiling—is the outstanding feature of this hostel. Homey touches add to the comfort factor: potted plants, beanbag chairs, and a large flat screen TV

(with Playstation and Netflix). There are also books from around the world to dive into in case you're relaxing on a rainy day.

The Yard has an excellent fully equipped kitchen if you're looking to save money on food, and there's a filling complimentary breakfast in the mornings. Coffee and tea are also available free of charge all day.

From drinking in the bar culture of Kallio to discovering the chic lifestyle of Punavuori or immersing yourself in the surrounding nature and city parks, you can explore the best parts of Helsinki with The Yard as a welcoming home base.

Good to know

PRICE RANGE
$ $ $ $ $
AMENITIES INCLUDE
linens; 24-hour
reception; self-catering
facilities; free coffee
and tea; lockers (locks
available free of charge);
adaptors available; free
take-out delivery for
customers from Wolt;
free walking tours.
Breakfast included.

Tip: From drinking
in the bar culture
of Kallio to
discovering the
chic lifestyle of
Punavuori, you
can explore the best
parts of Helsinki
from The Yard!

Hektor Design Hostel

Sleeping in Tartu's creative hotspot

The combination of a traditional hostel service at an affordable price for businessmen and backpackers plus a minimalist yet functional and unique design makes Hektor Design Hostel a truly revolutionary accommodation concept in Estonia and in the entire Baltic region.

The hostel is in a former commercial space dating from the 1950s. KAMP Arhitektid converted the office block into an inviting and convenient living space, preserving as much of the structure as possible and introducing black-and-white graphics for wayfinding.

Launched in 2016 with 112 rooms (large by local hostel standards), the hostel's impressive amenities include a high-quality lobby café, library, guest kitchens, gym and jacuzzi, laundry and ironing facilities, and a meeting room that can be used as a cinema or for corporate events.

The rooms have been furnished in a modern and sophisticated manner with eye-pleasing colors and natural timber. They are furnished with high-quality comfortable beds and fitted with kitchenettes and private bathrooms.

Local artists, architects, and craftspeople contributed creatively to the design. Martin Eelma from Tuumik Graphic Design created many of the graphic and interior design elements, and several independent manufacturers produced the custom furniture. Artwork by Ahti Sepsivart decorates the rooms, and street artists from Multistab left their mark in the basement.

Good to know

PRICE RANGE
$ $ $ $ $

AMENITIES INCLUDE
café; buffet breakfast; seminar room; sauna; gym; yoga room; library; lounge; laundry; communal self-catering facilities; bike hire.

Tip: Check out the Aparaaditehas next door, which like the hostel lives & breathes design, accessibility, and progress. You'll find artists' studios, design shops, and hip restaurants here, not to mention the Paper and Print Museum.

Local artists, architects, and craftspeople contributed creatively t *Hektor Hostel's* design.

Hektor Design Hostel has a 24-hour reception, free WiFi, parking, and a variety of extra services that include a café, buffet breakfast, gym and sauna access, seminar room, laundry, and bike hire. There is also space for business meetings in the library area and foosball in the lounge.

The hostel is located next to Aparaaditehas, an old factory complex that has been transformed into a cultural and creative hotspot with design stores, trendy restaurants, and the Estonian Print & Paper Museum (many of the creatives at Aparaaditehas contributed to the design of the hostel). The courtyard is a busy space in the summertime, offering a regular program of parties and concerts. Tartu Raekoja plats and the old town are also within walking distance. Hektor Design Hostel is a perfectly designed and cosy base to explore this vibrant Baltic city.

Hostel Café Koti

A Nordic dream without breaking the bank

Hostel Café Koti is located in the last frontier before the stark wilderness of the Nordic North: Rovaniemi, the capital of Lapland.

Surrounded by Scandinavia's natural beauty, it was a deep appreciation for nature that prompted two friends, Antii and Tuulia, to set up a hostel and café in their hometown. The vision was simple: to have a modern place for people to stay and eat, while using natural materials and "pure" food. The pair converted an old bank into their contemporary dream, Hostel Café Koti, though elements of the building's original purpose are still evident in its design.

This is an easygoing and welcoming spot. Every space is beautifully crafted, and the design is minimalist and elegant with a predominantly black-and-white palette.

Accommodations range from standard or superior twin rooms, triple rooms, family rooms (extra cribs available on request), and female or mixed dorms. Rooms have pristine en suite bathrooms, crisp white bed linens, and soft, pillowy mattresses.

There are a number of tours available: mountain biking tours to Finnish Lapland and Arctic photography expeditions are two of the unique experiences on offer. Café Koti serves up delightful local delicacies. Breakfasts are simple yet satisfying, and ingredients are locally sourced. Guests can enjoy porridge, natural yogurt, homemade bread and jam, boiled eggs, and more. There's a soup of the day, always accompanied by some homemade sourdough bread, a salad, and a fresh cup of tea or organic coffee. The salads are mouthwatering; think beetroot and goat cheese, or salmon and fennel. The café also serves a variety of cocktails, organic wine, and local beers. Overall, a stay at the Hostel Café Koti is full of exciting possibilities and new experiences.

PRICE RANGE
$ $ $ $ $
AMENITIES INCLUDE
café; bar; restaurant;
sauna; hot tub; rooftop
terrace (summertime).

*Tip: There are a number
of tours available.
Mountain biking tours
to Finnish Lapland
and Arctic photography
expeditions are two
of the unique
experiences on offer.*

◁

IN RYE WE TRUST

KYRÖ
DISTILLERY
COMPANY

GIN GIN
GIN GIN

7 Fells Hostel

Good to know

PRICE RANGE
$ $ $ $ $
AMENITIES INCLUDE
linens; fully-equipped
shared kitchen; cozy
lounge with fireplace;
sauna; studio
apartments; chalet
with private facilities.

Tip: The hostel is
a good starting point
for snowshoeing
and skiing during
winter months, or
hiking in warmer
seasons. After a long
day in the beautiful
outdoors guests can
pop into a communal
sauna to rejuvenate.

This new eco-hostel in beautiful Ylläs has opened up Finland's Lapland region to the backpacking community. Run by a retired backpacker, 7 Fells is the perfect place to take a break and immerse yourself in natural surroundings. From picking cloudberries and riding bikes around the nearby Äkäslompolo Lake during the summer's midnight sun phenomenon, to seeing the northern lights directly from your hostel bed in winter, this place is a one-of-a-kind experience. Thanks to its proximity to the Ylläs Ski Resort, the hostel is a good starting point for snowshoeing and skiing during winter months, or hiking in warmer seasons. After a long day in the beautiful outdoors guests can pop into a communal sauna to rejuvenate, or chill in the common lounge area by the log fire.

Depending on your budget, guest can choose from an excellent value four and six-bed dorm or upgrade to a private en suite double or studio apartment. All the furniture in the rooms is secondhand or up-cycled, which gives each room its own personal character.

Wombat's City Hostel

This hostel strikes a nice balance between social venue and somewhere to chill out and relax.

Guests benefit from the hostel's excellent location: right next to the main train station; it's also within walking distance of the old town and the Oktoberfest grounds (if you're here at the right time of year).

The star feature of the hostel is the air-conditioned, glass-roofed indoor patio. It's filled with potted plants, lots of beanbag chairs, hammocks, and beach chairs, giving a very relaxed, convivial air to the place. Guests get a complimentary welcome drink, and free linens and city maps. Dormitories are a cheerful affair; brightly painted, spacious, and comfortable. All rooms are en suite here, and the double rooms come with a private terrace. There's a kitchen for guests, and a breakfast buffet is available for an additional cost, which includes orange juice, tea and coffee, bread, spreads, cereal, fruit, cheese, and meats.

The place to meet fellow guests and kickoff your evening in the city is at the on-site bar; happy hour is usually from 6 to 8 p.m. For daytime activities, you're well situated to walk or take a train to a variety of sights, or take advantage of the three-hour walking tour the hostel offers in partnership with Gordon's Tours. ⌂

Good to know

PRICE RANGE
$ $ $ $ $

AMENITIES INCLUDE
free WiFi; en suite bathrooms; self-catering facilities; comfy common areas; private rooms; dorms with balcony; pool table; bar; parking available for a fee.

Tip: If you're planning to visit the Oktoberfest, the Wombat's is a good choice, since the hostel is within walking distance from both the old town and the Oktoberfest grounds.

Reyjkavík: a city shaped by nature

Most holidays in Iceland involve a stop in *Reykjavík,* Europe's northernmost capital city.

Most holidays in Iceland involve a stop in Reykjavík, but few tourists stay for long. Iceland is, after all, famous for its vast wilderness— a country dotted with volcanoes and dominated by Europe's largest icecap. While Reykjavik is, for many, little more than a gateway to Iceland, I have found that it offers more than enough to keep you occupied for a few days. Here are a few recommendations for those who are planning to spend a couple of days in Europe's northernmost capital city.

Where to eat

Once named by *The Guardian* as Europe's best hotdog stand, Bæjarins Beztu Pylsur (The Town's Best Sausages in English) has been feeding hungry locals and tourists from its chain of hotdog stands across Reykjavik for more than half a century. Billed as Iceland's national dish, these hotdogs have been given the thumbs up from various celebrities visiting the city, including Bill Clinton and Anthony Bourdain. Order the hotdogs with the works ("eina með öllu" in Icelandic), you'll get all the condiments, which includes ketchup, sweet mustard, fried onion, raw onion, and *remolaði,* a mayonnaise-based sauce with sweet relish.

Saegreifinn, or The Sea Baron, is a restaurant by the harbor that serves what it claims is the best lobster soup in the world. It's housed in an old green fishermen's hut and you can indulge in the lobster soup plus a choice of fresh barbecued seafood skewers.

Noodle Station is a spartan joint on Skólavörðustígur that serves up a choice of three noodle soups: with beef, with chicken, and vegetarian. Spicy and flavorful with strong notes of star anise and lemongrass, the

noodle soups are a fast and cheap option for visitors to the city. If you're feeling peckish at midnight, grab a quick, tasty, and greasy sandwich at Nonnabiti, also known affectionately as Nonni.

Where to drink

Kaffi Vínyl is a nice, relaxed place for a coffee and is also vegan and vegetarian friendly. The café houses a vinyl store with a selection of electronica, vintage grooves, and classic albums.

Bring your own drink when visiting the northwesternmost

» I recommend going to Skúli Craft Bar. It is a relatively new place that serves craft beer on tap. The regulars here are typically aged 30 years plus so it is a quiet and hassle-free environment. «

HÉÐINN

Where to party

For live music, karaoke, stand-up comedy, cult-movie screenings, and a weekly drag cabaret, Gaukurinn is definitely worth stopping by. Happy hour is from 2 p.m. until 9 p.m.

pay a visit to the hip and bohemian Kaffibarinn bar, part-owned by musician Damon Albarn and represented in the film *101 Reykjavik*.

Going for a walk

Jump on a bus from downtown or head out on a long bike ride to walk around Rauðhólar ("red hills") or the Heiðmörk nature reserve.

Reykjavík itself is a small and walkable city, and the best way to explore it is by foot. Reykjavík's harbor is a nice place for a relaxed stroll. If you follow the path along Sæbraut, you will start (or end)

point in Reykjavík, where the Grótta Lighthouse is located. From here, on clear days, you can enjoy the views over Flaxaflói Bay, Esjan, and even Snæfellsjökull glacier. Dip your feet into the warm geothermal waters of the Grótta footbath, which you can find amongst the rocks by the seashore, or grab a beer at Saemundur í Sparifötunum, a gastro-pub in KEX Hostel, featured in this book. Centrally located and with a big emphasis on live music, this place is a popular meeting point for locals and tourists.

Húrra, on the same street, is also a good pit stop for alternative-music lovers with the club hosting everything from jazz concerts to abstract electronic music nights. Paloma is a late-night dance club that draws hipsters into its Viking-style attic (complete with a Viking-ship bar) thanks to its unpredictable mix of alternative local bands and live DJs that play everything from electronic, techno, reggae, and pop, to dark, deep house music. Last but not least,

at the downtown area and one of the city's most distinguished landmarks, Harpa Concert Hall. Continue alongside the ocean to see the sculpture *Sólfar* (Sun Voyager). On a clear day you will get unhindered views of the Engey and Viðey islands and perhaps even the Snæfellsjökull stratovolcano.

The nearby Laugardalur (Hot Spring Valley) in downtown Reykjavík also offers multiple walking opportunities. As a major center for sports and recreation, there are plenty of

celanders love to read and write. In fact, one in ten Icelanders will publish a book in their lifetime. *Nexus* is the perfect place for soaking up the country's long-standing love affair with books.

aved paths weaving between the arious sporting arenas, along vith a botanical garden, camping ites, and a petting zoo.

The best places to relax

he Blue Lagoon geothermal spa s definitely worth visiting. Yes, it's typical tour-guide tip, but it really s worth it. Try to go early in the lay to avoid crowds—although even vith the crowds, it's a truly unique nd relaxing experience. You can lso go local and pay a visit to one f Reykjavík's many public baths. Intrance fees vary but can be s cheap as two euros. In most ountries people go to swimming ools to swim, but in Iceland hey are a place for relaxation nd meeting friends. The recently enovated Sundhöllin public bath n downtown Reykjavík is highly ecommended.

Best viewpoint

Hop over to Hallgrímskirkja, a 240-foot-tall rocket-shaped church located on top of the Skólavörðuhæð hill in the centre of Reykjavík. It is the largest church in Iceland and the tower offers fantastic panoramic views of the city and the little colorful houses in 101, the nickname for Reykjavík's center. A day hike to the volcanic mountain

Esja (914 meters above sea level) also provides a spectacular view that takes in Reykjavík, the town of Mosfellsbaer, and the surrounding countryside. For something different, and the chance to experience Iceland's rocky and mystical landscape from a unique perspective, go for a riding tour with Ishestar on one of the amazing Icelandic horses. Suitable for beginners and experienced riders, these horses can be booked for one- to five-hour riding tours in the Reykjavík area.

Secret places

You can visit renowned Icelandic filmmaker Hrafn Gunnlaugsson's house, a three-story building that looks like an unfinished sculpture and is made from rusty remains and junk. If you're lucky, Gunnlaugsson himself will be there to welcome you and give you a tour.

Icelanders love to read and write. In fact, one in ten Icelanders will publish a book in their lifetime. Nexus is the perfect place for soaking up the country's long-standing love affair with books. The local comic-book store offers a bit of everything, from a wide variety of board games to other essentials such as books and toys.

KEX Hostel

From biscuit factory to stylish hostel

With a lobby resembling a retro hipster lounge, Kex Hostel is one of the most stylish hostels in Europe—like something found in the glossy pages of an interior design magazine.

Kex (the Icelandic word for biscuit) is located in a former biscuit factory in downtown Reykjavík. The interior is furnished with salvaged materials and objects and blends a vintage industrial feel with an eclectic, contemporary touch.

Kex accommodates up to 215 guests with a variety of clean and comfortable rooms, including doubles, dorms, and female-only dorms. Some rooms have interesting wall decor, but it is the common spaces that have the real wow factor. The restaurant and bar, lounge area, heated outdoor patio, tourist information desk, old-school gym, and meeting room are beautifully designed. The large common room is filled with hammocks and comfy couches, and a library has leather chairs and a well-stocked bookshelf.

There are vintage maps on the walls as well as magnetic letters for creative poetry. There is also a 1940s-style barbershop in another corner.

The hostel has a bar and on-site restaurant where guests can order gourmet dishes such as roasted bone marrow served with crostini and a salad, followed by Icelandic-style tiramisu made with layers of tart skyr yogurt instead of mascarpone.

Kex is located in the center of Reykjavík, with a view across the bay to Mount Esja. The former biscuit factory is also home to The Living →

Good to know

PRICE RANGE
$ $ $ $ $
AMENITIES INCLUDE
gastropub; buffet
breakfast; WiFi; events
and open-mic nights;
book exchange; in-room
lockers; secure luggage
storage; 24-hour access
and security; meeting
room; lounge area;
heated outdoor patio;
self-catering facilities;
bike hire.

Tip: Make sure to
try one of the
restaurant's gourmet
dishes, such as roasted
bone marrow,
followed by Icelandic-
style tiramisu.

Kex is located in the center of Reykjavík, with a view across the bay to Mount Esja.

Art Museum and various studios of artists, dancers, and fashion designers. Nightlife, restaurants, shopping streets, cultural attractions, and other points of interest in the city center are within easy walking distance. It is also well connected to the public bus system allowing guests to reach destinations further afield.

The staff at Kex serve as travel agents, helping guests choose from and book the dozens of excursions on offer in the Reykjavík area. Nearly all excursions pick up and drop off at Kex. Many travelers to Iceland spend their days chasing high adrenaline activities such as glacier-climbing, rafting, hiking through the volcanic landscape, and snorkeling in near-freezing water. After a day outdoors, many guests simply want to curl up with a book or their computer. Kex understands that, and the hostel is outfitted perfectly. ⌂

Midgard Base Camp

Midgard used to be simply "Midgard Adventure," an Icelandic outdoor guiding company. But after a successful few years of helping visitors explore the country, the business expanded to include Base Camp—a friendly place with a family feel, where travelers can feel at home.

Midgard Base Camp is located in a contemporary industrial building on the outskirts of Hvolsvöllur. A creative young Icelandic design team transformed the building into a modern center with a warm and trendy feel. Elements from nature and adventure travel were incorporated into the design, but perhaps the best feature is the unobstructed scenic views to the mountains and Eyjafjallajökull icecap.

Midgard Base Camp offers dorms with bunk beds and private rooms. The bunk beds are designed with quality mattresses, privacy curtains, bedside lights, lockable drawers, and blackout blinds. There is also a family room that fits up to four. Midgard Base Camp has an on-site café and bar, and the daily happy hour is a great chance to mingle with travelers and locals who stop by. The on-site restaurant caters to all diets whether vegetarian, vegan, or meat and fish based. The hostel has a busy calendar of events, but you might be too busy relaxing in the rooftop hot tub.

Good to know

PRICE RANGE
$ $ $ $
AMENITIES INCLUDE
free WiFi; hot tub; sauna; café; bar; restaurant.

Tip: The hostel has a busy calendar of events. The company's guided adventures are worth checking out, there's something amazing on offer for every season. The on-site café and bar is a great place to mingle with travelers and locals who stop by.

YHA Ambleside

Good to know

PRICE RANGE
$ $ $ $ $

AMENITIES INCLUDE
wheelchair accessible;
free WiFi; self-catering
facilities; laundry
facilities; luggage
storage; parking; bicycle
storage; dining room;
drying room; grounds;
library; barbecue
area; board games;
TV; licensed bar and
restaurant; lounge;
private rooms.

*Tip: The hostel is
perfectly located,
with a number of
walking and cycling
routes in close
proximity. Rent a
kayak for the day, or
take a picnic down to
the waterside benches.*

Situated in the lap of nature on the edge of Lake Windermere, this is one of the most scenic hostels in the world. Staying here is simply a dream.

The hostel has been refurbished in recent years, so guests can expect clean, modern rooms, and excellent amenities, including a café serving local food, and a restaurant.

Accommodations are varied and suit all kinds of travelers, including friends or families. Many of the rooms have lovely views of the lake or the Langdale Pikes.

The hostel is perfectly located, with a number of walking and cycling routes in close proximity. The hostel also has its own jetty. Guests can rent

a kayak for the day, or take a picnic down to the waterside benches. There's a variety of watersports available at the lake too—ask at the reception for information about the lake cruise.

If you're staying inside for a day, there is a game room (perfect for kids) and a selection of books for guests to borrow.

Cape Town: breathtaking vibrancy

With magnificent Table Mountain as a backdrop, Cape Town lives up to the hype as *one of the most beautiful cities* in the world.

From the iconic V&A Waterfront to infamous Robben Island where Nelson Mandela was incarcerated for 18 years, the African penguins of Boulders Beach, and, of course, the Cape Winelands where you can sample some of the best wines in the world— Cape Town has it all.

Where to eat

» Kloof Street House is a culinary institution in Cape Town. Once you step through the fairy lights of the garden entrance and walk up the stairs to the main area, pure magic comes to mind. It is incredibly decorated, the team are excellently trained, and the food is cooked beautifully. «

MILOU STAUB
– The B.I.G.

One of the most unique dishes to try in Cape Town is waterblommetjie bredie, which literally means "small water flower stew." Prepared with lamb and potatoes, waterblommetjies, commonly known as Cape pondweed, are found in the dams and marshes around the city and Western Cape, and they have a distinctive taste. The stylish café Hemelhuijs is a good place to try this dish.

A great choice for affordable and genuine Mexican fare is El Burro in Green Point. It has great food, service, and ambience in a relaxed environment. You can build your own tacos with El Burro's signature ceviche, which is made with locally sourced sustainable white fish, or try the exotic mushroom and white bean quesadilla. Wash it down with a quality craft beer or famous tequila-based cocktail.

If you love beautifully presented food in a dreamy setting, then Irish chef Liam Tomlin's award-winning tapas restaurant Chefs Warehouse →

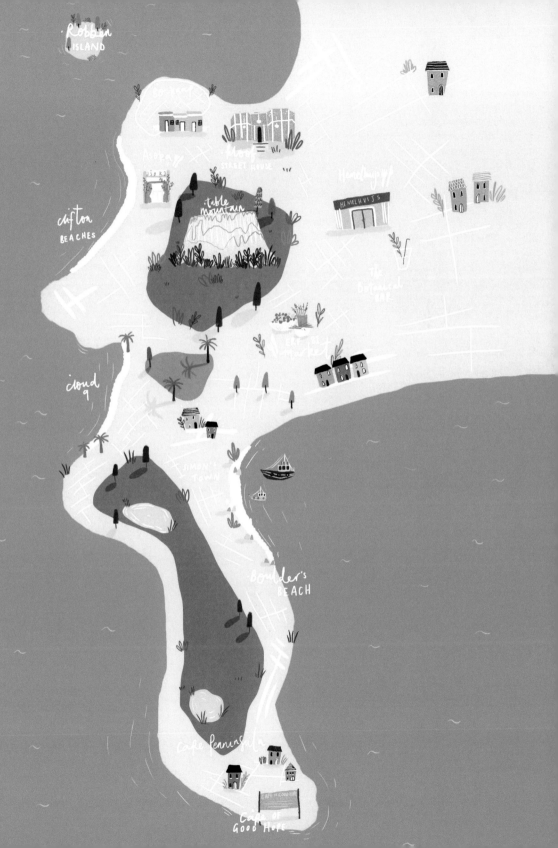

is a must. From beef tartare with a spicy Szechuan dressing to lip-smacking signature risottos, everything tastes great here. No prior bookings are taken, and you may have to queue for 30 minutes, but it is definitely worth the wait.

Where to drink

There are plenty of top-class bars and pubs worth visiting, but you will generally find these to be pricey and filled with tourists. Get off the beaten path and opt for the places where locals go. You'll enjoy good drinks and definitely have made friends with a few Capetonians by the end of the night.

Asoka is your first port of call for cocktails, and its Porn Star Martinis are apparently the best in the country. The bar is built around an olive tree next to which the DJ works his magic. Asoka is famous for its jazz nights on Tuesdays. If you're feeling peckish, the tapas kitchen stays open until midnight, which is rare for Cape Town.

» There are niche and specialized bars for gin, wine, and beer all over Cape Town. My favorite is The Botanical Bar, which serves delicious gin cocktails infused with local (Western Cape Province) botanicals that grow wild, such as fynbos (fine bush), buchu, and rooibos. «

SOPHIE BAGHERI
—*Once in Cape Town*

Where to party

Once in Cape Town's on-site bar Yours Truly is a great place to kick off a night out in the city. Set underneath jacaranda trees and immersed in greenery, it's a café by day and beer garden by night. Locals come here for the live DJ sets, which run from Thursday through Sunday, serving up a mishmash of house, hip hop, old-school vinyl, and R&B.

With a vintage feel and an emphasis on sharing the South African braai culture, The Village

Idiot is a fun inner-city neighborhood bar and restaurant that's popular with locals and tourists alike. Besides braai boards, you can feast on Durban-style chicken curry, boerewors burgers, potjie kos, biltong, and cheese platters. After dinner, there is often live music or a DJ to carry on the party into the early hours.

Going for a walk

Walking anywhere in Cape Town is an experience. It is perfect for people watching, and you will never cease to be amazed by the colorful characters you pass. The walk from Sea Point Promenade to Camps Bay is a favorite. It follows the coastline and is frequented by locals on their daily jogs or taking babies for a sunset stroll. Capetonians also love hiking the many trails that Table Mountain offers. A recommended one is Tranquility Cracks—you'll walk through forest-like terrain, and it's great for bouldering enthusiasts once you near the top.

» I love going for a walk in Deer Park on the lower slopes of Table Mountain, which is mainly frequented by locals with their dogs and mountain bikers. With lots of different paths there is something for everyone and you can find great fynbos with huge protea bushes, keurboom trees, and pin cushions, and observe a wide variety of birdlife. The best time to go is September, when the whole park is in full bloom. Views of the city from here are also incredible. It only takes five minutes to get there from almost anywhere in the city and you are immediately immersed in nature. «

LEE HARRIS
—*The Backpack*

From the iconic *V&A Waterfront* to infamous *Robben Island*, the African penguins of *Boulders Beach*, and, the *Cape Winelands* where you can sample some of the best wines in the world: Cape Town has it all.

Getting around town

You have both Taxify and Uber in Cape Town, which provide a reliable, cheap, safe, and quick way to get from A to B. The city is also pedestrian friendly, so you can soak up the vibes and roam aimlessly with no destination in mind.

The best place to relax

Head up to Signal Hill for sundowners. There's nothing better than watching the sun set over the sea with a delicious glass of South African wine in your hand.

    With its immaculate white sands, Clifton Beach is the heart of Cape Town's beach scene and perfect for people watching and catching the sun's rays.

Best viewpoint

There is a view to savor everywhere you walk in the city. Waking up in the morning and walking onto the street with the stunning backdrop of Table Mountain with misty clouds hanging over it always sends a shiver down my spine. Many love Milnerton Beach for its postcard view of the city, which is hard to beat—you never ever get tired of that sight, and you can bring your dog there too.

    Cloud 9 Rooftop Bar offers another great vantage point with unobstructed views of the mountains, sea, and town. It's the best place to find your bearing in the "Mother City."

» We call it our secret spot. From the viewpoint you can see the immense Twelve Apostles Mountain Range and Lion's Head mountain peak, imposing over the four Clifton beaches. This vantage point can be accessed from one of the wealthiest streets in Cape Town, and Africa for that matter, located high up on the slopes of the mountain range. There are boulders (millions of years old) that are scattered and perched on top of each other, some jutting off the cliff's edge. You have to walk past a house that was priced at $40 million! «

SOPHIE BAGHERI
— *Once in Cape Town*

Secret places

First Thursdays will bring you into contact with a part of the city you might not see otherwise. On the first Thursday of the month the galleries and cultural institutions of Cape Town throw their doors open until 9 p.m. with no entrance fee.

» Once home to a military base, the Erf 81 Food Market is a hidden gem with a wealth of local handmade, organic food produce to buy at various food stalls. Also, the views of the city will take your breath away, surrounded by Devil's Peak, Table Mountain, and Lion's Head. «

LEE HARRIS
— *The Backpack*

Once in Cape Town

The art of social connectivity and sustainable luxury

Once in Cape Town was founded in 2013 by five intrepid travelers who saw that the Cape Town lodging market needed a hybrid concept—one that could combine the affordability and fun factor of a hostel with the luxuries of a three-star hotel.

Located on Kloof Street, within walking distance of the bar and restaurant nightlife hub, Once in Cape Town is in the perfect location for exploring the city.

Compared to other backpacker hostels, Once in Cape Town is a fairly large property (sleeping approximately 150 guests). It has mostly private rooms, with some four-bed dorms, all of which have newly renovated en suite bathrooms. The rooms are comfortable and well designed, with crisp white linens, handcrafted room amenities, and local artwork.

The hostel has created a variety of communal spaces—conference facilities, co-working spaces, a meeting room, cinema room, communal kitchen, an on-site restaurant and bar—and a daily social calendar. During "No Power Hour," the hostel offers free beer to guests who leave their phones aside; the idea helps facilitate guests meeting new friends and like-minded travelers. Other experiences on offer include hikes, walking tours of public street art, yoga sessions, bar crawls, and beach and farmers' market excursion

The on-site bar, Yours Truly, is a Cape Town institution and is frequented seven days a week by locals and travelers alike. DJs play a mix of vinyl records, hip hop, R&B, house, and electro funk, making it one of the best places to get your groove on. Return there in the morning for a free light breakfast with barista-crafted coffee. An added perk: Once in Cape Town is the first hotel company in South Africa to receive fairtrade accreditation with 100 percent— a testament to the way in which sustainable and responsible business can be done successfully.

Good to know

PRICE RANGE
$ $ $ $ $

AMENITIES INCLUDE
24-hour reception; free WiFi; self-catering facilities; free parking; bicycle rentals; cinema room; braai (barbecue) facilities; tours and concierge desk; small conference facilities; meeting room; co-working space; bar; café-restaurant.

Tip: Make sure to visit the on-site bar. It is a Cape Town institution, and frequented by locals and travelers alike. DJs play a mix of hip hop, R&B, house, and electro funk.

Somewhere Nice

Reimagining luxury in Ghana with a sustainable focus

Somewhere Nice is the brainchild of Mathias Schwender, founder of Bohemian Hostels, a boho chic Prague-based chain. Now the same vision and values behind Bohemian's success—to create shared spaces which bring travelers from all around the world under one roof—have jumped continents to Accra, Ghana, and established Somewhere Nice as one of Africa's finest luxury hostels. Located in a beautifully restored colonial-era house in the lively neighborhood of Kokomlemle, Somewhere Nice guests can choose from dorm-style accommodations, private rooms, or stylish apartments uniquely furnished as an African home. The rooms are the ultimate in hostel luxury; en suite bathrooms and rainfall showers, private terraces with outside seating, ceiling fans and air conditioning to battle the heat, and recycled or locally sourced furniture to keep in line with their philosophy of using Ghanaian craftsmanship and goods wherever possible in the hostel. To work towards a cleaner, more environmentally aware Ghana, Somewhere Nice has integrated many sustainable practices, leading to some very unique ideas. The hostel itself is designed with many repurposed and recycled items: signs made from old doors, mirrors made from windows, and chairs and tables made from rubber and tires.

Other key features here include a swimming pool, garden, and a semi open-air lounge. Guests are offered a generous free breakfast and filtered drinking water. Reception is open 24 hours and there is a 24-hour security staff on-site.

Good to know

PRICE RANGE
$ $ $ $ $
AMENITIES INCLUDE
24-hour reception; reading light; pool; garden; air conditioning; free drinking water. Breakfast included.

Tip: To travel around Accra like a local, jump on the traditional tro tros, which are vehicles halfway between a bus and a taxi. There are several stops near the hostel, and the friendly staff will give you some helpful tips to navigate them.

Curiocity Joburg

Hospitality with an honest perspective

The best hostels are the ones rooted at the heart of the local community, offering travelers a gateway to experience the city or region. Curiocity Joburg, the brainchild of 25-year-old Bheki Dube, is one of those rare finds.

Dubbed the "Ministry of Tourism" in Johannesburg's Maboneng Precinct, Curiocity is the beating heart of the neighborhood. If you meet Dube, you will understand why. Before starting Curiocity, Dube used to run Main Street Walks, a tour company offering visitors an authentic, raw experience of Johannesburg's inner-city districts.

That no-nonsense perspective metamorphosed into Curiocity, where guests can look beyond the buzz of Maboneng and experience the true, gritty, beautiful spirit of "Jozi".

The converted industrial building in which Curiocity Joburg is housed has a checkered history. It was formerly the home of Pacific Press, the infamous printing house which produced anti-apartheid pamphlets such as the *Black Sash*. During periods of mass resistance, the building also served as a refuge for apartheid resisters, including Nelson Mandela and Desmond Tutu.

The hostel has 70 beds in a mix of private rooms and dorms. There's also a dozen trendy self-catering units

in a nearby apartment building, each designed by a local creative. Dorms have sturdy bunk beds, free WiFi, and lockers; bathrooms are shared. Hip private rooms offer en suite facilities and kitchenettes.

The hostel has a cool on-site bar called Hide Out (the name referencing the building's history), which is also a popular hangout for Maboneng dwellers. You can savor a frosty beer or a cocktail there, play a game of pool in the hostel's laid-back lounge, or strike up a conversation at the popular outdoor hot tub in the back courtyard. But one of the best things to do at Curiocity is to simply chill on the balcony and watch the ebb and flow of people in Maboneng.

Good to know

PRICE RANGE
$$$$$
AMENITIES INCLUDE
bar; courtyard; living
lounge area; splash pool;
bicycle rentals; yoga
facilities; surfing
excursion; night cycles;
city tours (walking and
cycling); hikes; scuba
diving; Kruger camps.

Tip: Savor a frosty
beer or a cocktail
in the hostel's cool
on-site bar Hide
Out, play a game
of pool at the laid-back
lounge, or visit the
popular outdoor
hot tub in the
back courtyard of
the hostel.

Once in Joburg

A vibrant hybrid hotel for adventurous flashpackers

Once in Joburg opened in 2015 in Braamfontein, Johannesburg's dynamic cultural precinct, aiding the urban regeneration of a previously dilapidated downtown neighborhood.

The hostel is centrally located, nestled between NGO head offices, universities, coffee roasters and coffee shops, restaurants, trendy fashion boutiques, and modern co-working spaces. With outdoor food markets and nightlife hotspots showcasing local South African talent, it's an area that shows off a more authentic side of central Johannesburg.

Once in Joburg's modern design is sleek and contemporary; many pieces of art made by local creatives are displayed on the walls.

Apart from comfortable and well-designed rooms with crisp white linen and handcrafted room amenities, local artwork and newly renovated en suite bathrooms, the hostel owners have created a variety of communal spaces (conference facilities, co-working spaces, meeting room, cinema room, large communal kitchen, on-site restaurant and bar) and a daily social calendar of events so that guests can interact. Schemes such as "no power hour," where free beer is offered in return for leaving phones behind, help facilitate

more interaction amongst guests. Other experiences include hikes, walking tours of public street art, yoga sessions, bar crawls, and excursions to the beach and farmers' markets. They also serve a free daily light breakfast with espresso coffee.

From shared dorms to private rooms, the accommodation here is modern and tailored to a variety of traveling needs. There's also a variety of common areas and facilities including a large communal kitchen, a cinema room, and an on-site bar and restaurant, so you can get the big group experience if you're traveling solo. Once in Joburg organizes plenty of ways to get to know this amazing South African city!

Good to know

PRICE RANGE
$ $ $ $ $

AMENITIES INCLUDE
24-hour reception; free
WiFi; self-catering
facilities; free parking;
bicycle rentals; cinema
room; braai facilities;
tours and concierge
desk; small conference
facilities; meeting room;
co-working space; bar;
café-restaurant.

Tip: Be sure to check
out all the amazing
excursions on offer.
From yoga and
walking tours, to bar
crawls or trips to the
beach. Plenty of ways
to get to know this
South African city!

The Backpack

A hostel fostering social change

The Backpack is an award-winning fairtrade hostel that invests in people, communities, and the environment in the hopes of providing meaningful travel experiences. The hostel is committed to the concept of "responsible tourism," taking measures to make water recycling, solar-heated showers, recycle bins, worm farms, composting, and water-wise gardening a normal part of hostel life.

Additionally, The Backpack is ideally located in the heart of Cape Town—so you have convenience on your side too. Guests can walk to Green Market Square, explore the cobblestone streets of the colorful Bo-Kaap area, or go for a stroll in Company's Garden. Surrounded by a number of bars and restaurants, guests are close to everything and just a short cab ride from Cape Town's V&A Waterfront and the Table Mountain Cable Car Station.

The design of the hostel is best described as trendy and urban. Located in a 100-year-old Victorian house, The Backpack has a private courtyard and gardens. There are an array of room choices, including dorms, single rooms, twin and double rooms with shared or private bathrooms, family rooms, and even a self-catering loft apartment.

Guests can enjoy a free continental breakfast in the morning—the food is plentiful, and you get spectacular views of Table Mountain as you savor your meal.

There are so many perks of staying at this conscientious hostel: a community craft shop, a bar that stays open until late at night, evening hostel activities, a swimming pool, a garden, free WiFi, and a self-catering kitchen to name a few. But with its ethical stance and mindful business practices, you can also be assured that staying here will feel like the right thing to do.

Good to know

PRICE RANGE
$ $ $ $ $
AMENITIES INCLUDE
café; bar; travel desk;
community art and
souvenir store.

Tip: Walk to Green
Market Square,
explore the
cobblestone streets
of the colorful
Bo-Kaap area, stroll
through Company's
Garden, or take a
short cab ride to Cape
Town's V&A
Waterfront and the
Table Mountain Cable
Car Station.

91 Loop

No order too tall at this chic abode

Nestled in the heart of Cape Town's city center, 91 Loop effortlessly combines luxury living with modernity. The hostel is cozy and comfortable and only a short walk away from Long Street and the historical Green Market Square. A former slave market, the square has become the site of local green markets and flea markets. It took a major renovation to take the previously run-down and derelict building and give it a facelift that resulted in this luxurious design: chic, modern, and minimalist.

The hostel's reception is staffed 24 hours a day, so guests are welcome to arrive around the clock. There are a total of 150 beds spread over two floors, with a mix of en suite private rooms (with extra long beds and the most comfortable mattresses), shared dorms, and the rather futuristic pod-style accommodations (which are air conditioned). The restaurant, The Honey Badger, is a bistro-style eatery, serving up fresh, seasonal cuisine sourced from regional produce. The food is simple but very satisfying and can be enjoyed in the outdoor courtyard. Breakfast is complimentary here and features locally roasted coffee and fresh produce. The staff of 91 Loop are happy to offer a variety of activities for guests, including free walking tours and movie nights. Make sure you take them up on these offers to get the most out of your stay here in Cape Town.

Curiocity Durban

Fill your days with a flurry of local activities

As with other Curiocity sites, Curiocity Durban is influenced by the rich history, heritage, and aesthetics of the neighborhood it's in. The hostel is nestled in the bustling Rivertown Triangle, housed in a historic 1930s British colonial-style building.

The location of the hostel is a short walk away from the beach, Durban International Convention Center, and Warwick Junction. The hostel features a mix of single rooms, tasteful doubles, and spacious four to eight-bed dorms. Most rooms here enjoy a private balcony lined with flower boxes, often with a hammock for lounging around in. Bunk beds come equipped with a power point, reading light, and a locker under the bottom bunk.

Guests take sanctuary on the canvas chairs under fairy lights in the inner courtyard patio lounge—everything from morning yoga and salsa dancing to Monday movie evenings takes place here. Guests and locals alike spend a lot of time in the excellent on-site Bar Curio, where you can enjoy local craft beers, South African wines, and a wide range of spirits.

There's a well-equipped shared kitchen, an on-site library, and a laundry service here. If you're working while on the road, you can catch up at the hostel's co-working space.

Perhaps the most exceptional feature of Curiocity Durban is the on-site spa. Nane is an urban spa offering holistic treatments using natural products. Sure to uplift mind and body, these therapeutic treatments are a luxurious remedy for the weary traveler, but non-guests are welcome too.

With an urban spa, daily city walks, cycle tours every Thursday, and daily surf trips with an awesome local NGO called Surfers Not Street Children, there's no shortage of experiences to fill your days here!

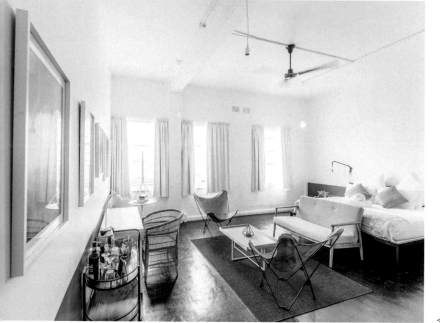

Good to know

PRICE RANGE
$ $ $ $ $
AMENITIES INCLUDE
bar; courtyard; lounge
area; splash pool; bicycle
rentals; yoga facilities;
surfing excursion; night
cycles; city tours
(walking and cycling);
hikes; scuba diving.

*Tip: The on-site spa
offers holistic
treatments with the
use of natural
products. Sure to
uplift mind and body,
these therapeutic
treatments are a
luxurious remedy for
the weary traveler.*

Rodamón Riad

An innovative design hostel turning tradition on its head

Step into your new home, a 100-year-old riad in the heart of Marrakech. Rodamón Riad, a hostel designed for a new generation of culturally curious world travelers, is an oasis of calm amidst the city's hustle and bustle.

Housed in a historic building, this modern hostel comes equipped with all the necessary amenities. Before Rodamón Riad, there were a ton of accommodations in traditional riad houses, but most of them were expensive affairs, not built for the budget-conscious traveler. Rodamón was the solution—take a traditional property and convert it into a fun design hostel. The renovation project took almost 12 months to complete, and the result is a simply mesmerizing luxury hostel.

Thoughtful attention to subtle details are evident in its design. The interior is decked in Iranian rugs, handcrafted furniture, and traditional Moroccan elements. The hostel's 24-hour reception has gray walls embellished with verdant emerald green tiles; it's an enticing and welcoming space.

The rooms at Rodamón are pristine, white-washed affairs with delightful local details. The decor is simple yet very practical, and the color palette is dominated by navy blue, yellow, and gray, with white walls. A variety of air-conditioned rooms are available, ranging from the superior suite, shared or

Good to know

PRICE RANGE
$ $ $ $
AMENITIES INCLUDE
bar; swimming pool;
rooftop terrace.

Tip: Take a dip in
the pool, relax
on a lounge chair,
sip on a flavorful
Moroccan mint tea,
or enjoy the panoramic
view of Jemaa
el-Fnaa square and
the imposing Atlas
Mountains on the
hostel's rooftop
terrace. The staff
is also happy to
organize entertaining
tours for you.

Rodamón Riad is not luxurious or flashy, but innovative, inspiring, enjoyable, and social.

private dorms, and private rooms. Common areas have a Nordic style about them, but plants and foliage are liberally scattered around the terrace and living room, giving the otherwise clean space a warmer feel.

The central courtyard features a swimming pool. If you're not in the water, you can relax on a lounge chair and sip on a flavorful Moroccan mint tea. There is a dedicated reading area with books that guests may borrow, or they can indulge in the relaxing delights of a typical Moroccan hammam. The hostel's rooftop terrace commands a panoramic view of Jemaa el-Fnaa square (just a 10-minute walk away) and the imposing Atlas Mountains (much further away).

The hostel can be a tricky spot to find on the first visit, but its location—in the heart of the medina—couldn't be better if you want to experience an authentic Moroccan medina and the mint and orange perfumed fragrance of the souks (marketplaces). As smartphone GPS coverage can be patchy here, ask the riad staff to meet you somewhere, or pay them for an airport pick-up—it can be frustrating trailing up and down alleyways with suitcases and dealing with unofficial "guides."

While the hostel doesn't host many activities, there's ample help available from the staff to get some organized for you. Such activities and events include: walking, biking,

or camel tours, or an evening tapas and craft beer tour.

The atmosphere at Rodamón Riad is calm and quiet, providing a space where guests are able to work quietly or chill—a home away from home.

With that said, there's no old-style hostel curfew here: With a 24-hour reception, guests can stay out late and enjoy the local nightlife, the hustle and bustle of the souks, and local eateries.

Rodamón Riad is not luxurious or flashy but innovative, inspiring, enjoyable, and social. Like its sister hostels, Rodamón Riad is rich in style and experiences, yet affordable and unpretentious.

S'TAY Hostel Apartment.

Welcome to Rhodes' very first design hostel

Located on a quiet side street of Rhodes' New Town and just a 10-minute walk away from the beach, STAY Hostel will delight cosmopolitan travelers and sun-seekers alike.

Launched by a Greek-German couple, Notis and Gesine, this sleek hostel was designed with functionality in mind. The top priority was to meet a modern traveler's every need. However, by mixing clean modern elements with upcycled ones—such as converting old clothes hangers into hooks and wooden pallets into seats

for the spacious in-house cinema— Notis and Gesine have also created a hostel with great personality.

With several common areas for guests to mingle, plus a regular program of social activities, meeting other travelers at STAY is super easy. Activities range from pizza and souvlaki nights, yoga and gym sessions, massage therapy, live music events, movie night, beach activities (swimming, sunbathing, and surfing), and a variety of other excursions. There is a bar with a happy hour every day, so you can have a few cheap drinks with guests before exploring more of Rhodes' nightlife scene. Weary travelers who might

prefer a quiet night at home can enjoy nightly movie showings. The outdoor terrace and library are additional places to chill. There is also a fully equipped gym and a spacious communal kitchen where guests can cook and enjoy each other's company.

For a small fee, guests can enjoy a nutritious breakfast in the mornings. It includes everything from Greek yogurt with muesli, honey and fruits, to a special selection of premade sandwiches.

With its emphasis on functional design, great facilities, and friendly owners, STAY is one of those hostels that feels more like a restful home than a foreign traveling hub. ⌂

Good to know

PRICE RANGE
$ $ $ $ $
AMENITIES INCLUDE
linens; towels; free
WiFi and internet;
self-catering facilities;
laundry service; bar;
daily cleaning; late
check-out; luggage
storage; mini market;
hairdryer; free locks,
plugs, and lights
by all beds. Breakfast
available.

Tip: Enjoy STAY
Hostel's pizza and
souvlaki nights, yoga
and gym sessions,
massage therapy, live
music events, movie
night, beach activities,
and a variety
of other excursions.

Caveland Hostel

A hostel carved out of volcanic ash? Welcome to the unique and wonderful Caveland Hostel on the photogenic island of Santorini.

As a volcanic island, Santorini's topography is made up of pumice stone, ideal for developing underground housing. This hostel complex is a continuum of cave houses that open out to the exterior through amazing terraces. The space is surrounded by picturesque gardens bursting with flourishing vegetation. Lemon, pomegranate, orange, pear, vanilla, and pistachio trees jostle for attention and create a charming atmosphere. Caveland is located in an old winery and has a pleasing shabby chic feel. The design is homespun with refurbished antiques and furniture.

There are a few choices for sleeping: dorm-style bunk beds, single beds, and private double rooms. If you're looking for an upgrade, then the "Historic Apartment" (the winery's old office) might fit the bill.

Good to know

PRICE RANGE
$ $ $ $ $
AMENITIES INCLUDE
wheelchair access (some caves too); towel rentals; free WiFi; laundry service; parking; luggage storage; vending machine; hair dryer; secure safe; excursions and events (yoga, barbecues, dinners); donation-based coffee bar; book swap. Breakfast included.

Tip: Enjoy the picturesque gardens around the hostel. Lemon, pomegranate, orange, pear, vanilla, and pistachio trees jostle for attention and create a charming atmosphere.

Hostel 1W

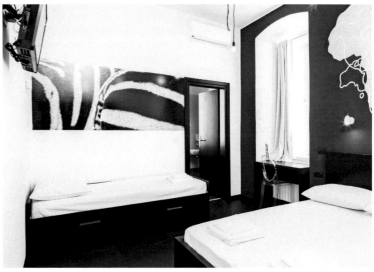

Situated in a nineteenth-century building that was built when Rijeka was ruled by the Austrians, Hostel 1W is a throwback to good old-fashioned Croatian hospitality with a twist of modern design. Beautiful rooms, a wonderful team of friendly staff, and a great location right in the heart of the Korzo (the town's main pedestrian zone) make Hostel 1W an ideal base for exploring Rijeka and the surrounding area.

Private rooms are designed for couples, families, and business people; they are all en suite and have cable TV and a desk. The dorms are spacious and have been designed with guests in mind. They have big lockers, air conditioning, curtains, reading lights, and a power point for each bed. Each dorm has a comfortable reading corner, and the female dorms have a separate makeup corner.

The hostel has a common living area where staff gather all guests in the evening for a free welcome drink of rakija (local brandy). There's a communal kitchen, an internet point, and several communal showers and toilets for dorm guests. In the morning you can have a croissant and coffee for free, and for a small fee you can order a full continental breakfast that includes cereals, bread, juice, and coffee.

Cape Town's iconic mountains and the rolling waves of the Atlantic provide a stunning backdrop for the stylish Backpackers in Green Point aka "B.I.G." After traveling the world and staying in some of the best (and worst) accommodations along the way, the owners of B.I.G. were keen to create a perfect hostel in Cape Town. Their experience is clearly reflected in the hostel's design and facilities.

The dorms here have spacious wooden bunk beds ("designed by adults for adults"), and rooms are serviced daily, so you can climb into a clean bed after each long day of exploring. The private rooms have smart TVs, where you can get your Netflix dose if you're suffering from a little jetlag. The hostel serves a delicious continental breakfast for free, with freshly brewed coffee ready to set you up for the day. With top-notch amenities and traditional South African barbecues or "braai" facilities, the completely perfect hostel experience can be found at the B.I.G.

Good to know

PRICE RANGE
$ $ $ $ $
AMENITIES INCLUDE
free WiFi and internet; swimming pool; parking; library and book swap; games rooms; TV, movies, and XBox; garden; braai (barbecue) facilities; airport transfers.

Tip: Enjoy a traditional South African barbecue called braai or go out and explore Cape Town's iconic mountains. You should also spend a relaxing day at the beach and watch the rolling waves of the Atlantic.

Abraham Hostel

Located in the hip Electric Garden district (Gan HaHashmal), Abraham Hostel is right in the heart of Tel Aviv's restaurant and nightlife scene. With live concerts featuring local musicians, Israeli cooking workshops, and organized pub crawls for dancing the night away, Abraham offers guests an authentic cultural and social experience. There are 350 beds at the Abraham Hostel with many different room options. During recent renovations the hostel partnered with local graffiti artists to decorate the walls. Their art combines colorful elements from Tel Avivian street life and draws on the hostel's multicultural nature; the result is vibrant and eclectic.

The lime, teal, and violet-colored corridors lead the way from a light-flooded lobby, past a spacious lounge and event space, and up to the hostel's beautiful rooftop overlooking the neighborhood. On long summer nights, both Tel Avivians and guests gather here to enjoy the spectacular views, Middle Eastern beats, and drinks with a Mediterranean flair.

There's also an excellent range of free tours on offer. Try a walking tour of Old Jaffa, or wander through modern Florentin where you'll learn about the edgy neighborhood's thriving street art scene.

Abraham Hostel

There's space for everyone under this welcoming roof

Abraham Hostel is the first quality backpacker hostel in Jerusalem. Created by two compulsive travelers, the pair of entrepreneurs were already running a tip-based walking tour business when they came up with the idea to create a place that gathers the best aspects of Jerusalem for travelers to experience. The result is Abraham Hostel, which fills the city's need for affordable accommodation with atmosphere, cleanliness, activities (both in and out of house), and quality customer service.

Located in the center of the city, the hostel is walking distance from many of Jerusalem's key landmarks. As founder Gal Mor says, "Abraham Hostel Jerusalem lies in the middle of it all, putting a multicultural cherry on top of the city's diversity-bursting cake."

Jerusalem, situated between green forests and the desert of the Jordan Valley, is home to a diverse population. It is considered holy to three of the world's Abrahamic religions: Christianity, Judaism, and Islam. It seems apt that a hostel—acting as a place of rest to countless travelers with a myriad of ethnicities from around the world—should carry this name.

This is a hostel that embraces curiosity and history and is more of a temporary home to a group of like-minded individuals than a thoroughfare. The first thing guests will see as they step into the hostel is the welcoming and brightly decorated lobby. Further into the hostel, along winding corridors and in the courtyard, you are continuously met by eye-catching graffiti of typical scenes from the life of a backpacker and familiar landmarks of Jerusalem.

Outside the doors of the hostel, the whole of Jerusalem's excitement, bustle, and culture lies in wait, just begging to be explored. The aroma-filled lanes of Mahane Yehuda Market are just minutes away. →

Good to know

PRICE RANGE
$ $ $ $ $

AMENITIES INCLUDE
free WiFi; self-catering
facilities; laundry
facilities; bar; lounge;
TV room; traveler center.
Breakfast included.

Tip: *Besides daily
free walking tours to
the Old City, the hostel
offers tours to the
West Bank, Egypt,
and Jordan, which
includes the option
of seeing Petra, Wadi
Rum, and an
overnight stay in a
Bedouin camp. Guests
can also try a yoga
session on the rooftop.*

Abraham Hostel lies in the middle of it all, putting a multicultural cherry on top of the city's diversity-bursting cake.

Make sure to spend time sampling the diverse cuisine and roaming the markets for spices, kitsch, and must-have items.

Another key benefit of staying at Abraham are the tours that take you beyond the tourist trail. Besides daily free walking tours to the Old City, the hostel offers tours to the West Bank, Egypt, and Jordan, which includes the option of seeing Petra, Wadi Rum, and an overnight stay in a Bedouin camp.

Back at Abraham, guests can relax in the airy, cozy lounge, or (in the summer) try a calming yoga session on the rooftop. There is a host of scheduled events on offer to keep

you entertained, ranging from open mic nights, hummus workshops, pub crawls, and Hebrew lessons. In the evenings, the guest kitchen becomes a social venue, where people gather to cook dinner in the company of hostel friends. In the warmer weather the rooftop hosts barbecues and sunset drinks. Speaking of which, the hostel lays claim to a well-stocked bar with happy hour running from 6 until 8 p.m.

There is a generous, free continental breakfast of cereal, salad, cheese, bread, and other condiments from 7 to 10 a.m. Towels and sheets are provided to all guests free of charge,

and there are free lockers in all dorm rooms—just remember to bring your own lock. To enable your explorations, the hostel offers free luggage storage during your stay and also on the day after you check out.

It's worth noting that Abraham Hostel Jerusalem has two sister hostels in Tel Aviv and Nazareth, with a new shuttle service between locations. The shuttle runs daily and drops you off at the door of the hostel you're traveling to. It's a much more convenient alternative to navigating public transportation and is available to Abraham guests and non-guests alike.

Fauzi Azar Inn

A rich history brings people together in this ancient city

Fauzi Azar Inn lays claim to being the first guesthouse in the Old City of Nazareth. This guesthouse-cum-hostel first opened its doors to travelers in 2005 and, since then, has provided innumerable guests with rest and restitution in the historical city associated with Jesus's birth. The building that houses the hostel is a beautiful 200-hundred-year-old Arab mansion, and it still retains the name of its previous owner.

Fauzi Azar Inn is the perfect base for exploring Nazareth and the Galilee. As you step into the hostel environs you can't help but feel you're stepping into a place steeped in history. Every morning, the grand-daughter of Fauzi Azar relates the building's unique story, and how what was once a vision of Jews and Arabs working together became a thriving reality today.

The hostel has an enviable location in the heart of Nazareth—only a minute's walk from the shuk (marketplace), a few blocks from both of Nazareth's two city centers, close to a host of restaurants and coffee shops, and to the attractions of the Old City. All of Nazareth's major attractions, including the Basilica of the Annunciation, the White Mosque, and St. Gabriel's Greek Orthodox Church are just 10–15 minutes away from Fauzi Azar.

Upon entering the hostel complex you come upon a rustic lounge that serves as both reception area and dining space. The hostel has a central courtyard with an old bubbling fountain surrounded by Ottoman arches and architecture. You can get to the lounge by following a narrow staircase up one floor. With stunning frescos, high ceilings, and marble floors, the upper level is breathtaking. Three enormous arched windows provide a spectacular view overlooking the Old City and the Basilica of the Annunciation.

→

Good to know

PRICE RANGE
$ $ $ $ $

AMENITIES INCLUDE
free WiFi; self-catering facilities; lounge; courtyard; free Old City tour.

Tip: The hostel hosts a series of daily events: a free walking tour of the ancient old town, a day tour to the Sea of Galilee, Golan Heights (which includes wine tasting and lunch), and a self-guided day tour of Haifa, Acre (Akko), and Rosh Hanikra.

» Operating from a region in conflict, we believe that our hostels facilitate cultural exchange and build economic relationships and can help encourage dialog and build bridges between ourselves and our neighbors. «

In the evenings the lounge turns into a convivial communal space where people come together to learn Arabic, enjoy music, or participate in cooking workshops.

The Inn has a well-equipped guest kitchen, as well as laundry facilities, and spotless showers and bathrooms. The complimentary breakfast with a choice of fresh fruits, vegetables, fried cheese, olives, feta, hummus, pita bread, pizza, omelets, salads, and delicious cakes, alongside fresh mint lemonade, tea, and coffee, is a highlight worth staying for. Additionally, you can gorge on the homemade cakes with free coffee, water, and tea on offer throughout the day. The hostel hosts a series of daily events. Explore the sights with a free walking tour of the ancient old town; you can sign up six days a week (excluding Sundays). If interested in going on a tour dedicated to the places associated with the life of Jesus, make sure to ask about the Jesus Trail tour at the front desk. Conveniently, the starting spot on the tour is right next to the hostel itself.

If you're looking to get further afield, ask about a day tour to the Sea of Galilee, Golan Heights (which includes wine tasting at a boutique local winery and lunch at Masada), and the self-guided day tour of Haifa, Acre (Akko), and Rosh Hanikra.

If you love hostels with history and lots of character, then you will love Fauzi Azar Inn. It is cozy and comfortable, and Nazareth is the perfect escape from the hustle and bustle of Tel Aviv. Wandering through the narrow streets of the Old City is a delight, with vantage points all over, including from the hostel, that afford you wonderful panoramic views of Nazareth.

The hostel is a beacon of peace, bringing together people of different faiths and origins. As a local symbol of unity in a once troubled neighborhood, Fauzi Azar Inn is a place where people of all faiths and backgrounds can work and live together.

It's worth noting the two sister hostels of Fauzi Azar Inn in Tel Aviv and Jerusalem. There's a daily shuttle service between locations that will drop you off at the door of the hostel you're traveling to. It's a much more convenient alternative to navigating public transportation and is available to guests and non-guests alike.

Co-working hostels

For digital nomads

Hostels are often a perfect base for digital nomads. Free WiFi, co-working spaces, the opportunity to meet people and socialize, plus the affordability of hostels compared to co-living spaces means you can travel longer, better, and with less stress on your bank balance. These hostels are perfect for digital nomads.

LetsBunk Poshtel, New Delhi

The hip and historic Long Story Short Hostel (p. 258) in Olomouc has a dedicated co-working space, Vault42, on the ground level. LetsBunk Poshtel (p. 247) in New Delhi is transforming the local hostel experience with a co-working space that also offers a gourmet cafe and a rooftop terrace overlooking a thirteenth-century fortification. Adler Hostel (p. 298) in Singapore has a diverse bunch of resident co-workers, including technopreneurs, investors, MMA fighters, and web developers, and digital nomads can tap into its great location and fab facilities. ONEDAY Pause & Forward (p. 280) is a new hostel and co-working space in Bangkok. The wood, brick, and foliaged interior with large windows and

beautiful polished concrete floors will trigger your creativity, and the high-speed WiFi, meeting rooms, and individual desks will provide everything you need to be productive. YellowSquare (p. 134) in Rome, one of Europe's best party hostels, is launching a new co-working space, complete with free iPad hire. So now you can balance your nightlife antics with work during the day, or simply use the space to fill in time between the hostel's walking tours and cooking classes. Set in a UNESCO heritage site in Lyon, Away Hostel & Coffee Shop (p. 126) is a trifecta of café, hostel, and office, making it a popular spot for travelers and locals alike. Although the café is not a designated co-working space, it effectively acts as one, with the added bonus of being able to enjoy homemade food, local products, and cocktails from the bar.

» Hostels are often *a perfect base* for digital nomads. Free WiFi, co-working spaces, and the opportunity to meet people and socialize. «

ONEDAY Pause & Forward, Bangkok

Long Story Short Hostel, Olomouc

Away Hostel & Coffee Shop, Lyon

Swanky Mint

Playful colors delight guests at this edgy abode

Mixing elegance with post-industrial chic, this hostel is a decadent and truly swanky affair in the heart of Zagreb. Think gorgeous sun terraces, beautifully designed rooms, fun and friendly staff, and a bar that's hugely popular with locals. The addition of Swanky Mint's new outdoor pool and bar last year confirms its status as Croatia's most exciting luxury hostel.

One of the eye-catching features of this hostel is its incorporation of

the building's heritage into a modern design. Once an old textile dyeing and cleaning factory, the exposed brickwork, pipes, and steel beams still make an appearance, while remnants of machinery from old drying technology can be found in the courtyard.

Swanky Mint offers guests a choice of rooms to suit any budget. If you're traveling with family and friends then the beautiful self-catering apartments are good value. These come with a living space (with sofa-bed), a small kitchenette, and a double bed on the mezzanine level. If you're a couple, there are

four very stylish private rooms with double beds and colorful en suite bathrooms. All of the doubles and apartments are equipped with satellite TV, air conditioning, and private bathrooms. Most of the beds and furnishings in the rooms have been recycled; for example, the dorm bunk beds are built out of chipboard. Dorms are also equipped with air conditioning and secure lockers.

All guests are given a proper Croatian welcome upon arrival— a potent shot of rakija, a traditional fruit brandy. This might lead you to the wonderful on-site Swanky Bar, the meeting point for both hostel →

ŠNAJDERAJ

Good to know

PRICE RANGE
$ $ $ $ $
AMENITIES INCLUDE
linens; 24-hour
reception; free WiFi;
self-catering facilities;
laundry facilities;
parking; airport
transfers.

Tip: Join one of the
hostel's free walking
tours. There's one
steampunk-inspired
journey into Croatia's
science history,
and another which
investigates the
underground
abandoned military
complexes in the
Medvednica mountain
area outside of the city.

Mixing elegance with post-industrial chic, *Swanky Mint Hostel* is a decadent and truly swanky affair in the heart of Zagreb.

guests and locals. The party never stops here—between concerts, live DJ sets, and art events, the bar is the star of the Swanky show. The fun spills outside onto a sunny outdoor terrace with lots of tables and cozy corners; the staff come around to take your order so there's no need to wrestle your way to the bar to get a drink. This place is always buzzing—morning, noon, and night. The danger of staying here is that you may never leave and see anything else in Zagreb.

Swanky Mint has many amazing features and continues to develop more. Last year the hostel announced the completion of a small pool and two new terraces in the backyard. Other features include a rent-a-bike station in the front courtyard and an airport transfer service (ask via email in advance).

Beside the outdoor bar there is a fully equipped kitchen for guests to use, but the bar also serves the mother of all hostel breakfasts. You can choose from a menu of toasted sandwiches, croissants, or burek (delicious stuffed cheese pastry), and in addition tuck into a breakfast buffet which includes cereals, waffles, bread, jams, Nutella, yogurt, and juice, coffee, or tea. The staff here are experienced

and very attentive towards guests' needs. If you need a hair dryer or adaptor, they can be borrowed from reception, and there is a secure luggage storage option if you're checking in early or leaving late.

The hostel also runs a bunch of acclaimed free walking tours. There's one of Zagreb, a steampunk-inspired journey into Croatia's science history, and another which investigates the underground abandoned military complexes in the Medvednica mountain area outside of the city.

Don't miss out on this stylish accommodation to make your visit to Zagreb extra memorable.

Czech Inn

A paradise for design lovers in Europe's art nouveau mecca

In a nineteenth-century art nouveau building at the intersection of the Vinohrady and Vršovice residential districts sits Czech Inn, a beautifully decorated hostel with unique decor. With a combination of bright colors popping against muted tones, vintage furniture, and odd baubles throughout the building, it is one of the most visually attractive and interesting hostels out there.

Each room at Czech Inn has a different design with lots of character. Guests can choose from luxurious private apartments and rooms that feel more like hotel accommodation, or dorms ranging from small shared rooms to larger ones with up to 36 beds. There are shared bathroom facilities, but having one en suite is also an option. The two premium dorms on the top floor share a communal kitchen and living room area, making it feel more like a private apartment.

Czech Inn has an on-site basement bar with amazing microbrew beer, and social options like movie nights, quiz nights, and sports screenings. There are also self-service laundry facilities on-site. Unfortunately, there's currently no kitchen but the hostel is planning to introduce one in the near future.

Breakfast costs extra or you can go to their coffee corner next to the reception desk for a cup of super high quality brew from La Bohème (one of the absolute best coffee shops in Prague) before heading out for breakfast at either Moment Vegan Café or Marthy's Kitchen at Francouzska. From the Czech Inn, you can easily walk to two interesting neighborhoods in Prague, Vinohrady and Žižkov. They both have incredible nightlife, beautiful architecture, and plenty of great restaurants. For an absolutely stunning sunset, take a 15-minute walk to Riegrovy Sady with a few bottles of beer, grab a spot on the lawn, and enjoy the fantastic view overlooking the city.

There's also an in-house social network called Comundu where you can arrange to meet other travelers.

Good to know

PRICE RANGE
$ $ $ $ $

AMENITIES INCLUDE
linens; towels; free WiFi;
power adapters;
hairdryer; free walking
tour; library; regular
events; communal
kitchen; café; bar.
Breakfast not included.

Tip: Visit the ultra
cool neighborhood
around the hostel
and look into the area's
unique little shops.
Have a Czech cider
from InCider Bar
(the only cider bar
in Prague) and
a cup of coffee from
Café V Lese there.

Sir Toby's Hostel

Good to know

PRICE RANGE
$ $ $ $ $
AMENITIES INCLUDE
linens; towels; walking
tours; locks and other
amenities available
at reception; library;
balconies; garden; bar.

*Tip: Explore the
hostel's artistic
neighborhood: DOX
Modern Art Gallery,
the notable Cross Club,
and Prague Market.
There's always plenty
of weird and
wonderful things
to see and experience
in this part of town.*

Sir Toby's is in an offbeat location: the industrial and gritty Holešovice district. While the area still has an industrial feel, it has transitioned to one that caters to the more artistically minded travelers. The area is home to the DOX Modern Art Gallery, the notable Cross Club, and Pražská tržnice (Prague Market)—there's always plenty of weird and wonderful things to see and experience in this part of town. Guests at Toby's can choose from five to twelve-person dorms (including female- and male-only rooms), or cozy and tastefully decorated private rooms equipped with interesting antiques. Each room has beautiful dark wood floors, richly painted or wallpapered walls, and gorgeous furniture, fixtures, and drapes. All beds come with big fluffy pillows. Smaller shared rooms are bunk-free, and smaller dorms have individual sockets, bed lamps, and lockers where guests can store their phones while charging.

The social scene at Sir Toby's is extraordinary thanks to their fantastic on-site pub, popular live music and trivia nights, and their garden terrace where they host complimentary barbecues.

Sophie's Hostel

ophie's is tucked away on a quiet side treet in Prague's New Town area. Housed in a nineteenth-century rt nouveau building on the edge f Vinohrady, one of the city's most icturesque neighborhoods, the hostel s a short tram or metro ride from the istoric city center and is surrounded y local shops, restaurants, bars, and afes. It's an excellent option for nyone who wants easy access to all f the main tourist attractions but still

wants a taste of local Prague life. With the assistance of Czech architect Olga Novotná, the hostel recently received a fresh design makeover. Expect a boho-chic feel with vintage furnishings and contemporary art complemented by stencil artwork of Prague's skyline from local artist, Zora Mazácová.

Accommodations include a mix of designer dorms, artsy apartments, and private rooms. The dorms here are

fantastic: They feature beautiful wooden floors, brushed steel bed frames, comfy mattresses, and big, plush pillows. The female dorms have separate beds—no bunks, spacious en suite bathrooms with railhead showers, plus a kitchenette, making Sophie's Hostel, a fantastic option for female travelers.

Sophie's Hostel has a lovely bar that's open 24 hours where guests can have a homemade breakfast buffet.

Good to know

PRICE RANGE
$ $ $ $ $
AMENITIES INCLUDE
linens; towels; maps;
free WiFi; self-catering
facilities; hairdryer; iron;
alarm clock; power
adapters; bar. Breakfast
not included.

Tip: One of the receptionists has a degree in history and art history, and puts on a tour once a week for guests looking to learn more about the surrounding area. Sophie's also has daily events like morning 10K river runs, and free pancake nights.

Hostel Old Plovdiv

Vintage charm off the beaten Bulgarian path

The historic design of this hostel reflects the spirit of Plovdiv, an old and colorful town. Originally owned by one of the richest tobacco merchants in Bulgaria, the hostel building was finished in 1868 during the Bulgarian Renaissance. It was in a state of total disrepair before being restored by the current hostel owners.

The wooden columns of the house are constructed from Lebanese cedar, the marble is from Ottoman Turkey, and there is even an original Roman fortress in the dining room. The rooms are just as impressive; they're furnished with hand-picked antiques and unique lamps, and painted in pastel shades that artfully balance out the rich mahogany. Details like having dried flowers on your pillow and black-and-white family photos on the walls add to the nostalgic charm.

Dorms have individual beds (no bunk beds), and the bathrooms and showers are spotless and well maintained. Personal lockers are inside antique suitcases—a nice touch. Free linen and towels are included for all guests, and WiFi is available throughout the building.

The sun-drenched courtyard is the cherry on top for Hostel Old Plovdiv, but the excellent free breakfast is a close second. So do both! Start your day with local meats and cheeses, bread, jam, fresh coffee, and tea, under the shade of a medlar tree with the delightful sounds of a water fountain in the background.

Plovdiv is a fun and beautiful place to spend time during your trip to Bulgaria. Under-traveled and well worth getting lost in, you can enjoy time away from tourists and really get to know this place. Hostel Old Plovdiv is central and an easy two-minute walk from the city's pedestrian area. Make sure to wander the beautiful, old cobblestone streets and take in the beauty. If you pass by any locals playing chess, watch them for a while. They may even invite you to play—no matter if you speak Bulgarian or not.

Good to know

PRICE RANGE
$ $ $ $ $
AMENITIES INCLUDE
linens; towels; free WiFi
and internet access;
lockers; free parking;
free tea, coffee, and
homemade lemonade;
garden. Breakfast is
included.

Tip: _Make sure to_
wander the beautiful
old cobblestone
streets of the city's
pedestrian area, which
is an easy two-minute
walk from the hostel,
relax and just take in
the beauty.

Long Story Short

A place where stories are made

Long Story Short Hostel & Café is just one of those places: You have to see it to believe it and particularly to feel it. The building itself has a special, balanced energy that makes it a very unique place. As founder Eva Dlabalová explains: "We didn't build this place with the intention of being a luxury hostel; we just did what felt right, only focusing on our values and what the space was asking us for, and in the end it turned out really well."

Located in the historical center of Olomouc, Long Story Short Hostel is perfect for travelers looking for something truly extraordinary.

The project was initiated by Eva Dlabalová, a local businesswoman who gained the inspiration for the hostel during her travels and longer stays abroad. Dlabalová partnered with an interior designer, Denisa Strmisková, and the property owner of the historical, seventeenth-century Podkova building to create a friendly and cosmopolitan accommodation for today's digital nomads.

The name "Long Story Short" alludes to the building's rich history— you can ask the friendly staff for the long version. It's also a "punny" reference to the building's layout, one with a long, continuous hall. Dlabalová transformed an entire floor of the Podkova horseshoe to create Long Story Short, a contemporary hostel. The design concept was created from scratch, including all its

Good to know

PRICE RANGE
$ $ $ $ $

AMENITIES INCLUDE
accessible facilities; free towels; free WiFi and internet access; laundry service; keycard access; private lockers; hairdryer; rainfall showers; baby changing facilities; garden; terrace; boomerang hangout space; book swap; movie nights; music jams; barbecues; meeting room; pétanque pit; friendly staff; breakfast buffet (with veg/gluten-free options).

Tip: Enjoy a peaceful and sun-filled morning with a cup of coffee from the café on the beautiful garden terrace!

Long Story Short Hostel & Café is just one of those places: You have to see it to believe it and mainly to feel it. We didn't build this place with the intention of being a luxury hostel, we just did what felt right.

furnishings. Strmisková worked on the hostel's design for two years; she wanted to highlight the genius of the building's historical elements and, with appropriate adjustments, marry it with a contemporary design. The original history of the Podkova has been nicely blended with modern touches of raw materials like wood, stone, and metal. To soften things up a bit, artwork from local artisans and creatives is on display and matched with delicate vintage

furniture. The hostel has a mix of privates and dorm rooms—and no bunk beds. As Dlabalová suggests, "We don't believe in bunk beds! We focus on comfort, quality, and experience in all that we do." Instead, the sleeping zones in each dorm room were created with mezzanine floors, which help create a sense of privacy and enough space for personal belongings—that's a luxury hostel idea, indeed. The premium double rooms are all en suite.

The wedding suite, with its extravagant bathtub, is no doubt the most unique room in the hostel.

The reception, which simultaneously functions as a common room and a café, is the heart of the hostel. An arched hallway leads from the reception to all the rooms, but watch as you walk down it—it appears different from every perspective and surprises you constantly as you go along. Furniture is carefully arranged into intimate seating areas, and →

the upholstery's pastel colors pop against the pure white plastering in contrast to the black detailing.

The majority of the furnishings are custom made. Beds, mirrors, lamps, and shelving, as well as the bathroom equipment, were made to measure in cooperation with local artisans. All of these sit elegantly alongside the classic modernist design of the previous century and more trendy conceptual details. From the interior lighting and the minimalist navigation system (based on the complex visual style of the hostel) to the original artworks by the Czech artist David Minarík, Long Story Short truly has a long list of curious and remarkable details to discover.

The hostel has many amenities: an in-house café and bar, a meeting room, free WiFi, an on-site meeting room for networking, a co-working space for nomads with deadlines, and more. Guests can relax on the beautiful outdoor garden terrace frequently used for various events like world-themed barbecues and live DJ shows. The terrace overlooks the pétanque pit (a game similar to bocce). Surrounded by plenty of trees from the nearby park, it's a delightful place to enjoy a peaceful and sun-filled morning.

The café prides itself on using local produce wherever possible. The breakfast, available for a small fee, is a buffet of fresh fruit, greens, tomatoes, eggs, cheeses, delicious red cabbage salad, toast, and, of course, great coffee.

Long Story Short Hostel is a special place and an often overlooked gem on the traveling circuit. ⌂

TwoWheels Hostel

Homely vibes in a Latvian biker's paradise

TwoWheels is a cozy little hostel that feels like it has a lot of stories to tell. It almost feels more like staying at a friend's family house than a hostel. The two-story timber building is wonderfully rustic, with creaking wooden floorboards, a twisting staircase, and sprawling pots of green ferns trailing from the windowsills. It is a quirky and interesting space that combines historical Latvian architecture with a familial touch. As you might expect from the name, it has a motorbike theme, with classic bike parts mounted on the walls and nestled in corners, and motorbikes also available for rent. The rooms at TwoWheels are secluded and cozy. The 20 bedrooms are individually designed and named after different cities around the world, including New York, Tehran, and London. There are plenty of unique design touches such as batik curtains, local artwork, colorful rugs, and eclectic ornaments scattered around the surfaces, as well as thick blankets at the end of the beds for added warmth. Each room also has multiple power sockets as well as end tables and wicker chairs, plus drawers and wardrobes in lieu of lockers. Most rooms have a private bathroom—a wet room with glass walls (which might be disconcerting if you are staying with a friend) and a great power shower. A buffet breakfast is laid out on the reception bar from 9 a.m. to 11 a.m. The reception area, which doubles as a common area, has wooden tables and chairs, and there are also comfy armchairs and sofas dotted around the hostel's two floors. The small balcony with tables and parasols is a great place to watch the sunset while enjoying an ice-cold Latvian beer—many of which are stocked behind the TwoWheels bar.

Riga has a wonderful café culture in amongst its striking Art Nouveau architecture, so it's worth spending time wandering the streets before stopping for coffee and cake.

Good to know

PRICE RANGE
$ $ $ $
AMENITIES INCLUDE
bar; small restaurant;
summer terrace; Harley
Davidson motorbike hire;
breakfast included.

Tip: The small balcony
of TwoWheels Hostel,
equipped with tables and
parasols, is a great place
to watch the sunset while
enjoying an ice-cold
Latvian beer—many
of which are stocked
behind the TwoWheels
bar. It almost feels
more like staying at
a friend's house than
a hostel.

Downtown Forest

A green haven on a budget

Downtown Forest Hostel & Camping beautifully reflects the Lithuanian soul, love for nature, and the bohemian spirit of hosteling. Located in the self-declared independent republic of Užupis in Vilnius's old town, you're in the artistic and alternative heart of the capital.

With a countless number of churches, Vilnius might have one of the prettiest old towns in Europe, but the key to enjoying this Baltic capital is looking for the alternative and quirky things around. Check out the Užupis district, and keep an eye out for street art, cute little angels, or the city's incredible cemeteries, for example.

Even while in the heart of the capital city, Downtown Forest is so calm and quiet it feels like a complete getaway. The rooms here suit travelers of all budgets; there's an even mix of bright, spacious dorms and privates—some of them have a private balcony too. The hostel is also the most centrally located place in Vilnius to put your tent or camper. Complimentary tea and coffee is available in the morning and the freshly baked croissants are a nice way to start your day.

On cold days you can relax in the small yet lovely common room and read one of the books from the exchange shelf. The hostel serves up local craft beer for you to try too.

Their outdoor terrace transforms into a bar in the summertime; locals come here to have a barbecue and chill—and every now and then concerts happen outside. This hostel is the perfect place for meeting people and to explore all Vilnius has to offer.

Good to know

PRICE RANGE
$ $ $ $ $
AMENITIES INCLUDE
free WiFi; complimentary
tea and coffee every
morning; bar; free
concerts; barbecue.

Tip: Their outdoor
terrace transforms
into a bar in the
summertime; locals
come here to have
a barbecue and chill,
and every now
and then concerts
happen outside.

Soul Kitchen

There's a little extra space for everything at Soul Kitchen

The concept of Soul Kitchen was built from the bottom-up by two avid hostel travelers. The goal was to maintain the privacy of a hotel experience but also integrate the social vibe of a youth hostel and cool interior design. The result is Russia's—and probably Europe's—finest design hostel, Soul Kitchen. Featuring en suite private rooms, custom-made bunk beds with curtains for privacy, and great design, this hostel is perfect for solo travelers, couples, and families alike.

The dorms are the ultimate in hostel luxury. Each dorm bed is almost queen size and has plenty of room for two people (if you desire). It comes with a reading lamp and an individual power outlet. The mattresses are comfortable, the spaces feel private, and you never have to worry about bright room lights blinding you at 3 a.m. thanks to a universal control switch at reception that keeps all the lights dim at night. Backpacks can be stored in lockers under the bed; lockers have power outlets inside for securely charging your electronics while you're out and about. Private rooms come in all sizes: double bed

en suites (with and without private shower), luxury en suites (with fireplace and shower), and family private rooms (shared showers). All rooms are secure with keycard entry.

The TV lounge is the ultimate hangout, and features a custom-built couch (with power points conveniently placed throughout) in front of a TV with about a thousand channels.

Breakfast is not included, but there is free tea and coffee available around the clock. The guest kitchen is beautiful, however, and so well equipped and inviting that self catering becomes yet another perk of staying here.

Good to know

PRICE RANGE
$$\$\$\$\$$

AMENITIES INCLUDE
free linens; free towels and internet access; free WiFi; free international landlines; free umbrellas to borrow on rainy days; board games; lounge; library; ample bathroom space.

Tip: The hostel is located in the most beautiful area of town, in walking distance from all the sights, and some rooms even have an exclusive river view!

Fabrika Tbilisi

A Soviet sewing factory in the heart of old Tbilisi

Located on the left bank of Mtkvari River in the old part of Tbilisi, Fabrika brings a once-forgotten, historical-cultural part of the Georgian capital back to life. The area is undergoing urban rehabilitation as both national and international visitors have become inspired to rediscover and appreciate the city's landmarks and iconic neighborhood spaces.

The hostel is the product of renowned infrastructure development company the Adjara Group. With a forward-thinking design, they wanted to promote both sustainability and authenticity regarding the hostel's roots. The façade of the building remains largely untouched except for some industrial and loft-style elements that create a stark contrast to the aged concrete exterior. The Fabrika has a wonderful blend of new and old character, and its lofty ceilings and large communal areas provide a great sense of space.

The lobby is large and decorated with many brightly colored oriental carpets that provide great texture. The room is liberally dotted with a variety of seating areas—armchairs, comfy sofas, and even a hammock or two. Every piece of furniture has been carefully selected to create a vibrant and comfortable communal space that encourages a dynamic social experience. Daylight streams through floor-to-ceiling bay windows on two sides of the room, while a bar tucked into a corner with blue and purple neon lights provides nightly promises of "Cocktails and Dreams." Alongside the funky lobby and dining area, the hostel has a number of multifunctional spaces and a social courtyard area—all bringing an interesting crowd together to →

Good to know

PRICE RANGE
$ $ $ $ $

AMENITIES INCLUDE
24-hour reception; tours
and activities; free WiFi;
self-catering facilities;
multipurpose event
room; luggage storage;
secure keycard access;
laundry facilities;
multipurpose event
room; common room;
self-catering facilities;
breakfast buffet;
restaurant; cocktail bar;
Fabrika shop.

_Tip: The courtyard
is loaded with
café/bars, artistic
studios, workshops,
concept stores,
co-working space,
and ever-changing
one-off events!_

Daylight streams through floor-to-ceiling bay windows while a bar tucked into a corner with blue and purple neon lights provides nightly promises of *Cocktails and Dreams.*

connect, exchange experiences, and set new stories in motion.

Fabrika has utilized the size of the building—which used to house a Soviet sewing factory—to good effect: The hostel has the capacity to accommodate 354 guests. Take your pick from dormitories, private rooms, and apartment suites—this hostel has it all. The dorm rooms are clean and minimalistic (think comfortable beds with crisp white sheets), and some of the private rooms have amazing views.

The breakfast buffet is a sumptuous feast and includes strong coffee, fresh fruit, homemade yogurts with a variety of jams and compotes, freshly baked bread, delectable baked treats, green salads, and hard-boiled eggs.

With hip urban design and sophistication, personable service, amazing facilities, and superb sleeping quarters, Fabrika is an affordable alternative without compromise.

LetsBunk Poshtel

Minimalist tones offer calm amidst the flurry of Delhi

Located in Delhi's hip Hauz Khas Village, LetsBunk Poshtel is central and surrounded by a rich history dating back to the thirteenth-century Delhi Sultanate. This "poshtel" is the first hospitality venture to introduce a mix of affordability, style, and sociability to India's accommodation industry and offers the right relaxing yet social environment to come home to after a hectic day exploring the urban chaos that is Delhi.

The intent of the hostel's design was simple: to blend the concept of boutique hotel with an upscale hostel while focusing on finer details of comfort, cleanliness, and a community vibe. "We wanted to make a place that is spacious, clean, and comfortable, with monochromatic colors and a dash of minimalism," says founder Gautam Munjal. With extensive use of wrought iron in the hostel's furnishings and a restrained color palette, the interior has a Scandi-minimalist vibe, rather than the vibrancy of color and texture usually encountered in Indian interiors.

LetsBunk has 11 rooms in total, ranging from female-only dorms to queen and king-size double en suites catering to couples and families. The spacious beds (7 × 4 ft) are a major plus.

Guests here can look forward to a busy calendar of social events, ranging from weekly barbecue nights with Indian beer tasting to movie nights, bar and café crawls, and outdoor activities like ultimate frisbee, slacklining, and rock climbing.

LetsBunk has fostered a strong connection to the local community. During the LetsBunk Socials, locals are invited to curate unique events, like filmmaking workshops, pop-up markets, and acoustic live mic sessions on the hostel's picturesque rooftop terrace.

Another major bonus of LetsBunk is the co-working space and café if you're looking to catch up with work while on the road.

Neat and orderly, LetsBunk is a great space to refresh yourself while visiting Delhi.

Good to know

PRICE RANGE
$ $ $ $ $

AMENITIES INCLUDE
free towels; air conditioning; en suite washrooms; free toiletries (private rooms and dorms); hair dryer; rooftop terrace; board games; access to partner gym and spa; daily tours and activities; free tea / coffee. Breakfast included.

Tip: Enjoy barbecue nights with Indian beer tasting, movie nights, bar and café crawls, and outdoor activities like ultimate frisbee, slacklining, and rock climbing.

Bangkok: a golden escape

The Thai capital is a fascinating *city of contrasts,* where past meets present among golden temples and yummy street food.

let your initial encounter with a taxi or tuk tuk driver teach you otherwise. Best of all, I enjoyed the study of contrasts in Bangkok, such as the history of the bedazzling Grand Palace side by side with the glam and glitter of the shopping centers. Here are my tips to help you make the most of your stay.

Where to eat

Bangkok's food scene wowed me the most. Apart from the innumerable, lip-smacking options on offer, you won't be left out of pocket by eating well. One cheap street food to try is the spicy papaya salad som tum. It's so good and usually only 20 baht (about 3 cents)! Avoid the shrimp or fish sauce if you're vegan or have food allergies. The street-food scene in Chinatown Street is amazing and you will be so full just tasting a few dishes. The food courts at the big malls such as Siam Square One and MBK offer a wider range of great value local dishes, and 50 baht will get you a sizable portion of delicious pad thai.

Koko, near Siam Square, is a small, unassuming eatery that serves well-cooked traditional Thai dishes. It's a good option for vegetarians, but I recommend the panang curry with pork if you are an omnivore.

» As a vegan, I love the massaman curry from Siam Ceylon, near Yim Yam. When I want to treat myself,

If, like me, you've made the mistake of taking an airport taxi, ambling along the highway at snail's pace, and being nearly scammed by the driver who refuses to use the meter, chances are that your first impressions of Bangkok haven't been the best. When I arrived at my hostel, breathless and with a few extra grey hairs, I was ready to call it a day. But after learning some tips from the locals, I felt better equipped to tackle the city. And in the end, my feelings about Bangkok completely changed. The gastronomy of the city is unparalleled, and Thai people are extremely polite and hospitable—don't

→

I go to Broccoli Revolution for its super-inventive healthy options, like smoothie bowls and veggie burgers, or Ethos for massive salads with homemade dressing or vegetarian Thai food. «

CARRIE
– Yim Yam Hostel

Where to drink & party

If you've ever been interested in the Bangkok nightlife scene, chances are you have heard about the thrills of Khao San Road. Apart from the ultra-modern dance clubs, there are a number of bars here that play soul-soothing live jazz and blues. Other venues play everything from hip-hop to house and acid jazz to rock ballads. Other party hotspots of note include Chinatown, in particular the area around Charoen Krung Road. The Tep Bar, Ba Hao, Teens of Thailand, Asia Today, Jua, Tropic City, Soulbar, and FooJohn Building are just some of the places to check out.

» My must for every friend who visits is Train Night Market Ratchada, open every day from 5 p.m. to 1 a.m. Located right behind Esplanade Cineplex on busy Ratchadaphisek Road, becomes crowded with market-goers from the moment it opens. Although Bangkok hosts flea markets almost every weekend around town, the Train Market's legacy is maintained with a guarantee of great food (at reasonable prices) and a bunch of lively live music bars and pubs. «

CHOTIRAT APIWATTANAPONG
– Yim Huai Khwang Hostel

The quirkily named Sorry I'm Gay is my pick of all the cocktail bars at the Train Market. With bar tables made from old Volkswagens, this tiny venue has DJs cranking out a mix of house music and Berlin-style techno beats every night. Continue the party at nearby Mustache Bar, which is establishing a reputation as one of the city's best after-hours party hotspots.

Going for a walk

Given the heavy traffic, walking in Bangkok is a good idea.

» I really enjoy walking from Yim Yam all the way to the Golden Mount temple, then along Khao San Road or to the Grand Palace area. It's a long stroll and good workout, but you'll pass lots of interesting local markets to keep you entertained. Plus walking can sometimes be faster than taking the bus or a taxi. «

CARRIE
– Yim Yam Hostel

A less strenuous option is weaving your way through the narrow streets of the heritage district of Talad Noi, next to Chinatown, where you can see colonial mansions side by side with centuries-old temples.

Chatuchak Market might seem like the antithesis of a relaxing stroll. However, you will find a variety of vendors from all over Thailand there selling plants, trees, and flowers on Wednesdays and Thursdays. There are other garden and outdoor products, such as ceramics, available too. The perfect time to walk around the Talad Tonmai is Wednesday afternoon as the sun is going down.

Getting around town

Bangkok is notorious for extremely bad traffic congestion, so walking can often be the best option. The Skytrain, although a tad pricey, is a great option for getting around town quickly and conveniently.

But locals know of a cheaper, faster, and more exciting mode of travel: the Saen Saeb canal boat. It takes you directly to Pratunam and Siam, the main shopping centers of Bangkok. The last stop is the Parn Fah Bridge, located within walking distance of Bangkok Old City and the Golden Mount.

The hop-on-hop-off Blue Flag Tourist Boat passes by most of the major tourist attractions, including Wat Arun and the Grand Palace. The all-day unlimited travel pass is worth purchasing, and enjoying the cool breeze on the Chao Phraya River while contemplating the city's glorious past is one of my favorite experiences in Bangkok.

Best viewpoint

The Executive Lounge on the 31st floor of the Millennium Hilton Hotel has excellent views, and you could spend the entire day watching the skyline of the heaving, busy city. However, →

Bangkok's *food scene* wowed me the most. Apart from the innumerable, lip-smacking options on offer, you won't be left out of pocket by eating well. The street-food scene is amazing and you will be so full just *tasting* a few dishes.

Secret places

Bang Kachao, the green lungs of Bangkok, is a little-known jungle in the middle of the city. Here you can relax in nature, escape the pollution, and feel like you've left the massive metropolis behind. Rent a bike to explore the jungle pathways through neighborhoods, floating markets, ornate local temples, and pretty parks.

you might want to consider other options that don't pull on the purse strings so much. River View Guest House in Chinatown also has a great view of the skyline and Chao Phraya River, and its rooftop bar is way more affordable than the more famous ones.

The Golden Mount Temple is hands down the best place to watch the sunset with a 360-degree view over the city. It's also a spiritual, quiet place to relax and feel grateful.

» <u>Lungs Luean Chicken Noodle</u>, established 60 years ago, is a one-of-a kind noodle spot located in the Huai Khwang area. The tasty chicken soup and bowl of fried chicken noodles with sweet sauce are highly recommended. The price tag is less than 50 baht. «

CHOTIRAT APIWATTANAPONG
– *Yim Huai Khwang Hostel*

ONEDAY Pause and Forward

A unique concept design hostel on Bangkok's busiest boulevard

Situated on the animated Sukhumvit Street, ONEDAY is a "co-working/living place," a conglomeration of a hostel, a co-working space, café, and restaurant. On a typical day, travelers can work (with good beverages), play, and sleep soundly all under one roof.

Previously an old warehouse, the hostel has a loft-style design that retains the backbone of the building's past. With tall, airy interiors and exposed brickwork, these reminders of the building's history add a distinct, modern industrial appeal. Various vintage decor elements—from the furniture, headboards, chairs, lamps, and various other small decoration pieces—add visual interest. Wherever possible, the hostel's Thai origins have been incorporated into embellishing details, such as Thai-inspired graphics, artwork, maps, and fruits.

The hostel rates are very reasonable for what you get in return: comfort and cleanliness—all you would expect from a home away from home. With fine quality bedding and linens, towels and blankets supplied for dorm guests, shampoo and shower gel, free WiFi, coin-operated washers and dryers, access to kitchen facilities lockers, instant coffee and tea— you can expect all the little things that make a hostel experience comfortable. There's even a theater room with a big TV and DVD player for in-house entertainment.

In the words of the creators, ONEDAY wants to be more than a hostel you pass through: "We aspire to make your ONEDAY in Bangkok as memorable as that special ONEDAY in your life."

Good to know

PRICE RANGE
$ $ $ $ $

AMENITIES INCLUDE
towels; free WiFi;
self-catering facilities;
free coffee and tea;
shampoo and shower
gel; laundry facilities;
iron and ironing board;
common area; TV
room/theater room;
lockers.

*Tip: After getting
some last-minute
work done at the
hostel's co-working
space, stroll around
the animated
Sukhumvit Street
or treat yourself with
a tasty cup of coffee
at the ONEDAY café!*

In the words of the creators, *ONEDAY Pause and Forward* wants to be more than a hostel you pass through.

ONEDAY | PAUSE
HOSTEL
—
02 108 8855
WWW.ONEDAYBKK.COM

PAJAMAS
ALL DAY!

Yim Yam Hostel & Garden

A bright welcome to the Land of Smiles

Symbolic of the new generation of hostels and backpackers looking for more than just a cheap bed, Yim Yam Hostel & Garden is a place for guests to discover the soul of this destination.

In the words of the founder Gun Phansuwon, "We really encourage and want our guests to experience the exotic culture and hospitality that Thailand is famous for. Visiting a foreign country should be a life-changing odyssey, creating memories and friendships that last a lifetime."

In order to help create those life-changing experiences, the hostel curates a jam-packed schedule of events. Guests can look forward to free yoga classes, trips to the city's famous weekend markets, or a food tour of Yaowarat Chinatown, one of the world's premier street food destinations.

This is a social but quiet hostel. A lot of the socializing tends to take place in the hostel's atmospheric communal lounge, which has been painted a special bright "Thai blue" to welcome you to the "Land of Smiles"; it has a wonderful retro quality. The locally sourced furniture, original stone flooring in the lobby, artwork, and a sea of colorful paper lanterns on the ceiling combine to give guests a feel of 1980s Bangkok. Other communal areas include an indoor courtyard and a co-working space.

The hostel offers a mix of private, semi-private, and dorm rooms, all with the added bonus of a generous free breakfast.

Overall, the fantastic value, convenient location in the center of the city, and the fabulous staff make this a great hostel to visit on your adventures through Thailand. ⌂

Good to know

PRICE RANGE
$ $ $ $ $
AMENITIES INCLUDE
guest kitchenette;
café; bar; common room;
rooftop yoga shala.
Breakfast included.

Tip: Guests can look
forward to free yoga
classes, trips to the
city's famous weekend
markets, or a food
tour of Yaowarat
Chinatown, one of the
world's premier street
food destinations.

Yim Huai Khwang

A family affair with world-class design

Yim Bangkok Hostel & Café is a wonderful melting pot of diverse cultures, people, and design concepts. As owners and co-founders Tem and Bee explain: "Bangkokians are very quick to absorb new cultures and trends. The charm of living in this city is that it is constantly reinventing itself, mixing together influences from different parts of the world."

The design of the hostel mirrors that spirit with an interesting contrast of color and different design concepts. From the outside, the sleek, dark modernist façade is reminiscent of Gotham City, while the public area

inside is a wonderful burst of color, which adds energy and excitement to the hostel and makes it a very happy place to wake up to. It contrasts with the 16 rooms, which are minimalist, simple, and white-washed. Female-only and mixed dorms feature capsule-style, spacious wooden bunk beds that give the rooms an earthy, relaxed vibe.

The coolest design feature is the large clock in the lounge, which partitions the dining area and reception and serves as a meeting point for guests. The idea originated from Tem and Bee's first backpacking trip to Europe, when they noticed travelers always gravitated toward the city clock towers to meet friends.

There is a quiet but social atmosphere in the lounge area, where hostel staff interact freely with guests, playing board games, and enjoying noodle soup. There is also a once-a-month potluck dinner where guests gather and share stories over food and drinks.

The hostel is very much a family affair. Tem's mother sneaks in fruit with dipping sauces and brings her sukiyaki hot pot or Thai curry in for the potluck dinner. Bee's brother-in-law, a self-confessed history geek, gives guests a free walking tour on Tuesday mornings. You will often meet Bee and her sister in reception, and, by the end of your stay, you too will feel like part of the family.

Good to know

PRICE RANGE
$ $ $ $ $
AMENITIES INCLUDE
common room; outdoor terrace; café; steam room; safety deposit box; hairdryers; washing machine.

Tip: The hostel is conveniently located near the hip and mainly locals-only Ratchada Train Night Market and the popular Chatuchak Weekend Market. There are great noodle soup joints nearby which cost 30 to 35 baht.

Lub d Siem Reap

Ladies and gentlemen, we are (almost) floating in space

The design of Lub d Siem Reap is based on traditional Khmer stilt houses and takes inspiration from the floating villages of Kompong Phluk located outside of Siem Reap.

The hostel has 150 dorm beds and 72 private rooms. The dorm rooms are spacious, and each bunk has a charging point, reading light, and a separate locker and changing area. Private rooms have en suite bathrooms, comfortable mattresses, and black-out curtains so guests can sleep in. They are also decked out with a smart TV, mini fridge, safety box, and a tea and coffee maker.

Guests can enjoy a filling breakfast or dinner in The Little Red Fox, one of the most popular cafés in Siem Reap and situated on the hostel premises. Food is prepared by some of the city's best chefs using fresh local produce wherever possible, which in turn supports the local community.

There is plenty to keep guests busy, especially around the pool. You can enjoy a dip in the water or chill out with a delicious cocktail from the poolside bar. It becomes a popular location for parties in the evenings with big-name local DJs, a lot of drinking games, and movies that are sometimes shown with a projector on a screen over the pool. If you're looking for a quiet stay, be warned that this is Cambodia's biggest party hostel.

The hostel also partners with Garage Society, which offers guests access to a fully equipped co-working space within the hostel, with WiFi and event-hosting capabilities. There are also events to educate guests about how to travel responsibly, respecting the locals and their culture and traditions.

Good to know

PRICE RANGE
$ $ $ $ $
AMENITIES INCLUDE
swimming pool;
co-working space;
meeting room; all-day
food and beverages;
smart TVs in private
rooms; hairdryers;
laundry; WiFi; 24-hour
reception; baggage
storage up to 60 days;
24-hour security
monitor.

Tip: *The pool becomes
a popular location
for parties in the
evenings with big-
name local DJs, a lot
of drinking games,
and movies that are
sometimes shown on
a screen over the pool.*

Nexy Hostel

Where fun-loving memories are made

Nexy Hostel is the first of its kind to be found in Hanoi. Combining the luxury aspects of a boutique hotel with the low cost and amenities of a hostel, it's the ideal retreat for stylish but budget-conscious travelers.

Located in Hanoi's Old Quarter, Nexy Hostel is fittingly described as "a place to sleep or not sleep at all." The hostel has a very social atmosphere but also the necessary environment to provide a good night's rest. The hostel has both private and shared rooms; rooms and dorms are minimalist and simple, but unique. Guests staying here will be assured of a comfortable bed and a clean room and bathroom.

Additional perks of the hostel include incredibly rejuvenating hot showers, complimentary WiFi, and the delights of enjoying superior design and great attention to detail—a mirror hanging in every room; placement of hooks to hang damp towels or jackets; a locker for storing valuables; a power outlet for charging phones at night; and privacy curtains for that much-needed quiet time at the end of the day. These details might seem small, but they make all the difference to a traveler sleeping under an unknown roof.

The hostel provides a simple complimentary breakfast in the morning. Start your day with cereal, toast, fresh fruit, tea, coffee, and juice.

There are several social spaces at Nexy: a bar, a game room, a café, a TV room, a library, and a rooftop terrace. The hostel staff are super friendly and encourage a spirit of conviviality. They want guests to leave having properly explored the delights of Hanoi, made new friends, and hopefully having created a few stories to share back home.

Good to know

PRICE RANGE
$ $ $ $ $
AMENITIES INCLUDE
bar; games room; café; TV room; library; rooftop terrace. Breakfast included.

Tip: If you want to meet other travelers, check Nexy's various social spaces: a bar, a game room, a café, a TV room, a library, and a rooftop terrace. The hostel staff are super friendly and encourage a spirit of conviviality.

Oxotel Hostel

The perfect base in northern Thailand

 With a great location near the city center and easy transportation to the international airport, Chiang Mai's new design hostel Oxotel is a great choice when visiting Thailand's biggest northern capital.

Located on Wua Lai Road, the venue of the famous "Saturday Walking Street Market," the hostel is flanked by local jewelers and silver shops.

Built in the 1970s, the building was abandoned before its recent renovation and transformation.

The owners took great care to retain some of the building's original features, and guests can admire the remainders of the past in its vintage panels, vent blocks, expanded metal doors, and the old-style stair railing. The period features are infused into a modern look with the addition of contemporary furniture, gleaming parquet floors, and industrial and raw materials such as wood, steel, exposed beams and brickwork, and concrete.

All areas flow with air and light. A full-frame glass wall in the lobby area and the second floor allows sunlight to cast a warm glow into the hostel and creates healthy, natural

ventilation. There's seven communal areas to hang out in, including a semi-outdoor space and a huge garden area.

With 12 bedrooms, Oxotel has a mix of dorms and private options. Dorms sleep six; and there's both mixed and female-only rooms. Private rooms have standard or twin beds, or guests can choose the superior double rooms which also have more features, like air conditioning, an individual washbasin, a TV, a radio, a clothes rail, and complimentary towels and linens. Dorm beds have individual night-lights, personal lockers, and power sockets. The standout room at the →

Good to know

PRICE RANGE
$ $ $ $ $

AMENITIES INCLUDE
free linens; free towels;
free WiFi; keycard
access; air conditioning;
luggage storage;
lockers (bring your own
padlock); free toiletries;
hairdryer; reading
light; personal power
socket. Breakfast
included.

*Tip: The fabulous
Artisan Café on the
ground floor serves
up hot beverages,
baked treats, and good
food. Bask in the
sunshine with a coffee,
this spot has elaxation
written all over it.*

Light, lively, and
with lots of character,
Oxotel is a great
place to rest and
exchange your favorite
travel stories.

hostel is the caravan in the rear
garden; it's perfect for a couple
and comes with a private bathroom.
There are separate bath facilities
for men and women, which have
good ventilation, lockable high-
pressure rain showers, and clean
lockable toilets.

Other key on-site features include:
free WiFi, a 24hour-reception, free
parking, daily housekeeping, laundry
facilities, a vending machine, and
a tourist information service.

The fabulous Artisan Café on the
ground floor serves up hot beverages,
baked treats, and good food. Bask
in the sunshine with a coffee; this
spot has relaxation written all over it.

Light, lively, and with lots
of character, Oxotel is a great place
to rest and exchange your favorite
travel stories.   ⌂

Lub d Patong Phuket

The biggest hostel in Asia is a knockout

Lub d translates directly to "good sleeping." True to the name, guests of Lub d will sleep well in the custom-made dorms with comfy beds decked out in fresh, clean linens. Guests also receive unlimited towels and an individual locker custom-made for easy accessibility. The "Junior" or "Deluxe" rooms are on par with any boutique hotel; each has an en suite bathroom, a balcony with a hammock, and extras like a Smart LCD TV, a coffee machine, and an electronic safe deposit box for storing valuables. All rooms come with air conditioning and have free WiFi.

However, Lub d offers so much more than a place to rest your head. There's a whole range of activities to try here: Take a dip in the swimming pool or chill in the hammock with a strawberry smoothie in hand. There's a full-size boxing ring in the hostel lobby where guests can try a Muay Thai training session with a professional fighter. As with all Lub d hostels, there's a regular program of evening social events if you're looking to party. Challenge your fellow travelers to a game of giant Jenga, beer pong, flip cup, or get a pool party going after the sun sets.

If you're traveling with work, you'll be pleased to know the hostel has partnered with Garage Society to provide guests with a co-working space, so you can continue to meet deadlines while you travel. With super fast WiFi, plus meeting room facilities, you'll stay connected and be able to take care of business.

Lub d is a new-age hostel, perfect for those in search of a place to work, play, and sleep, all rolled into one. ⌂

Good to know

PRICE RANGE
$ $ $ $ $
AMENITIES INCLUDE
free WiFi; co-working
space; Muay Thai
gym; swimming pool;
all-day dining; meeting
rooms; left-luggage
service; cool down
room; travel desk.

*Tip: Take a dip in the
swimming pool or
chill in the hammock
with a smoothie in
hand. There's a
full-size boxing ring
in the hostel lobby
where guests can try
a Muay Thai training
session with a
professional fighter.*

Adler Hostel

Singapore's first and only luxury hostel

Established on the memorable date December 12, 2012, Adler Hostel is Singapore's first and only luxury hostel. Conveniently located in the heart of Chinatown, the building the hostel occupies used to house a pawn shop and a teahouse. It's a heritage home dating back to the 1940s and showcases the city's history and art deco influence. Entering the hostel is a walk back in time to the city's colonial-era roots—a quirky fusion of antique furniture and ceilings featuring artwork of local flora and fauna. Adler Hostel has all the features that are normally the preserve of luxury hotels. These include 24-hour room service, all day Segafredo Coffee and Clipper Tea, a hot cooked breakfast, a turn-down service, complimentary passes to nightclubs, and personalized travel itineraries.

"Sleep is important, especially when we travel," is the motto of founder and owner, Adler Poh, a self-confessed avid flashpacker. While there are no private rooms in this hostel, all six dormitory suites feature pod-style sleeping cabins that allow guests to have their own private space. The spacious cabins are the ultimate in luxury hosteling, each featuring a built-in personal locker perfect for storing your backpack; feather down pillows; a 350 thread-count linen quilt; a clothes hanger; personal reading light; universal power socket; and privacy curtain. Each guest is given a fluffy towel, complimentary toiletries, and use of a hairdryer.

If you are a foodie, you will love the range of high-quality, affordable meal options nearby, including the world's cheapest Michelin star restaurant, Liao Fan Hong Kong Soya Sauce Chicken Rice & Noodle— a five-minute walk from the hostel. You can also visit Satay Street, "Singapore's largest outdoor barbecue," where you can feast on grilled meats with a variety of dipping sauces. ⌂

Good to know

PRICE RANGE
$ $ $ $ $
AMENITIES INCLUDE
linens; free city maps; towels; free WiFi and internet access; security lockers; keycard access; common room; air conditioning; adaptors; hot showers; reading light; parking; safe deposit box; washing machine. Breakfast not included.

Tip: If you're a foodie, the world's cheapest Michelin star restaurant, Liao Fan Hong Kong Soya Sauce Chicken Rice & Noodle is only a five-minute walk from the hostel.

The Mahjong Hostel

For the culturally inquisitive explorer

Set in a bustling metropolis, The Mahjong is one of the most hip accommodations in the Hong Kong hostel scene. Despite the frenetic pace of life in this urban jungle, The Mahjong is in Chinatown, a peaceful neighborhood that's quiet, but still close enough to the city's more popular attractions. Steeped in Oriental tradition, yet modern and forward-thinking, The Mahjong combines the best of all worlds.

This hostel takes its name from an ancient, traditional tile game going back to the late Qing dynasty. The game, mahjong, is considered a national pastime and is played literally everywhere by locals. There is a saying that goes, "Mahjong is small but has everything it needs;" this also exemplifies the ethos of The Mahjong Hostel.

If you like to swap stories with fellow travelers, you'll love The Mahjong. The hostel features a spacious and social common room, with a friendly atmosphere and a large window looking outside. It's the perfect place to have a chat or perch on a barstool, balance a cup of coffee on the ledge, and contemplate the day of sightseeing ahead. Quiet corners of the common room have large iMacs free for guests to use. There's also a small self-service area to warm food or make a cup of tea, and a small hostel café serving hot chocolate, lattes, and more. In fair weather, the garden courtyard is a wonderful place to unwind with a drink to hand.

There's a variety of very cool mixed and female-only dorms here, each featuring futuristic custom-designed pods. With individual privacy curtains, personal safes, reading lights, and power sockets, sleeping in a dorm never seemed so inviting! The bathrooms are shared but toiletries are included. Your stay at The Mahjong includes invitations to daily hostel events and activities.

Good to know

PRICE RANGE
$ $ $ $ $

AMENITIES INCLUDE
free WiFi; hotel-grade
mattresses; central
location.

Tip: The Mahjong
offers daily events and
activities. Indulge in
Hong Kong's gastronomic
delights with a foodie
walking tour, visit the
horse races, go hiking in
the coastal mountains, or
go out on the town for
ladies night, a Hong Kong
pub crawl, or a dim sum
extravaganza.

SPIN Designer Hostel

The perfect tropical escape

Spin Designer Hostel sits nestled amid tropical gardens on the outskirts of town, not far from the powdery white beaches for which El Nido is famous.

With sleek, concrete floors, and natural materials like bamboo incorporated into the building, the hostel has an earthy aesthetic that imparts a chilled, relaxed vibe—a distinct intention of the design. In fact, everything down to the gorgeous green landscaping surrounding the hostel is well thought out. The common areas are spacious with cool designer furniture pieces that encourage guests to mill around them and socialize. Guests can see examples of this "social design philosophy" throughout the property, from the reception to the rooms. A perfect example is an eye-catching centerpiece in the common area that features a spiral staircase surrounded by a cylindrical nest-like enclosure to hang out in.

There's a variety of accommodations at Spin. The no-nonsense mixed and female-only dorms have four bunk beds, and shared bathrooms and lockers. Bunk beds in the dorms are a few notches above your typical hostel bunk; they're wide and come with the comfiest blankets imaginable. There's a shelf and personal power outlets next to every bed, as well as a set of pockets to hold any personal items. Private rooms offer en suite facilities.

The excellent complimentary breakfast buffet has fresh fruit, cheese, bread, tea, and freshly brewed coffee. On top of that, a chef is on hand to whip up an omelet or pancake if you so desire. Other amenities here include a shared kitchen, a garden, and communal lounge areas. There are barbecues on the beautiful rooftop— perfect for mingling with the other "SPINners."

The staff at Spin are extremely knowledgeable and helpful. There's a board in the common area where you can sign up for a bunch of fun daily activities—there's something for everyone.

Good to know

PRICE RANGE
$ $ $ $ $
AMENITIES INCLUDE
free WiFi; laundry
facilities; common area;
dining and pantry area;
open-air patio.

*Tip: There's a board
in the common area
where you can sign
up for a bunch of fun
daily activities
varying from picnics
on the beach,
barbecues on the
beautiful rooftop,
and legendary pub
crawls—perfect
for mingling with
the other SPINners.*

36hostel

Celebrate peace amidst the cherry blossoms

36hostel is a cozy, family-run hostel in Hiroshima, the "International City of Peace and Culture."
The hostel started out as a café with a small library of books, and it still carries some of that enjoyable "biblio" character as a guesthouse.

It all started when the space next door to the coffee shop became available. The owners, Manabu and Sayaka, jumped on the chance to expand the business while keeping the original café running. The couple

had seen so many travelers interested in the history of Hiroshima and decided to create a comfortable environment in which to host them.

As a family-run affair, 36hostel has a close, intimate appeal. When you open the door, you're greeted with a smile from Haru, the couple's son, and a very cute, small, shaggy dog named Totto.

The design is derived from the owners' own hostel visits abroad. Initially, the hostel's look focused on capturing the bright light and colors of New Mexico, but the international inspirations grew

over time. With the assimilation of vintage decorations and pieces of art, the hostel has assumed an appealing character all of its own.

Tiny and beautifully kept, everything in the hostel fits together neatly; the owners have carefully considered every detail. The hostel's communal spaces are cozy and comfortable, and have a secure home-away-from-home atmosphere. Books and plants have been gathered with care, and many pictures adorn the walls. In the morning, sunlight streams in through a big window. There's something special about →

Good to know

PRICE RANGE
$ $ $ $ $

AMENITIES INCLUDE
free linens; free WiFi and
internet; air conditioning;
hairdryer; free city
maps; security lockers;
bicycle parking; guest
kitchenette. Breakfast
not included.

Tip: Try a delicious
coffee tasting at the
café, or go to a Hanami
during cherry blossom
season, which involves
a picnic with food and
drinks, celebrating
the cherry blossoms
when in full bloom.

36hostel is a cozy guesthouse where you can spend your time drinking coffee slowly, surrounded by books.

sipping on a cup of delicious, freshly brewed coffee while sitting in this pleasant space. In the evenings, the space is beautifully illuminated and a great spot to start talking to fellow travelers and to make friends with people from various countries.

The sleeping quarters are divided into private rooms, a female-only dormitory, and a mixed dormitory. The beds are very spacious and comfortable, and all guest rooms have air conditioning. Next to each dorm bed there is a locker, a reading light, and a power outlet; the space can become private with use of a personal blackout curtain. The shared showers and bathrooms are clean and almost always available. Free toiletries are included, and towels can be rented for a small fee. There is a small kitchenette with an electric kettle, a microwave, and a toaster for guests to use.

The hostel is secure with rooms that are keycard-access only. The entrance of the hostel is locked at 9 p.m., but can be accessed by a password you receive at check-in.

The hostel is in a super convenient location. It's only a 10-minute walk away from the Peace Memorial Park and also very close to Hondori Street, where you find all the shops, restaurants, and a shopping center.

Hostel events provide cultural entertainment as well. Try coffee tasting at the café, or go to a "Hanami" a. k. a. "cherry blossom party," which involves a picnic party with food and drinks, celebrating the cherry blossoms when in full bloom.

36hostel is a beautiful, tastefully designed accommodation, filled with books, plants, and a tranquil atmosphere that matches the ethos of Hiroshima—it is definitely a hostel to visit when in this area of Japan. ⌂

The Millennials

Futuristic traveling feels at home in Kyoto

Combining state-of-the-art technology with utilitarian social spaces, a stay at The Millennials Kyoto can be likened to a futuristic experience from a science fiction novel.

The key factor that scales this hostel up to the next level of luxury is the use of over 150 multifunctional smart pod units. The pods are spread over four floors in an area that is considered prime Kyoto real estate. Guests receive an integrated iPod Touch at check-in, which provides them with various controls to operate different functions of their individual smart pod sleeping unit. Functions include an alarm system, optional projectors, and adjustable bed elevation. Hostel guests can adjust ambient lighting, air flow, and mattress incline at the press of a button. Beds can be easily converted into sofas, a mini living space, or a home theater. Certain pods are equipped with projectors, enabling guests to hook up to them via personal smart devices. Each pod unit has substantial secure storage under the bed. The individual showers here are private as well, making this hostel feel respectfully discreet.

The Millennials offers a host of complimentary items to make the hostel stay more comfortable. Cosmetics, ear plugs, and hairbrushes are available at reception; guests can even rent sleepwear if needed. A simple breakfast is complimentary, too, and consists of a variety of baked goods and breads.

When not discovering the technological delights of the sleeping pods, you can enjoy the lobby and co-working space on the eighth floor. This is a spacious environment buzzing with local entrepreneurs who take advantage of the full office amenities provided—including unlimited coffee. Be sure to join in on the cheerful happy hour each evening.

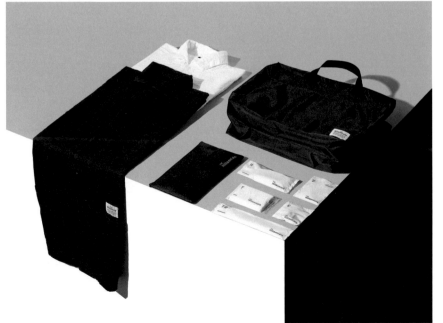

Good to know

PRICE RANGE
$ $ $ $ $
AMENITIES INCLUDE
lounge; bar; co-working
space; meeting room.

Tip: Be sure to join
in on the cheerful
happy hour each
evening at the lobby
and co-working
space on the eighth
floor; the draft beer
is complimentary
and flows freely!
It is a spacious
environment buzzing
with local
entrepreneurs.

The Blend Inn

Japanese aesthetics meets contemporary design

The Blend Inn is the latest creation from Tato Architects, a Japanese studio inspired to create a space with the perfect blend of local Japanese culture and contemporary architecture. Using a combination of materials—concrete, wood, and stainless steel—and elements of industrial design, they've designed one of the most unique hostels on the planet. The interior furnishings are cobbled together out of various things made by local elderly people and artists, creating a beautiful link between hostel and city.

Situated in the old downtown area of Baika in Osaka, The Blend Inn has seven rooms—both private and dormitory-style—an open shared kitchen, an eating and meeting space, and a small cultural space called "ParadaSan." The open design of the building creates "a communal space both to relax and to enjoy the company of others." The open design of the hostel extends beyond its concrete walls into the neighboring street. Originally a private road, it was integrated into the final design to engage hostel visitors with the surrounding community.

A typical day at the hostel starts at the on-site bakery Mirow. Between 8 a.m. and 12 p.m., guests can enjoy a complimentary breakfast sandwich (changes daily) plus a drink. On days with good weather, guests can eat out in the garden or on the rooftop, another beautiful space to unwind after a long day of sightseeing. There is also a handy free laundry service on the rooftop.

All facilities in The Blend Inn are communal; this includes washrooms, bathrooms, kitchen, and lobby. ⌂

Good to know

PRICE RANGE
$ $ $ $ $
AMENITIES INCLUDE
linens; free city maps;
free WiFi and internet
access; common room;
outdoor terrace;
elevator; bicycle parking,
air conditioning;
self-catering facilities;
stove; fridge/freezer;
utensils; microwave;
reading light; hot
showers; towels;
hairdryer; washing
machine.

Tip: Between 8 a.m.
and 12 p.m., guests can
enjoy a complimentary
breakfast sandwich
(changes daily) plus
a drink at the on-site
bakery Mirow.

A space with the perfect blend of local Japanese culture and contemporary architecture.

Party hotspots

For fun and friendships

If you are the kind of person who wants to meet the world in one place, perfect your beer pong skills, and cultivate friendships that will last longer hopefully than your hangover, then you won't regret checking into these hostels.

Swanky Mint Hostel, Zagreb

Yellow Square, Rome

Often dubbed the greatest party hostel on earth, YellowSquare (p. 134) offers some of the cheapest drinks in Rome. It hosts a regular program of events that includes the bizarre but bold Tonika dancers, as well as great local bands and DJs in the basement nightclub, Arcade. Amistat Island Hostel (p. 52) is the perfect base for enjoying Ibiza's famed nightlife. Located in the center of Sant Antoni de Portmany, it has a pool and bar and is close to the legendary venues Café del Mar, Golden Buddha, Kasbah, and Ibiza Rocks. Mixing elegance with post-industrial chic, Swanky Mint (p. 248) in Zagreb has a gorgeous sun terrace and outdoor pool and bar. It's a perfect starting point for enjoying the city's nightlife. If you're heading to Munich for Oktoberfest, look no further than Munich's premier party palace, the fantastic Wombat's Munich (p. 199) which is within walking distance from the festival grounds and old town plus home to the womBAR, cheapest place for beers in town and a popular meeting point between locals and backpackers. Native Hostel (p. 318) in Austin, Texas, is the perfect place for partying thanks to the popular Native Bar & Kitchen where you can sample the infamous Bloody Eddy Mary. Head to La Banda Rooftop Hostel (p. 45) in Seville for the best hostel rooftop-terrace dinner, cocktails, and live music night in Europe.

Casa Gracia, Barcelona

Quiet escapes
For a good night sleep

If you'd prefer a restorative night of undisturbed sleep, rather than a raucous night of after-hour parties, then look no further. We have the definitive list of quiet hostels that offer an oasis of calm tranquility.

*I*n the picturesque village of Capel Curig, at the foot of Snowdonia in Wales, <u>The Rocks at Plas Curig</u> (p. 106) is possibly Britain's most beautiful hostel. Guests can enjoy the soothing beauty of the Northern Lights in winter and the midnight sun in Summer at the <u>7 Fells Hostel</u> (p. 198) at Yllas in Finnish Lapland. Away from the tourist drag Las Ramblas, Barrio Gothic, and the menace of pickpockets, <u>Casa Gracia</u> (p. 62) is a calm oasis in Barcelona. It has a beautiful outdoor terrace to relax, plus a downstairs lounge and bar where you can sip on a beer and chill. <u>Mountain Hostel Tarter</u> (p. 46) is nestled in the heart of the Pyrenees mountains in Andorra and resembles more of a tranquil mountain lodge than hostel. Guests can enjoy a glass of wine from the cellar while taking advantage of the fantastic outdoor jacuzzi.

Plas Curig on the Rocks, Capel Curig

Native Hostel

A creative home for southwestern wanderlust

Native Hostel is self-described as an "experiential hostel," and it is certainly eclectic. The hostel building sits, hewn out of limestone, in the part of Austin where the artsy eastside of town meets the downtown entertainment district. Inside, the design reveals charred exposed beam, dark plaster walls, and materials like glass and steel for a contrasting visual experience.

There are a total of 65 beds spread over 12 rooms. They have cool, whitewashed and exposed brickwork with bright oriental rugs laid across the gleaming hardwood floors. The four and six-bed dorms feature oversized single beds. If you're in a large group, consider booking the Romper Room: a wonderful large space, able to sleep ten people, with three baths, eight bunk beds, and a large communal space perfect for partying.

The Native Bar and Kitchen serves up lip-smacking fare. Features include American diner-style meals like brisket sliders, buffalo wraps, waffle fry nachos, and Bloody Eddy Marys and margaritas at brunch.

Native Hostel emanates an air of excitement and hospitality, all under one stylish roof.

The Quisby

New Orleans cozy eccentricity at its best

"The Quisby is a hostel that was inspired by our travels around the world—both real and projected," explain the owners. "We are a bunch of misfits and lovable troublemakers. Hence the name Quisby, which can be interpreted in a few ways: 'misadventure,' one who is 'out-of-sorts,' or 'eccentric.' Some of us have always called New Orleans home. Others came for a few days and never left. What we share in common is a mission to create a new kind of hostel in New Orleans." Situated right on Charles Avenue in the Lower Garden District of New Orleans, the Quisby, true to the owners' mission statement, fuses modern convenience and comforts to create the Big Easy's first modern hostel.

The Quisby is located in a beautifully restored building, one of the few remaining examples of a three-story structure in the historic district. The building sat vacant for most of the 2000s and redevelopment began in 2010. The hostel draws heavily on the identity of its former incarnation: the historic Audubon Hotel that was built in the 1930s as rough-and-tumble temporary housing for the captains and deckhands of Mississippi riverboats. It changed ownership numerous times, and rumor has it that the hotel served as a brothel for the majority of its history. Later in the 90s, the Audubon served as a multipurpose space, functioning as a bar (a popular hangout for artists), club, gallery, and performance space on the ground floor with hotel rooms on the upper floors. The hostel's industrial yet warm design reflects →

Good to know

PRICE RANGE
$ $ $ $ $
AMENITIES INCLUDE
24-hour reception;
lobby bar; lounge area;
guest kitchen; guest
laundry; lending
library specializing
in vintage pulp
paperbacks; 24-hour
concierge service

Tip: All the major
parades during the
city's legendary
Mardi Gras cele-
brations file through
Charles Avenue and
pass in front of the
Quisby. So make sure
to book your room
here for a ringside
view of the action.

» *The Quisby* is more than a crash pad; it's a community where everyone is welcome. So come on by and check us out. «

its rich heritage. Guests visiting the hostel can still observe the Audubon Hotel sign and its perfectly preserved ornate frieze at the top of the building's façade. The hostel lobby's open floor plan has simple wooden features and retains the building's original green columns. There's an open plan bar, work area, and small living room. The tall front windows look out onto St. Charles Avenue. Throughout the building you will see artwork pieces from local artists like Milagros and Joseph Konert.

The hostel owners try to source everything locally. The sturdy bunk beds (each come with a private locker and storage space) were custom made for the hostel by the local furniture company Holz Works. The hostel's 30 rooms are a mix of shared and private dorms. With sunny windows looking out onto Canal Street, the light and spacious shared rooms are a safe bet.

All the rooms here feature en suite bathrooms, memory foam mattresses, plenty of reading lamps,

electrical outlets, USB ports for every bed, air conditioning, and high speed WiFi. Complimentary morning breakfast here is a simple affair of New Orleans-style chicory coffee and locally made pastries.

The 24-hour, full-service bar serves guests local spirits, brews, and seasonal cocktails plus a menu from which you can savor everything from pasta to bagged ramen. Additional amenities include 24-hour front desk, luggage storage, daily housekeeping, and bicycle parking.

The Upcycled Hostel

A colorful retreat in an actual oasis

The Upcycled Hostel is perhaps Huacachina's premier hostel for a variety of reasons. The proximity to the oasis, general cleanliness of the property, funky design vibe, and charming hospitality mean it takes pride of place out of the options on offer.

Huacachina as a town owed its inception to the popularity of the oasis or laguna found in the dry wilderness of the Atacama Desert. The oasis is hence one of Peru's most booming tourist destinations. It was unheard of to stumble upon a lush fertile oasis in the midst of one of the world's

most arid deserts. Nestled in a shroud of green palm trees that provide shade and a welcome respite from the onslaught of the beating sun, the oasis is one of Peru's—and in fact the world's greatest—geological wonders.

Huacachina is 186 miles from Peru's capital city Lima on the arid verges of the Atacama. In the 1940s there was a huge influx of rich property developers who built holiday homes around the oasis. With this development came the growth of the tourist industry in Huacachina.

The hostel is a little bit outside Huacachina itself. A 15-minute walk should find guests in the midst of the heady nightlife that Huacachina is famed for if that is what they are

seeking. Otherwise The Upcycled is a perfectly quiet, lovely place to spend an evening sipping on the famed pisco sours served at the hostel bar and chatting to hostel friends. The hostel proprietor Renzo, the affable hostel staff, and the hostel's charming dog Coco render The Upcycled Hostel a home away from home.

The hostel is also a 10-minute walk from the laguna and there are plenty of shops nearby. The hostel repurposes or "upcycles" what others may call junk into gorgeous furniture and creative decor. From a bar made out of wine bottles to bathroom sink bases made from Singer sewing machines—even the grass is repurposed lawn clippings. The Upcycled Hostel has a very →

Good to know

PRICE RANGE
$ $ $ $ $
AMENITIES INCLUDE
WiFi; pool; bar; garden;
restaurant; fire pit; living
rooms; hot showers;
hammocks. Breakfast
included.

Tip: The hostel staff
are happy to arrange
sunset dune buggy
rides for guests, which
are a wonderful way
to capture the unique
natural beauty of the
destination. Staff also
provide a late
breakfast for sleepy
guests recovering
from a night out.

The Upcycled Hostel is a mini oasis in the middle of the desert.

laid-back, relaxed charm. There is a very clean outdoor swimming pool to cool off in. Nearby is the central bar area with lots of couches and hammocks in the garden surrounding it. It is a nice place to chill, sip on a cocktail, sunbathe, and read a book.

The oasis is not the only activity of note to be indulged in whilst staying at The Upcycled. The hostel staff are happy to arrange sunset dune buggy rides for guests, which are a wonderful way to capture the unique natural beauty of the destination. Staff also provide a late breakfast for sleepy guests recovering from a night out, which is a very thoughtful personal touch.

Friendly staff, large clean dorm rooms and bathrooms, and a fantastic location make Upcycled Hostel a unique South American accommodation. It is a mini oasis in the middle of the desert and is the perfect spot to rest and recharge in a super relaxed atmosphere.

ANDORRA

MOUNTAIN HOSTEL TARTER
mountainhosteltarter.com
Sant Pere del Tarter, AD100 Canillo
+376 330 412
info@mountainhosteltarter.com
Photography:
Mountain Hostel Tarter
PP. 46–49

AUSTRIA

WOMBATS CITY HOSTEL
Vienna Naschmarkt
wombats-hostels.com
Rechte Wienzeile 35, 1040 Vienna
+43 1 8972336
bookvienna@wombats.eu
Photography: Luiza Puiu
P. 156

BELGIUM

THE CUBE HOSTEL
cubehostel.be
Brusselsestraat 110, 3000 Leuven
+32 16 89 45 85
hello@cubehostel.be
Photography: Cube Hostel Leuven
P. 79

BULGARIA

HOSTEL OLD PLOVDIV
hosteloldplovdiv.com
3 Chetvarti yanuari Str.,
4000 Plovdiv
+359 32 260 925
hosteloldplovdiv@hotmail.com
Photography: Hostel Old Plovdiv
PP. 256–257

CAMBODIA

LUB D CAMBODIA SIEM REAP
lubd.com
7 Makara St, Wat Bo Village,
Sangkat Sala Kamreuk City,
Siem Reap 17254
+855 63 968 900
contact.siam@lubd.com
Photography: Lub d Hostels
PP. 288–289

CROATIA

**BOUTIQUE HOSTEL
FORUM ZADAR**
hostelforumzadar.com
Široka ul. 20, 23000 Zadar
+385 23 250 705
info@hostelforumzadar.com
Photography:
Boutique Hostel Forum
P. 38

HOSTEL 1W
one-world.com.hr
Barčićeva 4, 51000 Rjeka
+385 51 401 757
info@one-world.com.hr
Photography: Hostel 1W
P. 235

SWANKY MINT HOSTEL
swanky-hostel.com
Ilica 50, 10000 Zagreb
+385 1 4004 248
mint@swanky-hostel.com
Photography: Petar Santini
PP. 248–251

CZECH REPUBLIC

CZECH INN
czech-inn.com
Francouzská 240/76, 101 00 Prague
+420 210 011 100
info@czech-inn.com
Photography: Dominik Holz
PP. 252–253

LONG STORY SHORT HOSTEL
longstoryshort.cz
Koželužská 945/31, 779 00 Olomouc
+420 588 008 278
reception@longstoryshort.cz
Photography: Josef Kubíček
josefkubicek.net
PP. 258–263

SIR TOBY'S HOSTEL
sirtobys.com
Dělnická 1155/24, 170 00 Prague
+420 210 011 600
info@sirtobys.com
Photography: Dominik Holz
P. 254

SOPHIE'S HOSTEL
miss-sophies.com
Melounova 2, 120 00 Nové Město
+420 210 011 300
info@miss-sophies.com
Photography: Dominik Holz
P. 255

DENMARK

STEEL HOUSE COPENHAGEN
steelhousecopenhagen.com
Herholdtsgade 6,
DK-1605 Copenhagen V
+45 3317 7110
reservations@
steelhousecopenhagen.com
Photography: Steel House
Copenhagen
PP. 180–183

ESTONIA

HEKTOR DESIGN HOSTEL
hektorhostels.com
Riia street 26, 50405 Tartu
+372 7405 100
hektor@hektorhostels.com
Photography:
Hektor Design Hostels
PP. 192–195

FINLAND

7 FELLS HOSTEL
sevenfellshostel.fi
Kartanontie 2, 95970 Äkäslompolo
+358 040 5229925
info@sevenfellshostel.fi
Photography: 7 Fells Hostel
P. 198

DREAM HOSTEL & HOTEL
dreamhostel.fi
Akerlundinkatu 2, 33100 Tampere
+358 45 2360 517
info@dreamhostel.fi
Photography: Studio Puisto
(186, 188 top left), Jarno Laine
(187, 188 top right, bottom right,
189 top), Dream Hostel & Hotel
(189 bottom)
PP. 186—189

HOSTEL CAFE KOTI
hostelcafekoti.fi
Valtakatu 21, 96200 Rovaniemi
+358 44 7961 333
info@hostelcafekoti.fi
Photography: Kota Collective
PP. 196—197

THE YARD HOSTEL
theyard.fi
Kalevankatu 3 A 45, 00100 Helsinki
+358 400 909118
booking@theyard.fi
Photography: YARD Nights Oy
PP. 190—191

FRANCE

AWAY HOSTEL
AND COFFEE SHOP
awayhostel.com
21 rue Alsace Lorraine, 69001 Lyon
+33 4 78 98 53 20
bonjour@awayhostel.com
Photography: Frenchie Cristogatin
(126, 127 top, bottom left,
bottom right), Gaetan Clément
(127 center right)
PP. 126—127

GASTAMA HOSTEL LILLE
en.gastama.com
109, rue de Saint André, 59000 Lille
+33 3 20 06 06 80
contact@gastama.com
Photography: Gastama Hostel
P. 124

GENERATOR PARIS
generatorhostels.com
9—11 Place du Colonel Fabien,
75010 Paris
+33 1 70 98 84 00
ask.paris@generatorhostels.com
Photography: Generator Paris
PP. 122—123

HO 36 LES MÉNUIRES
ho36hostels.com
Route de Val Thorens,
73440 Saint-Martin-de-Belleville
+33 4 79 55 08 40
hellomenuires@ho36hostels.com
Photography: ho36hostels.com
PP. 118—119

HÔTEL OZZ
hotel-ozz.com
18 Rue Paganini, 06000 Nice
+33 4 93 88 48 83
bonjour@hotel-ozz.com
Photography: Hotel Ozz
P. 128—129

LES PIAULES
lespiaules.com
59 boulevard de Belleville,
75011 Paris
+33 1 43 55 09 97
contact@lespiaules.com
Photography: Les Piaules
P. 120—121

GEORGIA

FABRIKA TBILISI
hostelfabrika.com
8 Egnate Ninoshvili street,
Tbilisi 0102
+995 32 2020399
info@fabrikatbilisi.com
Photography:
Nakanimamasakhlisi (270—272,
273 top, bottom right),
Bobo Lab (273 center left,
bottom left)
PP. 270—273

GERMANY

DIE WOHNGEMEINSCHAFT
die-wohngemeinschaft.net
Richard-Wagner-Straße 39,
50674 Cologne
+ 49 221 98593090
info@die-wohngemeinschaft.net
Photography: Natalie Bothur
(172, 173 top, 174 top, 175 top,
center left, bottom left),
Die Wohngemeinschaft
(173 bottom, 174 bottom,
175 bottom right)
PP. 172—175

DOCK INN HOSTEL
dock-inn.de
Zum Zollamt 4, 18057 Rostock
+49 381 670700
info@dock-inn.de
Photography: Dock Inn
P. 147

EDEN HOSTEL & GARTEN
eden-leipzig.de
Demmeringstraße 57, 04177 Leipzig
+49 1522 5181544
info@eden-leipzig.de
Photography: Stefanie Schmidt
(168, 169 top, 170, 171),
Anne Hutschenreuter (169 bottom)
PP. 168—171

GRAND HOSTEL BERLIN
grandhostel-berlin.de
Tempelhofer Ufer 14, 10963 Berlin
+49 302 0095450
info@grandhostel-berlin.de

Photography: Grand Hostel Berlin
P. 157

**JUGENDHERBERGE
NUREMBURG**
jugendherberge.de
Burg 2, 90403 Nuremberg
+49 0911 2309360
nuernberg@jugendherberge.de
Photography: DJH
Jugendherbergen Bayern e.V.
P. 115

MULTITUDE HOSTEL
multitude.de
Lützner Straße 7, 04177 Leipzig
+49 1590 1330851
info@multitude.de
Photography: Multitude Hostel
PP. 166—167

SUPERBUDE ST. PAULI
superbude.de
Juliusstr. 1—7, 22769 Hamburg
+49 40 807915820
stpauli@superbude.de
Photography: Christian Perl (150,
151 top, 152, 153 bottom left, center
right, bottom right), Steve Herud
(150 bottom), Eva Giolbas (153 top)
PP. 150—153

SUPERBUDE ST. GEORG
superbude.de
Spaldingstraße 152,
20097 Hamburg
+49 40 3808780
stgeorg@superbude.de
Photography: Christian Perl
PP. 154—155

THE CIRCUS
circus-berlin.de
Weinbergsweg 1a, 10119 Berlin
+49 30 20003939
info@circus-berlin.de
Photography:
Sebastian Neeb (162), Zoë Noble
(163, 164 right) Simon Becker
(165 top), Giacomo Morelli
(165 center left), The Circus
GbR (164 left, 165 bottom left,
165 bottom right)
PP. 162—165

**WOMBAT'S CITY
HOSTEL MUNICH**
wombats-hostels.com
Senefelderstraße 1, 80336 Munich
+ 49 089 59989180
bookmunich@wombats.eu
Luiza Puiu
P. 199

GHANA

SOMEWHERE NICE HOSTEL
hostelaccra.com
Cotton Avenue 9,
Kokomlemle, Accra
+233 54 374 3505
info@hostelaccra.com
Photography: Somewhere Nice
PP. 216—217

GREECE

CAVELAND SANTORINI
cave-land.com
Karterados 39, 847 00 Karterádhos
+30 2286 022122
info@caveland.com
Photography: Chris Spira
P. 234

STAY HOSTEL APARTMENTS
stayrhodes.com
Lochagou Fanouraki 19-21,
851 00 Rhodes
+30 22410 24024
stayrhodes@gmail.com
Photography: Stay Hostel
Apartments
PP. 232—233

HONG KONG

THE MAHJONG HOSTEL
themahjonghk.com
1/F, 10-16 Pak Tai Street,
To Kwa Wan, Kowloon
+852 27051869
info@themahjonghk.com
Photography: The Mahjong Hostel
PP. 300—301

ICELAND

KEX HOSTEL
kexhostel.is
Skúlagata 28, 101 Reykjavik
+354 561 6060
info@kexhostel.is
Photography: Borkur Sightorsson
(204, 206 bottom right, 207 top,
center left, bottom left),
Lilja Jónsdóttir (205, 206 top right)
Jess Kay (206 top left, 207
bottom right)
PP. 204—207

MIDGARD BASE CAMP
midgardbasecamp.is
Dufbaksbraut 14, 860 Hvolsvöllur
+354 578 3180
sleep@midgard.is
Photography: Midgard Base Camp
P. 208

INDIA

LET'S BUNK POSHTEL
letsbunk.live
T40, Hauz Khas Village,
New Delhi, Delhi
+91 81303 83199
bookings@letsbunk.live
Photography: Dinesh Madhavan
Photography
PP. 274—275

ISRAEL

**ABRAHAM HOSTEL
JERUSALEM**
abrahamhostels.com
67 Hanevi'im Street, Davidka
Square, Jerusalem 9470211
+ 972 2 6502200
infojlm@abrahamhostels.com
Photography: Abraham Hostels
PP. 238—241

ABRAHAM HOSTEL TEL AVIV
abrahamhostels.com
21 Levontin Street, Tel Aviv 6511604
+ 972 3 6249200
infotlv@abrahamhostels.com

Photography: Abraham Hostels
P. 237

FAUZI AZAR INN
abrahamhostels.com
Fauzi Azar Inn 2606,
Nazareth 16125
+ 972 4 6020469
info@fauziazarinn.com
Photography: Abraham Hostels
PP. 242—245

ITALY

DOPA HOSTEL
dopahostel.com
Via Irnerio 41 , 40126 Bologna
+39 051 0952461
info@dopahostel.com
Photography: Dopa Hostel
PP. 144—145

OSTELLO BELLO LAKE COMO
ostellobello.com
Viale Fratelli Rosselli 9,
22100 Como
+39 031 570889
info.como@ostellobello.com
Photography: Alice Gemignani
P. 142

OSTELLO BELLO MILAN
ostellobello.com
Via Roberto Lepetit 33, 20124 Milan
+39 02 6705921
info@ostellobello.com
Photography: Alice Gemignani
PP. 140—141

THE BEEHIVE
the-beehive.com
Via Marghera 8, 00185 Rome
+ 39 06 44704553
info@the-beehive.com
Photography: Maarten Mellemans
P. 143

THE ROMEHELLO
theromehello.com
Via Torino 45, 00184 Rome
+39 06 96860070
ciao@theromehello.com
Photography: Janos Grapow
PP. 138—139

WE_CROCIFERI
we-gastameco.com
Campo dei Gesuiti,
Cannaregio 4878, 30121 Venice
+39 041 5286103
hello@we-crociferi.it
Photography: Edoardo Pasero
(146 top), Riccardo Grassetti
(146 bottom right)
P. 146

YELLOWSQUARE
yellowsquare.it
Via Palestro 51, 00185 Rome
+39 06 446 3554
questions@the-yellow.com
Photography: YellowSquare
PP. 134—137

JAPAN

36HOSTEL
36hostel.com
36Hostel, 2-10-17, Tokaichimachi,
Naka-ku, Hiroshima-shi,
Hiroshima 730-0805
+81 070 5527 3669
info@36hostel.com
Photography: Masaru Yamamoto
PP. 304—309

THE BLEND-INN
theblend.jp
1-24-21 Baika, Konohana-ku,
Osaka-shi, Osaka-fu
+81 70 1745 1250
info@theblend.jp
Photography: The Blend-Inn
PP. 312—315

THE MILLENNIALS
the-millennials-kyoto-jp.
book.direct
235 Yamazakicho, Nakagyo Ward,
Kyoto 604-803
+81 75 212 6887
master@themillennials.jp
Photography: Global Agents Co.
PP. 310—311

LATVIA

TWOWHEELS HOSTEL
2w.lv
Balozu street 12, Riga LV-1048
+ 371 6746 8884
info@2w.lv
Photography: TwoWheels Hostel
PP. 264—265

LITHUANIA

DOWNTOWN FOREST
downtownforest.lt
Paupio str. 31A, Vilnius LT-11341
+370 686 84523
info@downtownforest.lt
Photography:
Antanas Miknevičius
PP. 266—267

MOROCCO

RODAMÓN RIAD MARRAKECH
rodamonhostels.com
Amssafah 32, Marrakech 40000
+212 5243 78978
Photography: Rodamón Hostels
PP. 228—231

PERU

THE UPCYCLED HOSTEL
facebook.com/theupcycledhostel
Urbanizacion La Estancia F-5
camino a Huacachina, Ica
+51 56 408911
upcyclehostelperu@gmail.com
Photography: The Upcycled Hostel
PP. 324—327

PHILIPPINES

SPIN DESIGNER HOSTEL
spinhostel.com
Balinsasayaw Road cor.
Calle Real, El Nido, 5313 Palawan
+63 917 566 7746
spinhostelph@gmail.com
Photography:
Spin Designer Hostel
PP. 302–303

PORTUGAL

GALLERY HOSTEL
gallery-hostel.com
Rua Miguel Bombarda, 222,
4050-377 Porto
+351 22 496 4313
info@gallery-hostel.com
Photography: Gallery Hostel
PP. 32–35

GOODMORNING HOSTEL
goodmorninghostel.com
Praça dos Restauradores 65,
1250-188 Lisbon
+351 21 342 1128
bookings@goodmorninghostel.com
Photography:
Goodmorning Hostel
PP. 12–13

HUB NEW LISBON HOSTEL
hostelshub.com
Rua de O Século 150,
1200-437 Lisbon
+351 21 347 1506
newlisbon@hostelshub.com
Photography: Hostels Hub
PP. 14–17

**SUNSET DESTINATION
HOSTEL**
followyourdestination.com
Praça do Duque de
Terceira, Estação Ferroviária
do Cais do Sodré, 1200-161 Lisbon
+351 21 347 0219
sunset@followyourdestination.com
Photography:
Sunset Destination Hostel
P. 39

TATTVA DESIGN HOSTEL
tattvaporto.com
Rua do Cativo 26–28,
4000-160 Porto
+351 22 094 4622
info@tattvadesignhostel.com
Photography: Tattva Design Hostel
P. 39

THE HOUSE OF SANDEMAN
Hostel & Suites
thehouseofsandeman.pt
Largo Miguel Bombarda,
4430-175 Vila Nova de Gaia
+351 21 346 1381
reservations@
thehouseofsandeman.pt
Photography: The House of
Sandeman Hostel & Suites
PP. 22–27

**THE INDEPENDENTE
HOSTEL & SUITES**
theindependente.pt
Rua de São Pedro de Alcântara 81,
1250-238 Lisbon
+351 21 346 1381
reservations@theindependente.pt
Photography:
Miguel Guedes Ramos
PP. 8–11

THE PASSENGER
thepassengerhostel.com
Estação São Bento, Praça
Almeida Garrett, 4000-069 Porto
+351 963 802 000
info@thepassengerhostel.com
Photography: Vasco Maia Lopes
PP. 28–31

RUSSIA

SOUL KITCHEN
soulkitchenhostel.com
Moika embankment 62/2 app 9,
190000 St. Petersburg
+7 965 816 34 70
soulkitchenjunior@gmail.com
Photography: Soul Kitchen
PP. 268–269

SINGAPORE

ADLER HOSTEL
adlerhostel.com
259 South Bridge Road,
Singapore 058808
+65 6226 0173
contact@adlerintl.com
Photography: Adler Hostel
PP. 298–299

SOUTH AFRICA

91 LOOP
91loop.co.za
91 Loop Street, Cape Town 8001
+ 27 21 286 1469
stay@91loop.co.za
Photography: 91 Loop
PP. 224–225

CURIOCITY HOSTELS DURBAN
curiocitybackpackers.com
55 Monty Naicker Road,
Durban 4001
+27 31 286 0025
stay@curiocitydurban.com
Photography: Curiocity Hostels
PP. 226–227

CURIOCITY HOSTELS JOBURG
curiocitybackpackers.com
302 Fox St, Johannesburg 2094
+27 11 614 0163
 stay@curiocityjoburg.com
Photography: Curiocity Hostels
PP. 218–219

ONCE IN CAPE TOWN
onceincapetown.co.za
73 Kloof Street, Cape Town 8001
+27 87 057 2638
book@onceincapetown.co.za
Photography: Selma Olsen
(214, 215 top left), David Hofmeyr
(215 top right, bottom),
Carl Holman (215 center right)
PP. 214–215

ONCE IN JOBURG
once.travel/cities/joburg
90 De Korte Street,
Johannesburg 2000
+27 87 057 2638
book@onceinjoburg.co.za
Leeroy Jason (220, 221 top),
Oliver Petrie (221 bottom)
PP. 220–221

THE BACKPACK
backpackers.co.za
74 New Church Street,
Cape Town 8001
+27 21 423 4530
backpack@backpackers.co.za
Photography: Russel Smith
(222, 223 top right, center
right, bottom), The Backpack
(223 top left)
PP. 222–223

THE B.I.G.
bigbackpackers.com
18 Thornhill Road, Green Point,
Cape Town 8005
+27 21 434 0688
info@bigbackpackers.com
Photography: The B.I.G.
P. 236

SPAIN

AMISTAT ISLAND HOSTEL
amistathostels.com
Santa Rosalía, 25,
07820 Sant Antoni de Portmany
+34 971 34 38 34
ibiza@amistathostels.com
Photography: Amistat
Island Hostel
PP. 52–53

CASA GRACIA
casagraciabcn.com
Passeig De Gràcia 116 Bis,
08008 Barcelona
+34 931 74 05 28
info@casagraciabcn.com
Photography: Casa Gracia
PP. 62–63

LA BANDA ROOFTOP HOSTEL
labandahostel.com
Calle Dos de Mayo 16, 41001 Seville
+34 955 22 81 18
bookings@labandahostel.com
Photography: Nicole Williams
(45 bottom left), La Banda Rooftop
Hostel (45 top, bottom right)
P. 45

OPTION BE HOSTEL
bedandbe.com
Calle José Cruz Conde 22,
14001 Córdoba
+34 661 42 07 33
cordoba@bedandbe.com
Photography: MarinaMLuna
(55, 56 top right),Theresa
Schlage – ResiDiBerlino
(54, 56 top left, bottom right)
P. 54–57

QUARTIER BILBAO HOSTEL
quartierbilbao.com
Artekale, 15, 48005 Bilbao
+34 944 97 88 00
recepcion@quartierbilbao.com
Photography: Quartier
Bilbao Hostel
P. 38

THE LIGHTS HOSTEL
lightsouthostel.com
Calle Torregorda 3, 29005 Malaga
+34 951 25 35 25
Info@LightsOutHostel.com
Photography: The Lights Hostel
PP. 36–37

TOC HOSTELS BARCELONA
tochostels.com
Gran Vía de les Corts
Catalanes 580, 08011 Barcelona
+34 934 53 44 25
bcn@tochostels.com
Photography: TOC Hostels
P. 64

TOC HOSTELS MADRID
tochostels.com
Plaza Celenque 3, 28013 Madrid
+34 915 32 13 04
mad@tochostels.com
Photography: TOC Hostels
P. 44

TOC HOSTELS SEVILLA
tochostels.com
Calle Miguel Mañara 18-22,
41004 Seville
+34 954 50 12 44
sevilla@tochostels.com
Photography: TOC Hostels
P. 65

SWEDEN

GENERATOR STOCKHOLM
generatorhostels.com
Torsgatan 10, 111 23 Stockholm
+46 8 505 323 70
ask.stockholm@
generatorhostels.com
Photography: Generator
Stockholm
PP. 184–185

THAILAND

LUB D PHUKET PATONG
lubd.com
5/5 Sawatdirak Road,
Kathu, Patong, Phuket 83150
+66 76 530 100
contact.patong@lubd.com
Photography: Lub d Hostels
PP. 296–297

**ONEDAY
PAUSE AND FORWARD**
onedaybkk.com
51 Soi Sukhumvit 26, Klong Tan,
Klong Toei, Bangkok 10110
+ 66 21 088 855
contact@onedaybkk.com

Architecture and interior
design: Begray
Concept: Yiwa Bhusirat
Photography: ONEDAY Pause
and Forward
PP. 280—283

OXOTEL HOSTEL
oxotelchiangmai.com
149-153 Wua Lai Rd, Chang Wat,
Chiang Mai 50100
+66 52 085 334
oxotelcnx@gmail.com
Photography: Oxotel Hostel
PP. 292—295

YIM HUAI KHWANG
yimbangkok.com
70 Pracha Rat Bamphen Rd,
Khwaeng Huai Khwang,
Khet Huai Khwang, Krung Thep
Maha Nakhon 10310
+66 80 965 9994
yimhuaikhwang@gmail.com
Photography: Wison Tungthunya
PP. 286—287

**YIM YAM HOSTEL
AND GARDEN**
yimyambkk.com
503/2 Petchburi Road, Phaya
Thai District, Ratchathewi
Bangkok 1040
+66 90 931 5077
info@yimyambkk.com
Photography: Gun Phansuwon
PP. 284—285

THE NETHERLANDS

CLINK NOORD
clinkhostels.com
Badhuiskade 3,
1031 KV Amsterdam
+31 20 214 9731
reservations@clinkhostels.com
Photography: Clink Hostels
P. 88

COCOMAMA
cocomamahostel.com
Westeinde 18, 1017 ZP Amsterdam

+31 20 627 2454
hello@cocomamahostel.com
Photography: Cocomama
PP. 70—71

ECOMAMA
ecomamahotel.com
Valkenburgerstraat 124,
1011 NA Amsterdam
+31 20 770 9529
hello@ecomamahotel.com
Photography: Ecomama
PP. 76—77

GENERATOR AMSTERDAM
generatorhostels.com
Mauritskade 57,
1092 AD Amsterdam
+31 20 708 5600
ask.amsterdam@
generatorhostels.com
Photography: Generator
Amsterdam
P. 78

HELLO I'M LOCAL
helloimlocal.com
Spiegelstraat 4, 2011 BP Haarlem
+31 23 844 6916
mail@helloimlocal.com
Photography: Anouk B
PP. 86—87

HOSTEL ANI & HAAKIEN
anihaakien.nl
Coolsestraat 47, 3014 LC Rotterdam
+31 10 236 1086
info@anihaakien.nl
Photography: Hostel
Ani & Haakien
PP. 84—85

HOSTEL ROOM
roomrotterdam.nl
Van Vollenhovenstraat 62,
3016 BK Rotterdam
+31 10 282 7277
info@roomrotterdam.nl
Photography: Hostel ROOM
P. 89

KING KONG HOSTEL
kingkonghostel.com
Witte de Withstraat 74,
3012 BS Rotterdam
+31 10 818 8778
info@kingkonghostel.com
Photography: Abraham Quintana
(73, 75 bottom right), Nuno Viegas
(75 bottom left), Annebel Eppinga
(75 top), Christian Escobar (74),
King Kong Hostel (72, 75
center left)
PP. 72—75

KINGKOOL HOSTEL
kingkool.nl
Prinsegracht 51,
2512 EX The Hague
+31 70 215 8339
info@kingkool.nl
Photography: Kingkool Hostel
PP. 90—91

UNITED KINGDOM

CLINK78
clinkhostels.com
78 King's Cross Rd,
London, WC1X 9QG
+44 20 7183 9400
reservations@clinkhostels.com
Photography: Clink Hostels
P. 114

**FORT YORK
BOUTIQUE HOSTEL**
thefortyork.co.uk
1 Little Stonegate, York YO1 8AX
+44 1904 639573
info@thefortyork.co.uk
Photography: The Fort
Boutique Hostel
PP. 110—111

**PALMERS LODGE,
SWISS COTTAGE**
palmerslodges.com
40 College Crescent,
London NW3 5LB
+44 20 7483 8470
Photography: Palmers Lodge
PP. 98—99